D1580463

The Secret World of Witchcraft

THE SECRET WORLD OF
WITCHCRAFT

JASON KARL

NEW
HOLLAND

First published in 2008 by
New Holland Publishers (UK) Ltd
London • Cape Town • Sydney • Auckland

Garfield House
86–88 Edgware Road
London
W2 2EA
www.newhollandpublishers.com

80 McKenzie Street
Cape Town 8001
South Africa

Unit 1,
66 Gibbes Street
Chatswood, NSW 2067
Australia

218 Lake Road
Northcote
Auckland
New Zealand

10 9 8 7 6 5 4 3 2 1

Jason Karl has asserted his moral right to be
identified as the author of this work.

ISBN 978 184773 069 5

Editors: Giselle Osborne, Steffanie Brown,
Julia Shone
Design: Alan Marshall at Heron Recreations
Production: Melanie Dowland
Editorial Direction: Rosemary Wilkinson

Reproduction by Pica Digital Pte. Ltd., Singapore
Printed and bound in India by Replika Press

Note:
The author and publishers have made every effort
to ensure that all instructions given in this book
are safe and accurate, but they cannot accept
liability for any resulting injury or loss or damage
to either property or person, whether direct or
consequential and howsoever arising.

DEDICATION

This work is dedicated to the witches who have gone before, to the silent teachers whose lives
were taken by the ignorant and in whose footsteps the modern-day witches walk…

"I saw what people would call the world of everyday reality, as unreal. Behind it there was
something else; that was real, and which was very potent, and it was there. I saw the world of
forces, behind the world of form. I've never forgotten it, and that I think shaped my life a lot.
That just for a moment I had experienced what was beyond the physical, and it was beautiful,
it was wonderful. It wasn't frightening."

Doreen Valiente (1922–1999)
Mother of Modern Witchcraft
Resting in the Summerland

CONTENTS

FOREWORD 6
By Morianna Ravenswood

INTRODUCTION 12
Something Wicca This Way Comes...

I
THE HISTORY OF WITCHCRAFT 16

II
DOUBLE, DOUBLE, TOIL AND TROUBLE 42

III
SEASONS OF THE WITCH 70

IV
AS ABOVE, SO BELOW 86

V
TOOLS AND SIGILS OF THE CRAFT 106

VI
WHICH WITCH IS WHICH? 130

THE GRIMOIRE 164
Words of The Witches (Glossary) 164
The Witches' Web – Internet Resources 176
Bibliography and Further Reading – The Witches' Library 182
Index 188
Acknowledgements 192

FOREWORD

By Morianna Ravenswood, High Priestess of Witchcraft

 am a successful businesswoman, author, wife, mother and witch! There, I have said it!

It is with some trepidation that I write this foreword. Despite having been a witch for over 35 years, apart from my fellow covenors there are only a handful of close friends and family who know. Why keep it secret? The title of this book speaks volumes, and upon reading the book you will gain an immediate insight into what it is like to be a witch, both now and throughout history. It will also give you a clear indication as to why some witches have always practised their craft in secret – and still do.

What is a witch? I was horrified to see that according to the *Oxford English Dictionary*, as a witch I am:

1   A woman thought to have evil magic powers.
2   A follower or practitioner of modern witchcraft.
3   An ugly or unpleasant old woman (informal meaning).

No wonder we still get such bad press!

The words "witchcraft" and "witch" derive from Old English "wiccecraeft": from "wicca" (masculine) or "wicce" (feminine) (pronounced "witchah" and "witchuh"), which translates to "one who engages in sorcery"; and from "craeft", meaning "craft" or "skill". Therefore we are "someone who is skilled in the art of sorcery". But is that all it is to be a witch? Someone who can perform spells – and evil spells at that – at will? I think not. I am still reeling from the dictionary definition, but largely because I think that after all these years nothing has changed in terms of what the majority (thankfully not all) of society believes we are and what we do.

Is it any wonder that the title of this book reflects why most witches, both in the past and even now, often remain anonymous?

One can look back through time and see that the condemnation of witches is not a recent phenomenon. Almost all of us know something about the witch-hunts that ravaged the United Kingdom in the 16th and 17th centuries, sometimes known as "The Burning Times", although in fact witches were mostly hung, not burned. The hysteria that swept through certain parts of the country, and indeed abroad, was later accredited to nothing more than mass hysteria and neighbours' disputes. One suspects that many true witches kept silent vigil during those turbulent times and went further underground in an attempt to avoid detection.

"Real" witches have been around for centuries, and much has been theorized as to exactly when and how witchcraft was born. It is my belief that in order to trace the birth of witchcraft you have to look at the birth of humanity in terms of its evolution from the amoebic primeval swamps, to the heady heights of *Homo erectus*, to Neanderthal man, who had command over fire and made the very first tools.

Early cave drawings found at Lascaux, France, dating back approximately 17,000 years, show man's homage to the animals he hunted. In the now famous Trois-Frères cave in the Montesquieu-Avantès area of southwestern France, we see what scholars now believe to be the first depiction of shamanistic artwork. Here, in this secret chamber – which is extremely difficult to access unless crawling along on all fours – is the first possible representation of the god witches call Cernunnos, or the "Horned God". There is no doubt that some form of magic or ritual was utilized at that time to ensure a good hunt. It was the shaman who had the knowledge and skills to communicate with the spirit world and their ancestors, and who was able to take on the spirit of the animals they had killed.

The shaman was the tribes' priest, medium, healer and magician. He had the ability to control energy and to invoke it; to manifest it in the world of men. All that we know about our early shaman ancestors reflects the desire to have power over what they perceived as a dangerous and sometimes inexplicable world. Did they endeavour to "worship" the animals they hunted, or are the early cave drawings merely depictions of the shaman himself as he undergoes a transformation of self during his trancelike state? Today, the modern witch also utilizes ritual as a means of communicating between the worlds of the gods and the world of man.

But it was not only animals that were worshipped in ancient times. The moon was also revered, as most hunts occurred at night – a full moon on a clear night was a godsend, literally! Theories today suggest that Stonehenge may have been more than a temple of worship; that it was in effect an astronomical calculator enabling ancient man to observe the celestial movement of the planets and stars, and to predict the solar and lunar eclipses. Later, as man became a farmer as opposed to a hunter, he practised rituals to ensure a good crop, the remnants of which we still see today in the Christianized version of the harvest festival. From these early, humble beginnings, man sought to feed himself and the tribe and to keep himself safe from harm and illness. This was reflected through ritual or spellwork, using all that nature provided from the earth, air, water and eventually, fire! This was man's early magick...

As the millennia rolled by, early man became the forefathers, and mothers, of true witchcraft. For me, part of being a witch is the ability to connect with nature, the universe and all the inhabitants of this wonderfully diverse planet. It is that first primeval pulse that still beats in my own heart and soul; a belief in a great power that connects each and every one of us to the earth and manifests itself in the form of the ancient gods and goddesses with whom man has aligned himself for centuries. It is these ancient gods whom we connect to daily, monthly and throughout the Wheel of the Year. Unlike some other religious groups, our gods do not require "worship"; they require empathy with Mother Nature and her consort, the Horned God. The sacred sites of the witches are not grand cathedrals or churches, but rivers, seas, mountains and woodlands.

Wicca, or contemporary witchcraft, is believed to have emerged from ancient magickal roots. Although there are many different "traditions" to this tangled web, in truth, each witch, Pagan or Wiccan must find his or her own path. It is this flexible, eclectic and transient nature of The Craft, as it is often called, which many find appealing. Largely, there is no set dogma or rules, save for the Witches' Creed of "An harm ye none, do as thou will", meaning that today's followers find it easy to slip into modern witchcraft as it allows the individual to form a set of beliefs based upon their own understanding and experience of what being a witch is.

Witchcraft goes beyond empathy and respect for all things connected to the earth (today we call this being "eco-friendly" or "green"). It is also the ability to harness the unknown power that the universe and our planet, Gaia, exude – this is spellcraft, or magick.

But why should the world of witchcraft be secret, even now, in our multicultural, politically correct and supposedly tolerant society? The answer may be more complex than I can explain in a few sentences, but I will give you an insight into how and why I became witch, how it has enriched my life and, I'd like to think, that of those around me. Then I will tell you about the prejudice that sadly still prevails over us.

Some people are "born" witches, that is to say they are "hereditary witches" or witches whose skills and knowledge have been passed down from generation to generation and from one soul to the next. Others, like me, find themselves drawn naturally towards this Pagan religion. But what does being a Pagan mean and what is the difference between being Pagan and being a witch? Some people say, "I am a Pagan, not a witch", and it is here that things can become quite complicated in terms of true definition. Most New Age Wiccan groups worship both the Goddess and the Horned God, and they observe the festivals of the eight Sabbats of the year and the full-moon Esbats (celebrations). They utilize specific rituals – some handed down through the generations, some new – and they all believe firmly in a code of ethics.

Paganism is defined in most dictionaries as, "any non-Abrahamic religion e.g.: Judaism, Catholicism, Islamic, … etc.", and usually refers to any number of pre-Christian and European religions. It also means in a more literal sense "heathen"; that is, "a person of the heath", a country dweller that might follow the Old Ways. But what then of the followers of the Hindu faith; are they not Pagan too, having a belief system rooted in the worship and belief in many gods? The truth is that some witches believe in many gods and goddesses, while others hold a more pantheistic view and believe that the Horned God, Goddess and the universe are one and the same thing. This is not a theosophical discussion, but there is no doubt that defining the terms "witch" or "Pagan" is difficult. For me, as soon as I began to read about what used to be termed an "alternative" religion, it felt right, and I became interested in The Craft of the wise.

In my day, as a teenager in the late 1960s and '70s, many people in England were going public as writers and practitioners of witchcraft – Aleister Crowley, Gerald Gardner, Doreen Valiente, Alex and Maxine Sanders, Janet and Stewart Farrar, Patricia Crowther and Sybil Leek, to name but a few. Some of the first books I bought were *What Witches Do: A Modern Coven Revealed* by Stewart Farrar; *The Book of Thoth* by Aleister Crowley; and *The God of The Witches* by Margaret Murray. From the USA came other accomplished writers, including Raymond Buckland, who later became known as the "Father of American Wicca".

I performed my first spell at the tender age of 16. I wasn't part of a coven, I didn't have any other friends who were "witches" and I didn't get the spell from a book of spells. I made it up. To some extent what I did then reflects much of what being a natural witch is all about. A witch instinctively knows what is right and what is wrong. Yes, you read and learn much, but most importantly you practice (and practise some more!) the art of witchcraft.

Throughout my teens I settled in to my own version of witchery, and that felt right. I bought the books, I read and I practised magick. I observed the festivals, or Sabbats, following the witches' Wheel of the Year and also took delight in celebrating the Esbats. In effect, I had become a "hedge witch". Rae Beth's book, *Hedge Witch: A Guide to Solitary Witchcraft*, came too late for me, as it was published in 1992. Like many others, I did not begin my spiritual journey with hereditary initiation or through involvement with a coven, but through simply having a "feel" for the still-evolving practice of witchcraft.

As I began my journey of discovery early in my life I have had plenty of time to change and grow in confidence and knowledge. Over time, I realized my special affinity with the Egyptian deities more than any others. For some years I was drawn naturally to Isis and her counterpart Osiris. Egyptology in general held a haunting fascination for me, and Isis became my chosen Goddess deity. It was in Isis' name that I dedicated my offerings and rituals, and I called upon her many times for help and guidance. As a Triple Goddess representing the Maiden, Mother and Crone – which is so important in The Craft – she encompassed then, and still does now, each passing phase of my mortal life. Even though I used these ancient gods as a focus for my work, I still felt that doing so was a direct link or channel to the higher power that my forefathers had believed in many millennia before.

I was lucky enough to travel the world during my early twenties and thirties, and had the great fortune to visit not only Egypt, but also India and the Far East. My spiritual home is Bali. The people there follow a form of Hinduism called Agama Hindu Dharma – it is a religion that has evolved over time, incorporating elements of Hinduism and Buddhism. I found the Balinese tradition of worship refreshingly similar to "my" own religion. They believe that all gods are encompassed into one supreme being, their daily rituals and offerings given in the belief that their god will protect them and bring them happiness and prosperity. These beautiful people have a philosophical and simple approach to life: nature and ritual is important, as is magick. Indeed, it could be said that their beliefs are the same as those in witchcraft. I lived in Bali for several years, and had a wonderful, spiritually rewarding time. I also learnt a lot, mostly about religious tolerance and to not only see, but also respect, another person's viewpoint or belief.

On my return to England, I continued to practise my secret art alone, for I was still reluctant to share everything that I believed and practised with just anyone. I had already become the subject of ridicule to some people I had told. My lesson was learned and I kept my religion to myself. Being a solitary practitioner is not a problem, nor is it a new concept. In fact, in her book, *A Witch Alone: Thirteen Moons To Master Natural Magic*, Marian Green, like myself, advocates that most natural witches began life this way. She believes that, "the solo occult path is a traditional one, following in the footsteps of the oracle, the hermit, the shaman or the Druid priest". In real terms, it was easier to keep quiet rather than try and explain to people what witchcraft was really about. I became a self-initiated witch in my thirties, and felt no lesser a witch than if I had been brought into The Craft by a high priest or priestess of a coven. My own personal, spiritual and emotional fulfilment served as testimony that I felt more enriched after self-initiation; I needed no one's approval.

Only recently, since meeting other like-minded souls and being invited to form a coven here in my native Lancashire, have I realized the equally important role of being a high priestess and leading others less experienced than myself. Having said this, I would not now decry the way I found my path here. It has been a long, fruitful and interesting journey of self-discovery. Wicca is very much concerned with the individual's right to make their own way, and it is this philosophy that I personally find the most uplifting.

The coven to which I belong is a small, eclectic group whose covenors consider themselves a variety of things – Druids and followers of Isis, Arianrhod, the Morrigan and, of course, Pan. We proudly boast a diverse variety of genders and sexualities, with several gay and lesbian covenors who each lend their own energies to the work at hand. Our greatest attribute is that we all appreciate each others' differences and beliefs, yet we work side by side. At the special times of the month and the year we come together to revere our gods and goddesses, seeing them as the embodiment of the power of nature and the universe around us.

Do gods and goddesses exist in actual terms, and do they require us to worship them? In truth, this is down to personal belief and such is the fluidity of The Craft. I personally believe that the reverence we hold towards our chosen deities is simply a way of manifesting and focusing something towards that greater power. The impressive power of nature itself is, of course, disembodied, and therefore some of us do find it easier to give a "body" or name to that power as we perform rituals and spells.

As I sit at my desk in my semi-rural location, I know that I am indeed privileged to be so close to nature on a daily basis. A river runs behind my home and I have several acres of garden, a wild wood and, yes readers, my very own stone circle. My sacred circle offers a peaceful haven after a hard day's work, and the closeness of nature that I feel in the trees, the water and the winds prevailing from the north serve to remind me that these elements will survive long after I have departed this world. I reflect daily on how much the God and the Goddess are around me, in whatever omniscient form. I dedicate my personal altar to both the feminine aspect, represented in the guise of Isis and the Morrigan, and the masculine as Cernunnos – all are forces of nature in the broadest sense of the word.

In time, as we become even more eco-friendly and more environmentally aware, we will recognize the need to secure the future of our species on this unique and beautiful planet. To date, no inhabited worlds have been found in our or any other solar system. Do we not realize how privileged we really are? Much of the damage we have done during the last century is being realized now in terms of global warming as we continue to deplete the world's resources. I firmly believe that in the end we may, in fact, come full circle and revert back to being more in tune with the Earth, listening to Mother Nature and what "she" has to say. If we do not, we will have only ourselves to blame.

I believe that as modern-day witches we should not be judged by our ability to remember old spells or outdated rituals, nor should we be required to believe exactly the same things as the next witch or Wiccan. We have no firm set of rules, no book akin to the Bible or the Koran that we are required to follow doggedly and unquestionably. In fact, we should welcome new ideas, for this is an ever-changing and evolving religion, and one which must, for some people, always remain a part of their "secret world".

Blessed Be

Morianna Ravenswood
High Priestess of the Coven of All Hallows Haven

ΙΝΤRΟDVCΤΙΟΝ

Something Witchy This Way Comes

*"When dormant senses come wide awake,
male or female, a witch they make."*

 have always been under the spell of witchcraft. Since climbing to the pinnacle of mist-clad Pendle Hill, haunt of the Pendle Witches, aged just eight, and wandering among the ruined metropolis of Olympia in Greece, where great gods and goddesses once commanded vast kingdoms, I have always felt an affinity to the hidden worlds around us. As a young child I remember being drawn to a small picture of a faun on the spine of a book; it somehow spoke to me in a deep, subconscious way, and although I did not understand it at the time, it was the horned one calling me.

I was brought up in a Christian family, where good values, fairness and truth were paramount. But for me there was something missing, a gaping chasm that could not be filled by biblical fantasy and stories of Christ. As I grew up in rural Oxfordshire, where rolling hills and lush woodlands surrounded our home, I felt a kinship with nature and a "draw" to the wild places where field meets fell. Visits to the nearby Rollright Stones and the rugged coastline of Cornwall made my soul dance. It was in these places of ancient power that the spirits of the trees, sea and sky welcomed me. I was at home.

When I was 16 years old I met a witch. She was a wonderful influence on my life and showed me how, through learning, I could connect with the true force of nature around us.

With stones and plants she showed me how the wise ones made magick. She told tales of the Mother Goddess, spirit of the Earth; and the Horned God, her consort, lover and child, who together made all things; and she told me of the Green Man, the ever present force of life in the Green. The idea of Mother Nature as the Goddess and the sun as the Horned God creating the world appealed to me. It was a power I could see in mountains, touch in leaves, feel in cold wind and smell in freshly cut grass. It was accessible and devoid of dogmatic rules and structures. It was then that I realized I was Pagan through and through.

Witchcraft is a frightening word. It conjures up images of cackling hags soaring through a stormy sky to meet with Lucifer and mix poisonous brews at a secret Sabbat. These images are far from the truth. With the onslaught of Christianity, followers of the Old Ways and the old Pagan gods were frowned upon – or worse, feared. Over time, the Church demonized the Horned God as "Satan"; the Goddess, being female, was largely forgotten and the "wicce" (Anglo Saxon for "wise"), who were the herbalists, healers and Cunning People, were despised by the new priests. Witchcraft was no longer just an act against God, but also against the Crown. With the coming of "The Burning Times", when witches were burned alive or hung for practising The Craft, witches were forced into hiding, disappearing in all but the most rural places where the 17th-century witch-finders would not tread.

But witchcraft survived. Passed down from mother to daughter, father to son, the Cunning ways of magickal folk continued. In 1951 the Witchcraft Act of 1735 was repealed and witches came out of the broom closet. A resurgence followed, with the revival of the Old Ways and the development of new "traditions" of earlier magickal belief. With the diversity of worldwide culture and mass communications, it became apparent that The Craft had survived not only in England, but further afield. Stregherians, followers of Italian witchcraft, met with Traditional Witches of England who followed the ways of country magick, who in turn met with the contemporary revivalists in the shape of Gardnerians and Alexandrians, themselves followers of new "traditions" that had developed in the British Isles. Dianic witches, worshippers of the Roman goddess Diana, mixed with followers of the Celtic or Faery traditions. Although diverse, witchcraft was alive and well.

Witchcraft is a form of Paganism, a polytheistic religion that encompasses a variety of beliefs in the divine, manifesting as the Goddess and Horned God. It is one of many Pagan belief systems, which include Druidry, Shamanism, Odinism and Heathenism. There are currently more than 100,000 Pagans in the United Kingdom and more than 10,000 witches.

Why are people drawn to witchcraft? Is it for the elaborate theatrics of ritual, the fascination with magickal power or the closeness with nature? It is probably all of these things and more. Witchcraft is an imprecise term that encompasses so many things and has no true dogma, so it can be whatever the witch wants it to be. The modern revivalist laws of the witch are the Witches' Creed, "An harm ye none, do as thou will", and the Threefold Law, which states that what you give out will return to you three times. With this Law in mind contemporary witches rarely, if ever, use magick to harm.

What is the difference between witchcraft and Wicca? Witchcraft in its true sense means British Traditional Witchcraft, and relates to forms of magick practised by Cunning Men and Women in centuries past; it is devoid of ceremonial ritual and elaborate garb. In comparison, "Wicca" is a term primarily derived from 20th-century witchcraft revivalist Gerald Gardner, who was responsible for the contemporary popularity of The Craft.

This book is a general guide to the secret world of witchcraft, Wicca and everything in between. Rather than your typical book of spells, rituals or history, this is an overview of the witching world. Imagine it, if you will, as a cauldron filled with different ingredients that together make something, yet singly nothing. I have assumed that the reader believes, or at least has the potential to believe, in magick, which you will notice I spell with a "k" at the end. This is not because I am trying to be deliberately arcane for the sake of it, but to make the distinction between the magic performed by a stage magician and the magick performed by a witch.

In a commercial world where spirituality sometimes takes second place to the hustle and bustle of everyday life, it is interesting to note where magick plays its part. Traces of the Old Ways survive in modern culture – touching sacred woods has become "touch wood" for luck; the upturned horseshoe representing the Horned God is hammered up for luck; turning money in our hands when the moon is full and "Friday the 13th" still makes us think twice. We read our astrological predictions in the newspaper and watch mediums contact the dead on television; these are all acts of witchcraft. Magick is all around us, seeping into our lives without us even noticing.

As I sat down to write this book, I asked the Green Man to guide me. He has faithfully sat upon my desk, grinning from the foliage, throughout my journey through the world of witches. Now I invite you to join me and the Green Man as I unlock *The Secret World of Witchcraft*, but not before a final word from the witches themselves:

"Flags, Flax, Fodder and Frig!" Translated, this means, "I wish you a roof over your head, clothes upon your back, a full belly and love". In short, it is a blessing, wishing you everything you need in life.

Jason Dexter Karl

www.jasondexterkarl.com

I

THE HISTORY OF WITCHCRAFT

IT IS IMPOSSIBLE TO GIVE A COMPREHENSIVE HISTORY OF
witchcraft in a single chapter. There are centuries of tales, tall and true;
hundreds of individuals who have played their role and deserve inclusion
and countless accounts of witch trials, each as valid as the next. Instead,
I have plucked a variety of noted and not-so-noted subjects from the
cauldron. There are many excellent works for the scholar or academic to
seek out, but for the inquisitive, this chapter is an introduction to some
of the famous people and episodes from history that have helped to
shape witchcraft as we know it today.

"Hanged and burned, tortures untold,
The witches history, will now unfold."

 n the King James Bible, Exodus, chapter 2, verse 18, it is written "Thou shalt not suffer a witch to live". This phrase is often quoted by Christians as a powerful condemnation of witchcraft from God. Although still widely accepted today, doubt has been cast on its validity, with the likelihood that the quote is in fact a misinterpretation of the original text, resulting in a fundamental change to the intended original meaning. The original text gave the word "chaspah", which in Hebrew meant "poisoner", but when it was translated into English the equivalent word also meant "witch", and thus the translation altered the meaning. What was originally written as "thou shalt not suffer a poisoner to live" was thus changed to the famed quote, above, often referenced today.

The practice of witchcraft, whether it be for the conjuration of spirits, divination or indeed to cause harm, has been illegal in England since the first *Witchcraft Act* was passed in 1401 at the instigation of Archbishop Thomas Arundel (1353–1414). The creation of the Act redefined the cultural acceptance of magick – in 1135, under King Henry I (1068–1135; reigned 1100–1135), it had not been a capital offence to practice witchcraft, but it *was* one to kill a faerie! Over the centuries a variety of amendments and new acts were passed in England until in 1951, the final Act was repealed, making it no longer against the law to practise witch-craft in England.

The 1401 Act was called *De Haeretico Comburendo*, and stated that all forms of sorcery, witch-craft and divination were forms of heresy, and therefore against the beliefs of the Church. It further stated that anyone practising these arts would be burned at the stake unless they renounced witchcraft. (This Act was created under ecclesiastical law, and therefore the practice of witchcraft was not considered a felony in common law terms.)

Those who were thought to be practising witchcraft were brought before an ecclesiastical tribunal, where their individual case would be heard. If found guilty in line with the Act, the accused would be sentenced to death. In an attempt to avoid actual bloodshed, witches were burned alive at the stake, which was more acceptable to the Church.

In 1541 penalties for practising witchcraft in England were dramatically increased. A new Act proclaimed, "It shall be a felony to practise, or cause to be practised conjuration, witchcraft, enchantment or sorcery to get money, or to consume any person in his body, members or Goods; or to provoke any person to unlawful love; or for the despite of Christ, or lucre of money, to pull down any cross, or to declare where goods stolen be". Like the earlier Act of 1401, anyone found guilty would be punished by sentence of death.

During his reign, Henry VIII (1491–1547; reigned 1509–1547) added a statute proclaiming that anyone found "invoking or conjuring evil spirits" would be sentenced to the same fate by fire, but his son, Edward VI (1537–1553; reigned 1547–1553), repealed his father's statute, leaving the earlier Act of 1541 in place.

In 1563, during the reign of Elizabeth I (1533–1603; reigned 1558–1603), the most legendary witchcraft Act was introduced. This Act stated that anyone who should "use, practise or exer-cise any Witchcraft, Enchantment, Charm or Sorcery, whereby any person shall happen to be killed or destroyed", was guilty of felony without benefit of clergy and was to be put to death. This signalled a radical change in trial venues, which now took place in common law courts rather than in the ecclesiastical courts. When Elizabeth's successor, James I (1566–1625; reigned 1603–1625), took the throne he amended the Act, adding that anyone who invoked evil spir-its or communed with magickal familiars would be punished by death without the benefit of clergy. (James was a witch-fearing king largely due to the fact that he had witnessed a trial in 1590 in which a group of witches were found guilty of attempting to bewitch a vessel upon which he was travelling.)

The Acts passed by Elizabeth and James changed forever the way in which witches were tried. Gone were the religious tribunals under which so many were burned at the stake, and in their place came a common-law court that provided the accused with the same rights as any other law breaker. Out, too, were the public witch-burnings; the hangman's noose now awaited those who were convicted.

By making witchcraft a felony in the law courts, those who were convicted found that ownership of their land and goods was forfeited by default to the monarchy. With a new financial motivation for finding witches to convict, local officials began witch hunts in earnest. One such man was Matthew Hopkins, who carved himself an extremely financially rewarding career as England's notorious Witch-finder General.

During the reign of King George II (1683–1760; reigned 1727–1760), the *Witchcraft Act* of 1735 indicated a change in attitude towards so-called witches. Those found guilty of witchcraft were no longer hanged; instead they were fined and imprisoned as con artists. The belief in witchcraft that had once struck fear in the nation was waning. The criminal offence was no longer to "conjure evil spirits", but rather to "pretend to conjure evil spirits". The tone had thus changed from "actual" to "pretend" conjurations.

In 1944 Helen Duncan, the well-known medium, spent nine months under lock and key after she was found guilty under the *Witchcraft Act*, and later that year Jane Yorke was the last person to be convicted. After centuries of fear, witchcraft was finally decriminalized in 1951 when the last *Witchcraft Act* was repealed. (It was still in force in the Republic of Ireland until 1983, however, when most old English laws were repealed.)

It is no longer against the law to practise witchcraft in England – nor, it seems, was it ever against the laws of the Bible, if the misinterpretation theory is to be believed.

THE WITCHES OF PENDLE

One bright, sunny morning in spring 1612, Alizon Device was making her way to the village of Trawden to beg for spare change. She happened upon a handsome traveller on the road near Colne, on the edge of the Forest of Pendle. The traveller told her that he came from Halifax, that his name was John Law and that he was a peddler by trade.

Alizon was plain and rather scruffy in appearance. When she enquired of the traveller if he might have a pin with which to tie up her hair, he cast her aside and continued walking without so much as a nod of his head. Scorned by the merchant and enraged by his dismissal of her, Alizon screamed a curse upon him. At once he was struck down, falling to the ground as paralysis wrenched through his body while the frightening image of a black dog with eyes of fire filled his mind. Lying in a crippled heap on the dirt track he fell into a deep trancelike state, but he was not dead.

Grief-stricken, Alizon ran from the scene back to her home at Malkin Tower, near Lower Well Head Farm, where she lived with her family. She was filled with remorse for what she had done. The traveller was found and taken to a nearby tavern where, after regaining consciousness, his son Abraham Law was summoned to tend him. Upon being questioned he remembered meeting a beggar woman on the dirt track and that she had cast a spell on him, summoning a hell hound to attack him. After he described the woman, it was clear to the innkeeper that he was describing Alizon Device, granddaughter of 'Old Mother Demdike' – a blind old crone who was hated and feared throughout the Pendle district because she practised witchcraft.

Alizon was brought to John's bedside and asked to explain what had happened. Filled with fear (for she was a simple girl), she admitted to calling a magickal curse upon him that she had been taught by her grandmother Demdike. She pleaded for forgiveness and John obliged her, but his son had already informed the authorities and accompanied Alizon to Read Hall where, on 30 March, she stood before Magistrate Roger Nowell. She was to answer to the charge of practising witchcraft with the intent to kill, an offence punishable by death since 1604.

Accompanied by her mother Elizabeth, herself a deformed widower spurned by society, and her brother, James Alizon admitted under examination that she had used witchcraft to strike John Law down, and that an evil familiar in the shape of a black dog had helped her do it. When asked how she had learned the arts of the Devil, she answered that her grandmother, Demdike (whose real name was Elizabeth Southern), had tutored her in the ways of witchery. Her naivety was to be the downfall of her family, for she also stated that her mother and brother were versed in the arts of magick as well. Needing no more evidence, Nowell set about examining the rest of the Device family and, one by one, they sealed their own fate.

Nowell continued his investigations of witchcraft in Pendle at Ashlar House, in Fence. On 2 April, under intense interrogation, Demdike confessed that she had practised witchcraft, and that she had sent her familiar, named "Tibb", to pester a local miller's daughter after he had refused them scraps of food. She claimed that Tibb had first appeared to her in Newchurch in Pendle, where it took the form of a young boy that transfigured into the shape of a dog, which suckled blood from her shrivelling body. (Elizabeth and James were also questioned by Nowell, but he did not detain them.) Thus far there had been no threats of torture, and Demdike's confessions were willingly given, perhaps in an effort to gain favour with the magistrate. But if this was the case, it was a plan that would backfire in the most spectacular fashion.

It was Demdike who first named "Chattox" as another local "witch". Anne Whittle, known locally as "Chattox" (after her maiden name "Chadwick") had once been a friend of Demdike's, but the families had fallen out with each other years earlier and they were now vehement enemies. Chattox's family, who lived in a dirty hovel in Greenhead, were summoned by Nowell. The Chattox family was as

A PERFECT RECORD

The story of witchcraft in Pendle is unique in that a perfect record of the events was recorded at the time by Thomas Potts in his book, *The Wunderfull Discoverie of Witches in the Countie of Lancaster*. This text, which is still in print, is the most authoritative source of facts that we have surrounding the incidents of 1612.

disliked locally as were the Devices, and as they entered the furore the two opposing families began to destroy each other with accusation and counter-accusation. Nowell examined Chattox and her daughter, Anne Redfearn, and both willingly admitted to practising witchcraft, claiming that it was Demdike who had led them into "devilment". In an attempt to incriminate Demdike further, Chattox stated that she had been initiated into witchcraft by Demdike 14 years earlier. She also confessed that, like her arch enemy, she had a magickal pet that had told her its name was "Fancie".

Nowell then detained Demdike, Chattox and her daughter, Anne Redfearn. Together with Alizon Device, who had been detained earlier, they were sent to Lancaster Gaol to await trial on 4 April, each charged with murder by witchery.

The following week, on Good Friday, friends of the accused gathered at Malkin Tower to try and find a way of helping the accused and their families. This secret meeting was reported to Nowell as a "witches' Sabbat", and it was claimed that a brood of cohorts were planning to rescue those that had been imprisoned in Lancaster. Upon investigation, magickal charms, including clay poppets, were discovered at the Tower, and Nowell instigated a further period of questioning in order to find out exactly what had taken place at the meeting.

On 27 April, Magistrate Nicholas Bannister joined Nowell in questioning Elizabeth and James Device, who had been interrogated earlier, and Jennet Device, sister of Alizon. It was nine-year-old Jennet that confirmed to the magistrates that during the meeting plans were made to break into the jail, do away with the jailer and free the accused. They were also asked to name all those who were present at the meeting at Malkin Tower, and thus another seven people were branded suspected "witches", including Alice Nutter of Roughlee Hall (a respected pillar of the community), James and Jane Bulcock, Margaret Pearson, Katherine Hewitt, Isobel Robey and Jennet Preston. They were all sent to Lancaster Gaol to await trial, except Jennet Preston of Gisburn, who was sent to York to await her trial for the alleged murder by witchcraft of Thomas Lister. On 29 July, after being found guilty, Jennet was executed by hanging.

The Official Trial

The Assize court judges visited Lancaster twice yearly, and the official trial of the Pendle witches began on Tuesday 18 August 1612. Sir Edward Bromley presided over the proceedings, with Roger Nowell continuing his role as prosecutor for the court. Chattox was first in front of the judges; she was accused of causing the death of Robert Nutter by magickal forces. Although she denied the charge, she was found guilty as she had previously confessed to it in the presence of Roger Nowell. Second to face the Assize court was Elizabeth Device, who was charged with three counts of murder. Along with James Device she was found guilty partly on the evidence given by her own daughter, Jennet. At the end of day one, three people had been found guilty of murder by witchcraft and were sentenced to death.

On Wednesday 19 August, Anne Redfearn, who had been acquitted of her first charges the previous afternoon, faced the court on a second charge of witchcraft; this time for the murder of Christopher Nutter 18 years previously. She was found guilty. Alice Nutter was found guilty of killing Henry Mitton because he had refused to give Demdike a penny when she had been begging. Margaret Pearson was accused of bewitching the horse of a neighbour and causing its death. She too was found guilty. Katherine Hewitt was convicted for the murder of Ann Foulds, and Jane and James Bulcock, mother and son, were found guilty of causing madness. All were sentenced to death by hanging.

The judge said "You shall go hence to the castle from whence you came; from there you shall be carried to the place of execution for this county, where you shall be hanged until you are dead, and may God have mercy upon your souls." On Thursday 20 August cheers rang out around Lancaster as the ten witches were executed on Gallows Hill. Demdike was the only one to escape the hangman's rope after she perished in the dungeon beneath the Well Tower at Lancaster Castle, her age and the terrible conditions in which she was kept finally killing her.

Modern scholars and experts analyzing the accounts are divided in their opinions as to why the trials were unfairly biased in favour of finding "witches", and against finding the "truth". It has been suggested that the "witches" were nothing more than innocent dupes, sacrificed by ambitious judges to find favour with the monarch, James I, a known witch-hater. (The king had written a huge treatise on demonology, sorcery and witchcraft; hundreds of women in Scotland were put to death as witches as a result of this document.)

Malkin Tower was demolished shortly after the witch trials, but remnants are known to have survived until as late as 1900. Sadly, nothing of the building can be seen today. The area has a thriving Pagan and witchcraft community, however, and on Halloween scores of enthusiasts, historians and modern-day witches gather around the hill to remember those that were hung in the name of witchcraft. An evocative landscape, it is easy to get swept up in the magickal melancholy of the place where the "Pendle witches" once lived.

THE WITCH–FINDER GENERAL

Possibly the most famous witch-hunter of all time, Matthew Hopkins, self-styled "Witch-finder General", left a blood-soaked legacy throughout East Anglia between 1645 and 1646. Hopkins was a cruel opportunist who persecuted the old, the unpopular and the naive and had them executed as "witches", profiteering as they were killed by a paranoid society.

This was a time when witch hysteria was at its height in England. Fear of the Devil and of those who were perceived to be in league with him was rife. Matthew, son of James Hopkins, vicar of Great Wenham in Suffolk, was born around 1619. He was the sixth child of a deeply orthodox, well-heeled family that owned land throughout Norfolk, Suffolk and Essex, most notably around Ipswich and Framlingham. He was at an impressionable age when his father died in 1634 and, following a religious upbringing, the seeds of his path to fame as England's most notorious witch-hunter were sown.

His early education is somewhat of a mystery, although it has been suggested that he travelled to the continent early in his life – including to Holland, his family having connections with the maritime industry. Upon his return, it is believed that he became involved with the legal side of the shipping industry. His knowledge of English law became vast, setting him in good stead for his later career.

As a young man Hopkins lived in the village of Mistley, in Essex, where he resided in an inn that stood on the site of the current Mistley Thorn Hotel. It was from this building that he undertook his crusade against witches.

Hopkins's Crusade

It was one night in March 1645 that Hopkins allegedly overheard the activities of a witches' Sabbat taking place in the dead of night at nearby Manningtree. The notion of becoming a witch-hunter had already occurred to him, but this experience (which may in fact have been fabricated) gave him the impetus to instigate his new career. He had developed an extensive knowledge of the intricacies of the *Witchcraft Act* after having studied it at length, and saw an opportunity to make money by exploiting the law for his own gain.

His first victim was Elizabeth Clarke, a one-legged crone whose mother had been executed as a witch – a prime candidate for exploitation. After publicly accusing her of practising witch-craft, claiming that he had heard her cavorting with imps at the Sabbat, she was thrown in jail, now under suspicion.

Accompanied by John Stearne, his sadistic assistant, the pair set about extracting a confession from Clarke, but none was forthcoming. Torture was illegal in England at the time, but Hopkins devised subtle "methods of interrogation" that might otherwise have been classed as torture had they not been viewed as "necessary tests" for witchery. With his knowledge of the law, he managed to stay within its confines while still inflicting torture in what was to become a killing spree.

They stripped the poor woman naked and commenced "witch pricking" her with a dagger-like bodkin to ascertain whether or not she had the "mark of the Devil" upon her body. If there were any patch of skin where the pricker drew no blood, this was taken as evidence that she was under protection from Satan. Next she was examined and found to have three teats with which, according to Hopkins, she had suckled her imps. She was then deprived of sleep, food and drink for three days and nights until, weakened and psychologically broken, she confessed to being a witch and named five other women as being her accomplices – Anne Leech, Helen Clarke, Elizabeth Gooding and Anne and Rebecca West.

In her confession it is claimed she had five familiars. These were probably nothing more than household pets, but they were given elaborate names and elevated to satanic status. They were a white kitten named Holt, a black rabbit called Sack and Sugar, a polecat named Newes, a spaniel called Jarmara and a greyhound with an oxlike head named Vinegar Tom.

As the hysteria grew, Hopkins stirred more suspicion, turning hearsay and gossip into formal accusations of witchcraft. With more and more names added to the list of "witches" he was forced to add to his twisted staff, and hired Edward Parsley, Frances Mills and Mary Phillips, whose job it was to find "witches' marks". John Stearne was elevated to Hopkins's second in command, and together they interviewed over 100 witnesses in their attempt to out the "witches". 32 women confessed under Hopkins's tortuous regime of interrogation. They were sent to Chelmsford, where their trials began on 29 July 1645. The Earl of Warwick, Robert Rich, presided over the trials, and 29 of the 32 women were convicted and sentenced to death under the *Witchcraft Act*. Ten were hung at Chelmsford, while the others were made a public spectacle in their hamlets, fuelling further the already prevalent witchcraft paranoia.

The cases received wide publicity, and soon requests for Hopkins's services were coming in from further afield. He proclaimed himself "Witch-finder General", and began charging high fees to rid villages of witches. Of course, his glorified status of "saviour" was a far cry from the grim reality: that he was nothing more than an evil opportunist. Yet, together with his team of rogues, he allegedly received a special commission from Parliament to "rid the country of witches", and his reputation grew to new heights.

As his success spread, a trail of dead bodies lay in its wake. Soon Hopkins, high on his power trip and heavy with his ill-gotten gold, instigated a new form of interrogation: "witch swimming". This had been in use in some parts of the country since 1612, and had become more widespread after King James I mentioned it as a form of witch-testing in his book on the subject of demonology. Victims of this ordeal were stripped and bound. After being bent double, their thumbs were tied to their big toes before they were flung into a local river or pond and held under water three times. The ideology behind this archaic test was that if the accused was indeed a witch, she would float, the water having rejected her; while if she did not float she was pronounced innocent (in many cases the women died while undergoing the test).

Another noted victim selected by Hopkins was John Lowes, the 70-year-old minister of Brandeston. An outspoken and unpopular character, he was easily exploitable, and was promptly accused and interrogated. Lowes initially denied the charges levied against him, but after being subjected to Hopkins's vile trials of torture he finally gave in, confessing that he had covenanted with the Devil, bewitched cattle and caused a ship to sink killing 14 people. He later retracted his confession during his trial, but was found guilty and taken to the scaffold on 27 August 1645.

This second high-profile sensation allowed Hopkins to continue his profitable rampage throughout East Anglia, but amid his self-glorification he made a fundamental mistake. As part of his plan to rid England of witchcraft Hopkins claimed to be in possession of a secret grimoire, *The Devil's List*, in which the names of all the witches in the land were written. How he came to have this book was not initially questioned, but this claim came to be his downfall.

The Demise of the Witch-finder General

Hopkins's activities were eventually noticed by those in high places, and questions started being asked as to whether he really had been commissioned by Parliament. With over 200 "witches" awaiting trial in various places, Hopkins was ordered to cease "witch swimming" and a new court was formed with the specific task of tackling the backlog of those accused. The court consisted of Edward Calamy and Samuel Fairclough, both local clergymen, Sergeant John Godbolt and two local justices. East Anglia was, of course, in the grip of witchcraft hysteria, and in quick succession the "witches were dispatched to the hangman's noose". Rather than investigate Hopkins's claims in a more objective fashion, the new court merely sped up the convictions.

Hopkins had in the meantime cast his net further afield, and in July he condemned 20 witches in Norfolk. In September and December the citizens in Yarmouth received his attentions, while Kings Lynn, Ipswich, Aldeburgh and Stowmarket were also on his tour of terror. His reputation preceded him, and word of his nefarious interrogation techniques had travelled far and wide.

It was John Gaule who finally spoke out against Matthew Hopkins. Gaule was the vicar of Great Stoughton, and, upon hearing that Hopkins had plans to visit the village, he bravely preached against him to his flock. Gaule also expressed his abhorrence for Hopkins's unfair trials of the weak in a pamphlet called "Select Cases of Conscience Touching Witches and Witchcraft", which he wrote in 1646. In it he suggested that Hopkins might be a witch himself. Hopkins decided not to invade the village, and shrewdly steered clear of Gaule. By the end of that year, Hopkins's credibility had diminished, and with requests for his services at an end he disbanded his team and returned to Manningtree.

It was then that fate finally caught up with Matthew Hopkins. One day while passing through Suffolk he was set upon by enraged villagers, who had previously suffered at his cruel hand. After accusing him of witchcraft and suggesting that his grimoire had been handed to him by the Devil, with whom he was in league, Hopkins was subjected to his own ordeal of "witch swimming". Some accounts claim that his life ended at the hands of those angry villagers, while others say that he survived and was hanged following a trial (although there are no records of such). Many historians believe it is more likely that he died of consumption.

The first evidence of Hopkins's burial was published over 200 years after his death in the *Notes & Queries* first series, volume 10, published 7 October 1854; this publication states that he was buried at Mistley on 12 August 1647. Clearly, Hopkins was an evil man who exploited society for his own ends; he was personally responsible for condemning 230 witches in his career as a witch-hunter.

Interestingly, even ardent and noted witch-haters disliked Hopkins. Montague Summers (1880–1948), an eminent Catholic priest, accomplished scholar and devout condemner of witches described Hopkins thus: "an orthodox Puritan of narrowest views, which were certainly adopted for convenience rather than from conviction, he was energetic enough so far as his own pockets were concerned, and his crusade up and down the eastern counties, which created something like a reign of terror at the time, has caused his name to stink in the nostrils of all decent persons ever since".

THE WITCH'S GARRETT

Charles Paget Wade (1883–1956), an architect originally from Suffolk who inherited a family fortune thanks to his father's West Indian sugar estates, was an archetypal English eccentric. He devoted his life to collecting antiques – amassing over 22,000 examples – and had a deep interest in witchcraft and ritual magick. Wade kept his collection at his former home Snowshill Manor, a Cotswold mansion in Gloucestershire. In 1951 he gave the Manor, along with his collection, to the National Trust.

Following Wade's death, the National Trust called in Cecil Williamson (1909–1999), an "elder stateman of The Craft". Although Wade had actually lived in the small Priest's House located across a courtyard from the Manor, it was obvious to Williamson that Wade had spent many nights practising witchcraft in a tiny attic space that is now known as "The Witch's Garrett". Williamson told *Talking Stick* magazine that Wade's attic space was the most sensational magician's den he had ever seen. The feature states that the room was only discovered after a National Trust architect realized that there was a void in the attic, and soon thereafter a secret chamber was discovered, accessible only by a secret panel. After the Trust's staff had opened the chamber they quickly shut it again, finding it to be filled with magickal paraphernalia and arcane symbols. It was then that they called in Williamson (who was then based in Bourton-on-the-Water, which was not far away) and asked him to come and investigate the secret room. When he arrived there were 26 people eagerly awaiting his opinion on what the chamber might have been used for. No one

WADE'S COLLECTION

The Museum of Witchcraft (*see page 38*) in Boscastle, Cornwall, shows some of the peculiar artefacts acquired by Cecil Williamson from the Witch's Garrett. These include the "Wondrous Candle", which, according to Wade's notes, renders the bearer invisible to others, along with an ornate magician's chest that was used to hold Wade's ritual regalia.

had entered the chamber, and it was reported that mystical circles adorned the floor, skeletal remains had been hung from the rafters and a fetid smell hung heavily in the air.

Williamson explains what happened next: "I popped through the panelling into the room and asked if anyone wanted to come in – nobody did. Once inside, it was quite clear that somebody, male or female, had been doing something in there because a very nice chair had been thrown over and a bottle had been smashed on the floor. There were the skeletons of two rats and a lot of herbs, which had all rotted. There were two other bottles with two sets of human liquid in them, and there was a whole lot of other clutter. The floor was beautifully polished and decorated with a circle of Key of Solomon symbols, and there were some on the wall. Over on the left-hand side of the wall were some very definitely Caribbean symbols. So I came down and told them it was a magician's den and that somebody had been scared and had left in a hurry. They asked what could I do? I said I would strongly advise them to keep their mouths shut and they went into a huddle and then came back and asked if I would be prepared to clear the room!"

"So I thought, 'goody gumdrops', something for nothing; no questions asked, so I said yes I would be there at 9am the following morning. By around 9 o'clock the next night the room was absolutely cleared, though I never did put any of the stuff on show."

I have seen the original notes and hand drawings of the contents of the Witch's Garrett. They are indeed fascinating, and include details on mandrakes, a wrought iron "Fire Devil", a dried porcupine fish and two machines for creating electricity by friction. One of the most interesting artefacts is "The Wondrous Candle". According to Wade's notes, "you must have a big candle composed of human tallow and it must be fixed into a forked piece of hazel wood. If this candle, when lighted in a subterranean place, sparkles brightly with a good deal of noise, it is a sign that there is treasure in that place. The nearer you approach the treasure, the more the candle will sparkle, yet it will go out when you are quite close. Thus one must have a supply of candles so as not to be left in the dark."

Years later, the Museum of Witchcraft in its current home does show some of the peculiar artefacts acquired by Cecil Williamson from the Witches Garrett; they include the aforementioned Wondrous Candle, two monkey skulls, a wooden mortar and a 17th century ornate oak Magician's Chest which was used to hold the ritual regalia of Charles Wade. Unfortunately this was badly damaged in the devastating floods which hit the building in 2004, but the carvings of four female figures, green men and the horned god have survived and can be seen by visitors today.

Strangely, no mention is made of Wade's occult interests, the Witch's Garrett or what was discovered behind the panelling in The National Trust's descriptions of Wade's Manor House and his collections. The Trust must have taken Williamson's advice in 1951 and decided to "keep their mouths shut"!

THE WHITE WITCH OF HELSTON

Thomasine Blight (1798–1856), more commonly known as Tamsin Blight, was a Cornish Pellar who is well documented in Cornish magickal literature. Born in 1798, she was descended from a magickal family. Though much of her early life is a mystery, she is thought to have begun practising pellarcraft (the ways of Cornish Cunning Folk) around 1830.

Her reputation as a magick-maker quickly grew, and people travelled long distances to visit her in order to obtain an amulet or charm to cure sickness or defend against the "evil eye". According to some accounts, some seekers travelled from places as far away as the Scilly Isles, St Ives and even Swansea.

In 1835 Blight married a widower named James Thomas, also a Pellar. Together the pair made a formidable magickal double act, whose reputation grew rapidly throughout Cornwall. Tamsin and James then moved to Helston, where they continued to practise their magickal activities with great success – until James's latent homosexuality brought a raft of negative publicity upon the pair.

Widely reported in the pages of the *West Briton*, a newspaper of the time, and re-published in several other volumes since, James reputedly used his reputation as a master of magick to seduce a sea captain and a tradesman, satisfying his carnal desires by exploiting young men who knew no better. Other cases of indecent suggestion also came to light, and soon Tamsin parted from her husband with her reputation severely dented.

The pair remained estranged for the rest of their lives. James fled from the glare of public scrutiny, and little is known of his later life; his obituary was published on 26 February 1874. Tamsin continued her Pellarcraft as best she could after moving to the village of Breage. As testament to her residency, the lane where she once lived with her daughter is known as "Pellar Row". After suffering increasing ill health in her later years, but nevertheless continuing to see clients even while bed-bound, she died aged 58 on 6 October 1856.

SALEM – A TOWN POSSESSED

It was in early January 1692 that the tragic tale of the Salem witch hunts began. Over the coming months, 141 people would be accused of practising witchcraft, and 20 would subsequently lose their lives as panic and fear struck the small American town of Salem, in Massachusetts. The lives of those that survived the ordeal would be changed forever and a terrible lesson would be learned.

It began four years earlier, in 1688, when town elder John Putnam had persuaded Samuel Parris to move his family from Barbados to Salem in order to take up the role of village minister. Together with his wife, Elizabeth, his daughter Betty, his niece Abigail and a slave named Tituba, an Arawak Indian who had been bought by the family, Samuel had accepted the yearly salary of £60 in exchange for his services.

Preferring to sit and tell stories of her life in the West Indies rather than carry out her household chores, Tituba created a name for herself as a storyteller in the village. It wasn't long before the parsonage was attracting the likes of 12-year-old Ann Putnam, 17-year-olds Mary Walcott and Elizabeth Hubbard, 18-year-olds Elizabeth Booth and Susannah Sheldon and 20-year-olds Mary Warren and Sarah Churchill. Huddled around the fireplace, Tituba would secretly regale the girls with tales of voodoo and magick from her native home, and taught them how to divine the future using eggs. The girls would re-enact some of the rituals she described, uttering arcane incantations and attempting to enter into trances. On occasion they were joined by a servant from the Putnam household named Mercy Lewis.

The Frenzy Begins

The turning point of village life in Salem occurred on a dark night in 1692, when seven-year-old Betty Parris and her cousin, Abigail Williams, were struck down by an unknown illness. After one of them had "seen" the shape of a coffin in Tituba's divination ritual, they began writhing around on the floor and barking like dogs. Despite prayers being said for them, the convulsions and apparent pains continued. They were attended by Dr William Griggs who, after examining the girls, and without any other obvious explanation, suggested that the cause of their ailment might have something to do with witchcraft. It was the timing of this fateful attack of alleged illness – which in contemporary terms could be explained as a possible epileptic fit or hysteria – that was to instigate a chain of events that resulted in the needless killing of 24 so-called "witches".

A recently published book, *Memorable Providences Relating to Witchcrafts and Possessions*, penned by Puritan minister Cotton Mather in 1689, had in the meantime been receiving much public acclaim across America. Its contents described a case of the suspected bewitchment of another local family named "Godwin" some years earlier. The symptoms described in Mather's text seemed to be replicated in Betty Parris's and Abigail Williams's behaviour, and thus a comparison was made between the two cases.

Small-town mentality ensured that talk of witchcraft spread like wildfire, and when three further cases of unexplained illness were confirmed, fears that the Devil had infiltrated the seaside town took root. The witchcraft epidemic had begun, and now 17-year-olds Mary Walcott and Mercy Lewis and 12-year-old Ann Putnam appeared to be in its dangerous clutches.

Soon Ann Putnam, Elizabeth Hubbard, Mary Walcott, Mary Warren and Mercy Lewis were all struck down with the same afflictions. The one-time friends had now become a "gang of juvenile delinquents" according to one historian. The girls were exhibiting a variety of grotesque postures and unnatural behaviour, and complained of being bitten and pinched by unseen spirits. By now, efforts to find the cause of the 'devilment' in Salem had become an obsession – the witch, it was agreed, must be found and stopped.

Suspicion and Scapegoats

Suspicion fell almost by default on to Tituba's head. When she followed advice from neighbour Mary Sibley, who told her that she should mix a "witch cake" of rye and urine to uncover the witches, the family dog ingested the "witch cake" by mistake. With the "countercharm" working, the afflicted girls were now able to identify the witches. They pointed at Tituba, villager Sarah Good and the elderly Sarah Osborne. All three were in a weak position in the eyes of 17th-century society – Tituba was a mere slave, Sarah Good was a homeless beggar and Sarah Osborne had not attended church for a year, a clear indication that she had turned from God.

On 29 February the first arrests were made. Tituba, Sarah Good and the bedridden Sarah Osborne were placed under lock and key by county magistrates John Hathorne and Jonathan Corwin. Their trials were set for 1 March.

On the morning of the "witches'" examinations, news of the trial had travelled far and hundreds turned up to watch as they were questioned. In fact, there were so many people that the trial had to be moved from a local inn to the nearby meeting house. Betty, Abigail and the other accusers displayed the same disturbing behaviour that had sown the seed of suspected devilment months earlier. They described how they had been visited by the witches in spectral form, causing their contortions and pains.

Although it is apparent that the magistrates clearly thought that the women were guilty from the nature of their questioning, this may well have been the end of the saga had it not been for Tituba. In fear of being used as a potential scapegoat, Tituba decided to confess that she was indeed a witch, and claimed that she had been visited by a tall man in black from Boston who she believed was Satan himself. She further claimed that he had made her sign his book, and had forced her to make a pact to carry out his work, adding that the names of other women from Salem were already marked on the page. This admission by Tituba silenced those that up to now had been sceptical of claims of witchcraft in Salem, and all but guaranteed that a full-scale witch-hunt to rid the town of evil would begin without delay. Tituba returned to jail, but she was not hung.

Over the next three months, more women were accused of being in league with the Devil: Mary Eastey, Rebecca Nurse and Martha Corey were each formally accused by the afflicted girls. Goodwife Cloyce was also named by Ann Putnam, who claimed that she had seen her spirit form sitting upon a beam suckling a yellow bird during a church service.

All four women, some of whom were respected members of the community, were thrown in jail to await trial. They were soon joined by Dorcas Good, daughter of Sarah Good who, at the age of four, was the first child to be accused of witchcraft. Three of the afflicted accusers had claimed that the spirit of Dorcas had visited them and that it had bitten them.

By now it was clear that the witches must have a ringleader, a kind of soldier of Satan. The man accused of playing this role was ex-minister George Burroughs. Burroughs had moved from Salem to Maine, but was arrested in early May and brought back for trial. Identified as their leader, Burroughs was dubbed "The Black Minister" by several of the afflicted. The most vociferous evidence against him came from the mouth of Mercy Lewis. She described how he had "flown her to the top of a mountain and, indicating the surrounding lands, promised her the entire kingdom if only she would sign his book". She further testified that she had replied, "I would not writ if he had throwed me down on 100 pitchforks". Burroughs was convicted and hung, protesting his innocence to the last breath and screaming out the Lord's Prayer as the noose was tightened around his Puritan neck.

The "Witch" Trials

By the end of May the hysteria had gathered momentum and the authorities stepped in. Sir William Phipps, newly appointed governor of Massachusetts, established a special court of "oyer and terminer" to hear the rest of the cases. (The name derives from the medieval Anglo-French "oyer et terminer" meaning "to hear and to determine" and refers to courts who try cases of serious criminal offences.) The court consisted of five judges, including colleagues of Cotton Mather.

SALEM'S PAST

In the 18th century Salem village split from Salem town and was renamed "Danvers", but this new name cannot erase the troubled past that still haunts the area. There are many who even now make the pilgrimage to Salem out of sympathy for the "witches" who lost their lives. The names of those convicted and put to death were:

Bridget Bishop
George Burroughs
Martha Carrier
Martha Corey
Mary Eastey
Sarah Good
Elizabeth Howe
George Jacobs
Susannah Martin
Rebecca Nurse

Alice Parker
Mary Parker
John Proctor
Ann Pudeator
Wilmott Redd
Margaret Scott
Samuel Wardwell
Sarah Wildes
John Willard

May they rest in the Summerland in eternal peace.

With the jail filled to capacity, the court heard its first evidence on 2 June 1692. The judges carefully examined the accused. They had wanted someone who they could be relatively sure would receive a guilty verdict to take the stand first, and had chosen Bridget Bishop. A controversial member of the community, she had been married three times, ran drinking houses and had been previously accused of witchery.

As the case got underway a variety of peculiar evidence that, in modern terms, would be dismissed, was accepted at face value. "spectral evidence" – the testimony of the afflicted that the spirit of the accused had tormented them – was accepted. Also allowed was the "touch test", whereby the accused was requested to touch the afflicted to see if it would cause their symptoms to cease – proving that they must be a witch. Accepted too was the examination of the bodies of those accused in order to find "witches' marks", believed to be areas where the witch's familiar might suckle. In common terms, this meant that any large moles or birthmarks might be accepted as "evidence" of a union with Satan.

A farm worker stated that he had seen Bridget's spectre stealing food, and another, a villager by the name of Samuel Grey, announced that she had attacked him in his bed in the dead of night. Examination of her body found that she had marks of the Devil upon her. As the villagers gave testimony against her, the rope was being prepared for her departure into the next world.

After hearing her character assassination and "evidence" that a poppet stuck with pins had been found in her previous home, Bridget Bishop was found guilty of witchcraft and hanged at Gallows Hill on 10 June 1692.

Following her death, Nathaniel Saltonstall, one of the judges, resigned from the court, horrified at the conduct he had witnessed. An intelligent man, he had realized that the "evidence" used to convict Bishop was flawed, and that the admission of "spectral evidence", which had no precedent in other courts of law, was unfair.

The accusers now numbered more than 40. As the court heard each case, confessions, seen as the only way to escape hanging, came thick and fast. Deliverance Hobbs confessed that she was a witch, saying that she had pinched the afflicted under Satan's guidance and had flown to a field upon a pole to celebrate a witches' Sabbat.

As the hot summer sun shone down upon the courtroom, the "witches", who had allegedly brought darkness to the town, were slowly tried. Next in line was 70-year-old Rebecca Nurse. A pious and respected old lady, she escaped death at first after more than 30 townsfolk signed a petition stating that they had seen no evidence of her practising witchcraft. However, a long-standing family feud between the Topsfields – of which Nurse was a member – and the Putnams, to which Ann Putnam, one of the main accusers, belonged, ensured that Nurse's reprieve would be temporary. After the court delivered a verdict of "not guilty", Ann began writhing in agony on the courtroom floor and accused Rebecca Nurse of sending her demons upon her. In the light of this new evidence Nurse was questioned further, but because of her poor hearing was unable to answer to this new charge. She was soon convicted, found guilty of witchcraft and hanged on 19 July. Her body was secretly buried later by her children in an unmarked grave near to her home.

The witch craze was now at its height. Those who viewed the accusers with suspicion were themselves vulnerable of being named as "witches", but one brave soul did speak out. John Proctor, an opinionated innkeeper, let it be known that he did not believe the testimonies of the afflicted. He paid dearly for this opinion. Ann Putnam, Abigail Williams and a slave girl who was employed at a competing inn accused him and his wife, Elizabeth, of practising witchraft. Proctor was the first man in Salem to be tried as a witch. After being found guilty, he was dragged to Gallows Hill, where he was hung. His wife was spared the hangman's noose as she was pregnant at the time.

The madness that had swept through Salem was drawing to a close by early autumn 1692, when farmer Giles Corey, who had spent five months in jail along with his wife after they had been accused of witchery, was killed. He wasn't hung, but rather pressed under stones until his body collapsed from the weight, expunging his final breath. Seeing the futility of the trials and possessing a savvy knowledge of the law, Corey knew that if he refused a trial, and thus a possible conviction, his land would not be granted to the State, but rather to his two sons-in-law. (The penalty for refusing trial was *"peine forte et dure"*, or "death by pressing".) Defiant to the end, his final words, laced with tragic humour, are recorded as "put on more weight". Three days later, on 22 September 1692, Giles's wife, Martha, along with seven other "witches", were the last to be hung in Salem. The witch-hunt was finally over.

The End of Hysteria

For some time doubts about the "witch" accusations had been developing in the minds of Salem's educated elite. Minister John Hale had said, "It cannot be imagined that in a place of so much knowledge, so many in so small a compass of land should abominably leap into the Devil's lap at once". The publication of Increase Mathers's (father of Cotton) book, *Cases of Conscience Concerning Evil Spirits Personating Men*, asked further questions about the truth surrounding the witch craze. The book argued that "...it is better that 10 suspected witches should escape than one innocent person should be condemned". The author advised the court that speculative forms of testimony should be excluded from trials, and subsequently "spectral evidence", the "touch test" and the seeking of the marks of Satan on the bodies of the accused were abolished by Governor Phipps. The court of oyer and terminer was dissolved on 29 October 1692, and the last witch trials were held in January 1693 under new rules. With no solid forms of evidence, 28 of the last 33 trials resulted in acquittals.

In May 1693, sixteen months after Betty Parris and Abigail Williams had become mysteriously ill, Governor Phipps officially pardoned all the remaining accused. Those awaiting trial in jail were released without charge; this included Tituba, who then disappeared into obscurity and was never heard of again. It was an end to a tragic tale of needless murder in which lies, deceit, hatred and fear had resulted in 24 people and two dogs (which had been killed under the belief that they were "familiars") losing their lives. 19 people had been convicted of witchcraft and hanged on Gallows Hill, one had been crushed beneath stones and at least four had died in jail awaiting execution.

Upon reflection, could the entire episode have been avoided if Tituba had not introduced Betty and Abigail to harmless fortune telling? Were any of the accused actually practising witches? Modern historians have suggested that Bridget Bishop and Rebecca Nurse might have been Cunning Folk, whose knowledge of herbs and charms were their eventual downfall. Would so many innocent people have been executed if it were not for the words of a Puritanical minister's book? Was it all a vengeful plot planned by jealous rivals? Or was it down to ergot, a grain fungus poison that causes convulsions and that may have been growing in the fields near to the village, as has been suggested by modern researchers? Whatever its origins, the "witchcraft craze" in Salem is a grave lesson that illustrates the dire consequences of what can happen when fear and ignorance replace reason. On a more positive note, it is believed that the events at Salem marked the beginning of the end of the witchcraft trials in England and Europe.

THE WITCH OF WOODPLUMPTON

In the heart of rural Lancashire, where legends and folklore are still celebrated, one can find a curious stone boulder sitting among the decaying gravestones of St Mary's Church, in Woodplumpton. It is known as the "Witch's Grave", and is avoided by the superstitious.

The tale of the "Fylde Witch" is dismissed by many as a mere story, but it might in fact be based in truth, although the story has been embellished over time into a contortion of the original facts. The "witch's" real name was Margery Hilton, and she came not from Woodplumpton, but from Cottam, a village nearby. Margery lived alone in a "wretched hovel called Cuckoo Hall" – according to *The Haydock Papers*, written by Joseph Gillow in the late 19th century – and she made a name for herself making a nuisance in the surrounding area. She was known as "Meg", but this name is thought to have been changed over time, for some accounts refer to her as "Mag Shelton", possibly a derivation of "Marg".

Tall tales told of Meg Shelton can be traced back over a century, with local misfortune blamed on her to this day. The most widely reproduced story claims that she was a "shapeshifter" who was able, by magickal powers, to transform herself and inanimate objects into different things. By night she would supposedly steal produce from the local farmers. It is said that on one occasion a farmer noticed that there were more bags of grain in the barn than he had filled. With a pitchfork he stabbed each bag in turn, and after a high-pitched screech filled the building, one sack turned into Meg, who flew off in a temper back to her cottage.

Another anecdote tells the tale of a different farmer who spied a woman and a goose feeding in his field. As he watched, white liquid spilled from the goose's mouth and so he walked up to it and nudged it with his foot. The goose shattered into pieces, spilling stolen milk all over the ground. It seemed that Meg had changed her pitcher into the likeness of a goose!

Perhaps the most famous tale of Meg concerns the Lord of Cottam, who was promised a hare to chase during a hunt on condition that he provided Meg with a small cottage on his lands. Meg gained the Lord's agreement that a particular black dog would not be allowed to take part in the hunt, and the deal was done.

On the morning of the hunt the hare appeared just as Meg had promised, and the hunt ensued. In the excitement of the event, however, the hound, which Meg had expressly forbidden to take part, was released by mistake and quickly caught up with the hare. Chasing it across field and fell, the hound finally snapped at the hare's legs as it made a dash through the window of Meg's cottage. The account in Gillow's book states: "...it was significant that ever afterwards Mag Shelton limped".

The death of Meg is surrounded in mystery. After she had not been seen for several days, the Lord's men broke into her cottage and found that she was dead, her body crushed between a barrel and a wall. She was buried in 1705, but local legend has it that she crawled from her grave on two occasions. She remained beneath the ground only when she was buried beneath a heavy boulder upside down in a 1.8-metre (6-foot) shaft.

What exactly happened to Margery Shilton is unknown. Perhaps she was indeed a witch, practising the magickal arts with herbalism and folk magic? Perhaps she was a beggar hated by those around her? Time has twisted the truth, as it so often does. Yet if indeed her mortal remains are buried beneath the stone at Woodplumpton, surely she deserves to be laid to rest after all these years?

I visited the grave with a modern-day witch one overcast afternoon in 2007. It was a peaceful Sunday, and an aura of quiet pervaded the churchyard, as it does in so many places of burial. A sense of a terrible miscarriage of justice can be felt around the stone, as if an echo from centuries past still lingers at Meg's grave. We picked some fresh wild flowers, laid them upon the stone and wished her peaceful rest in the Summerland.

THE MYSTERIOUS MOTHER SHIPTON

There is some controversy surrounding the mysterious folk figure known worldwide as "Mother Shipton". Whether she ever existed at all is disputed, but if one were to make one's way to the cave where she was allegedly born, they will tell you that she was indeed real – and a powerful prophetess as well.

The tale of Mother Shipton's Cave and the Petrifying Well has been replicated time and time again throughout the literature of witchcraft; indeed over 50 books on Mother Shipton's life and prophecies have been written over the years. Much of the tale derives from a work edited by Richard Head, which is said to be a true account of her birth, life and prophesies, and which was uncovered in an old monastery in Yorkshire. The rest of the stories are derived from hearsay and legend, passed by word of mouth over the centuries.

The widely accepted story states that Mother Shipton, whose real name was Ursula Southeil, was born in 1488 in a cave on the outskirts of the Yorkshire market town of Knaresborough, near to a mystical pool which turned everything that was placed into it to stone. The tale surrounding her birth is where the mystery begins, for it is said she was born of the Devil. Her mother, Agatha, may have been a "woman of ill repute", for she was a slothful young woman of 15 years when she bore Ursula. It is said that one of her lovers, a charmer, had lain with her on numerous occasions and that he had the "cold touch" of Satan himself.

A rumble of thunder is said to have ripped the sky as Ursula was born in the cave one hot night in July 1488. The stench of sulphur filled the cavern as a huge, misshapen baby was born. The storm overhead announced the arrival of England's most famous seer.

Unable to cope with her misshapen child, Agatha gave her up to a foster mother and spent her remaining years in a convent. Ursula grew up discovering that she was "different" from the other children. She was called "the Devil's child" – possibly because of her lineage and appearance, or maybe because she could cause harm to others at will. When the other children taunted her for being "ugly", she would send her magick upon them. Despite her unattractiveness and unholy reputation, she was wooed by a young carpenter named Tobias Shipton. They were married in 1512, when Ursula was 24 years old.

Ursula's reputation as a witch and soothsayer began when a neighbour, who had been the subject of a theft of expensive clothing, came to ask her for help. Ursula promised that the clothing would be returned the very next day, and indeed upon the very next morning, the thief returned the items to the neighbour, declaring that she had taken them.

Word spread of Ursula's prophecy – had she simply foreseen the future, or had she sent some Devil upon the thief and made her repent? As time passed Ursula's reputation grew. Visitors came from the town and further afield to hear her claims of what was to come and to seek her magickal help.

Ursula's prophecies, some of which came true in her own lifetime and some beyond, are world-famous. She is said to have predicted the Dissolution of the Monasteries, the Great Fire of London, the Spanish Armada and even modern-day inventions such as cars and iron ships floating on water. She even predicted the end of the world in 1881 (this one clearly did not come true!). After a life of fortune telling, magick making and prophesying, she died in 1561.

An enigmatic folk figure and beloved Yorkshire legend, the tale of Mother Shipton, as she later became known, persists even today with thousands of visitors flocking to the place where she was allegedly born over 500 years ago.

CECIL WILLIAMSON AND THE MUSEUM OF WITCHCRAFT

Born in Paignton, Devon, on 18 September 1909, Cecil Hugh Williamson was a folklorist and witch who was instrumental in creating the Museum of Witchcraft, now in Boscastle, Cornwall. It is an international archive and study centre that houses the largest collection of magickal artefacts, books and documents in the world. Although Williamson's name is not often quoted in lists of famous witches, without him the museum that so many witches and Pagans know and love today would not exist.

Williamson's father was an officer in the Royal Navy, and his family enjoyed the status that came with employment in the military. He was educated at Malvern College in Worcester, and sent to Rhodesia by his father when he came of age to learn the business of tobacco farming. Throughout his life he had brushes with the world of magick, and the first incident is said to have occurred when he was just seven years old. In a television documentary made just before his death in 1999, Williamson described how, while staying with his uncle in the village of North Bovey, Devon, in December 1916, he had witnessed a group of people getting very excited on the village green. He went over to see what the commotion was about and saw four very burly agricultural labourers taking the last shreds of clothing off a 78-year-old woman who they had accused of being a witch, and having put the "evil eye" on their cattle. The reason they were stripping her clothing was so that they could prove that she really was a witch – by showing that she had a witch's mark in the form of a third nipple or some other such hideousness. Williamson, gripped by impulse, fought his way through the jeering crowd and flung his arms around the naked woman on the ground. He was beaten and kicked until finally the fracas disbanded, but he held on to her in an attempt to protect her from the village vagabonds.

Some weeks later, while walking into the village, he came across the old lady and she invited him into her cottage. It was the beginning of his journey into witchcraft as she opened his eyes and soul to the ways of magick.

His next brush with a village wise woman was in 1921, when he was 12 years old and had been suffering from bullying at school. The witch told him how to deal with the bully, and after Williamson had carried out her instructions the bully was involved in a skiing accident that left him crippled and unable to continue school. This experience had a profound effect on Williamson, and the seeds of a life that was to be spent searching for occult truths were planted.

During breaks from college, Williamson was dispatched to France to stay with his grandmother. She had a close friend named Mona Mackenzie, a medium who subsequently taught Williamson the arts of scrying. In Rhodesia, while learning the business of tobacco farming under his father's instructions, he met another occultist, a house servant named Zandonda who was a witch-doctor and who introduced him to African magick.

When Williamson returned to the United Kingdom in 1930, he entered the film industry as a production assistant. It was through his work that he met Gwen Wilcox, a make-up artist who was to become his wife. Williamson's obsession with witchcraft was still growing at this time, and he began to amass a collection of artefacts and literature on the subject. It wasn't long before his interest reached the ears of MI6, possibly because of his father's military connections. In 1938, just before the outbreak of the Second World War (1939–1945), Williamson was asked to form a special branch of the Foreign Office to carry out research into the occult interests of the Nazis. After setting up the Witchcraft Research Centre, Williamson was instrumental in the capture of Hitler's deputy officer, Rudolph Hess. By planting hoax occult information and allowing it to reach Hess, he managed to lure Hess out of Germany and to Scotland, where he was later arrested.

After his success in the war effort, Williamson's deep interest in witchcraft needed a further direction, and he decided to set up the country's first museum of witchcraft. Williamson's first choice of site, Stratford-upon-Avon, had not worked out as local uproar, coupled with the still active *Witchcraft Act*, had forced him across the sea and to the Isle of Man, which seemed to be a perfect location. In 1948, together with Gerald Gardner, who he had met at the Atlantis bookshop in London, Williamson opened the Folklore Centre of Superstition and Witchcraft and the Witches Kitchen restaurant. Both the Centre and restaurant were housed in a disused mill that quickly acquired the title of "The Witches Mill".

Gardner acted as "resident witch" to the museum and began courting publicity, something Williamson did not agree with. In 1952, following the repeal of the *Witchcraft Act*, Williamson sold the Mill to Gardner and moved his collection back to England – it was time to try again!

Windsor was the next location for Williamson's collection of the arcane. His new museum enjoyed initial success, but after the tourist flocks died down local opposition rose up and he was forced to move on. In 1954 he re-opened the Museum in Bourton-on-the-Water, Gloucestershire, but here he was subjected to the most vehement rejection of all. After an arson attack, harassment and even a dead cat being delivered to his doorstep, Williamson decided to move once again. This was to be the final move for the Museum, and it took him back to his beloved West Country.

In 1960, the Museum of Witchcraft opened in Boscastle, Cornwall, and it has remained there for the last 47 years. Williamson continued to run the business and practise magick upon the cliffs surrounding the fishing village until his retirement in 1996, when, at the exact stroke of midnight, he sold the building and most of its obscure contents to Graham King and his partner, Elizabeth Crow. Williamson then moved to Witheridge, near Tiverton, Devon, where he lived out his final years in this world, departing to the Summerland in 1999. His 90-year lifelong hunger for knowledge and quest for the truths behind witchcraft has left an incredible and unique legacy for those that follow The Craft today. Updated and recently renovated following the terrible floods of 2004, the Museum is a lasting tribute to the life of a remarkable witch.

THE RINGS OF BONE

During early 2007 I was staying with friends at The Highwayman Inn, an historic old inn on the edge of Dartmoor, Devon owned by Sally and Bruce Thompson, with whom I have been friends for many years. My friends and I were due to spend a weekend in Boscastle, Cornwall, and had stopped off to spend one night with Sally and Bruce.

As talk turned to witchcraft, Sally asked if we would be visiting the Museum of Witchcraft during our stay in the West Country. We answered with a resounding "yes" – it was to be one of the highlights of our weekend! She then disappeared, and when she returned she held in her hands a small package that looked like a scrap of fabric. She told me that many years ago she had attended a sale at the old museum in the days when Cecil Williamson (*see page 39*) owned it (this would have been prior to 1996). Cecil had been auctioning off some smaller items from his collection to raise money for charity, and she had bid on and won a peculiar set of mag-ickal bone rings that she had kept hidden away in a drawer ever since.

I was very excited that we were about to examine some items that had once belonged to such a learned witch. Rather than show them to me, however, Sally asked me if I would like to keep them, saying they would be better off with me rather than sitting gathering dust in her drawer! I was delighted and thanked Sally before opening the pouch and taking a peek at the contents.

Inside the pouch were four peculiar bone rings of different sizes and materials. Two were obviously formed of shell, and the others possibly of bone. Upon closer examination it was clear that the largest ring had symbols carved around its edge, while another had an uneven surface. They exuded a strange aura that some found a little disconcerting, and we decided to wrap them back up until we could give them the attention that they deserved.

When we got to the museum the following afternoon I showed the rings to Graham King (*see page 39*) to see if he could shed any light on what they might be. After looking at the carvings, he told me that the symbols were for protection, and that two rings were made of shell and two from what he thought was human bone. Cecil had apparently owned many different occult tools that were made from bones, and it would not have been unheard of for him to have had rings of human bone in his collection.

I still don't know exactly what the rings were intended to be used for. It has been suggested to me that perhaps they were cast over a piece of leather or slate marked with symbols to divine the future or to answer questions, or perhaps the sound of them clicking together as one rocks them gently on one finger was intended to induce a trancelike state (I have tried this and it does work!). For now their true purpose remains a mystery, but if you, dear reader, have any suggestions as to what they might be, please do get in touch!

GERALD GARDNER AND THE MODERN WITCHCRAFT REVIVAL

Witchcraft is commonly believed to be the survival of an ancient belief system in which nature is revered as deity and magick is worked by the practitioner to create change in the world around us and within us. The modern term "Wicca", however, which dates only from the 1950s, is sometimes misused to describe all forms of witchery. The word orginated with Gerald Brousseau Gardner, a charismatic, eccentric English witch who is credited by some as the father of modern witchcraft.

Born near Liverpool on Friday 13 June 1884, Gardner was born into a successful family of timber merchants. A studious individual who immersed himself in books, he later worked in the Far East for the British Government as a rubber plantation inspector and customs official, generating enough income to support his deep interest in archaeology. After retiring from government work in 1936, and having married in 1927, Gardner returned to England and began to study the archaeological histories of Asia, Europe and Cyprus (where he believed he had lived in a former life incarnation, having dreamed of the place many times).

After settling in the New Forest area, Gerald became acquainted with The Fellowship of Crotona, a group of performers who produced public plays with occult themes in "England's first Rosicrucian Theatre" while secretly practising an ancient form of witchcraft passed down through generations by word of mouth. Gerald was invited to join the coven, and in 1939 was initiated into The Craft in the home of the enigmatically named "Old Dorothy Clutterbuck".

In 1947, Arnold Crowther introduced Gardner to Aleister Crowley, an infamous master occultist who provided Gerald with much of the magickal material which later formed the basis of his witchcraft tradition: "Gardnerian witchcraft". It was from this material, together with an eclectic variety of other sources (including the New Forest coven's own material) that Gardner created "The Book of Shadows", which followers of Gardnerian Witchcraft still use today.

In 1949 Gardner published *High Magic's Aid,* – a book of magickal workings dressed up as a novel and written under the pseudonym "Scire" (the practice of witchcraft was still illegal at the time, and publications of magickal practice would have caused an uproar at the very least).

After the repeal of the *Witchcraft Act* in 1951, Gerald broke away from the New Forest coven and formed his own coven in 1953. He initiated Doreen Valiente, widely beloved as the Mother of Modern Witchcraft, into the coven. Valiente re-worked Gardner's Book of Shadows, extracting much of Crowley's material and shifting the emphasis onto the Goddess (emphasis had previously been on the Horned God).

In 1954 Gardner published *Witchcraft Today*, his first work of non-fiction. The book inspired the formation of new covens all over the country, and Gardner took centre stage as he was dubbed "Britain's Chief Witch" by the media. This attention, much of it negative, caused a rift in the coven, however, and Valiente left to go her own way.

After the death of his wife, Donna, in 1963, Gardner met Raymond Buckland, who went on to introduce The Craft throughout the United States. Gardner died of heart failure in 1964, and was buried in Tunis, Tunisia.

II

DOUBLE, DOUBLE, TOIL AND TROUBLE

WITCHES AND THEIR CRAFT ARE COMPLEX AND EXTENSIVE
subjects and cannot possibly be fully described in one book, let alone a
single chapter. Instead of attempting the impossible task of providing you,
dear reader, with an exhaustive explanation of The Craft, I will share a few
of its select secrets, and will introduce you to the hierarchy of a modern
witches' coven. In this chapter you will learn about different types of
magick for healing and harming, and discover how past Cunning Men and
Women used charms to ward away evil. As the cauldron bubbles and
burns, I will stir up the secrets of the magickal arts, introduce you to
otherworldly beings and let you take a peek into another world…

"Double, double, toil and trouble;
fire burn and cauldron bubble."

 coven is a group of witches who learn and work together in ritual and spiritual development. The traditional maximum number is 13, although any group of three or more witches is known as a coven. To create harmony and balance, a mixture of male and female covenors is desirable, but this is not always possible and in modern groups you will find an eclectic mix of genders, sexualities and traditions.

Like any organized group of people, a coven usually has a variety of different roles to share responsibilities and activities, however not all covens have the same roles and many have none at all.

The High Priest or Priestess

The high priest and/or priestess are the leaders of the coven. They must ensure that all covenors receive support, teaching and guidance. They also lead rituals and plan celebrations.

The Maiden

The maiden assists the high priest and priestess as they conduct rituals; she also decorates the sacred space with candles, statuary and herbs.

The Summoner

The summoner is responsible for keeping records of all covenors' contact details. He/she sends out information about gatherings, celebrations and, if the coven is a teaching group, classes.

The Wayfarer

The wayfarer organizes field trips to sacred sites and gatherings away from the covenstead. This might include visits to stone circles, museums and sacred sites, as well as bonding weekends.

The Archivist

The archivist keeps coven records, books and documents and ensures that everyone has access to them when needed.

The Scribe

The scribe is responsible for writing records of magickal rituals and spells that have been undertaken by the coven, and notes the results. This information is written in a "Coven Book of Shadows", to which only covenors have access.

The Pursewarden

The pursewarden looks after the financial records held by the coven and keeps track of coven spending on ritual tools, supplies, food and drink. He/she also collects monies from covenors.

The Bard

The bard is the sacred storyteller and musician who entertains the rest of the coven with drama and music. He/she might play an instrument, sing or dance.

INITIATION

In many traditions of witchcraft, initiations are a central part of coven development. Whether someone is a solitary witch or a member of a group, initiation can be an important part of leading a magickal life. It can be argued that the witches of old, who practised folk magic and charming, are unlikely to have been initiated into a hierarchical system, and this may indeed be true. Initiation is evidently more common in contemporary witchcraft traditions, but, as with every part of The Craft, just because something is not old does not mean it is unimportant.

In modern witchcraft initiations are turning points and important rites of passage that mark learning, achievements and development. Many traditions, primarily Gardnerian, operate a three-degree system. The first degree is traditionally given after the postulant has completed a minimum of a year and a day's training and learning. After receiving a first-degree initiation from a high priest or priestess, the newly initiated witch begins to learn the deeper mysteries, acquires their own magickal tools and becomes adept at using them.

The second degree is bestowed upon those that have walked the path of the wise for a considerable time, and have learned a great deal. A second-degree witch will be comfortable writing magick and planning and leading others in ritual. He or she will have chosen witchcraft as a lifestyle choice and not merely as his or her spirituality, living every day through the Goddess and Horned God.

Few are initiated as third-degree witches. At this level the witch may lead his or her own coven or training group, or teach on a more personal level. He or she will have a learned knowledge of the magickal arts, and will have earned the respect of those around them. A third-degree witch will have explored the mysteries in the world (both seen and unseen) and within themselves, and will have a variety of skills in different magickal practices.

Many witches disregard the degree system, and that is fine too. To be part of a long line of initiated witches can bring a sense of belonging that might be beneficial to the witch, and to be able to prove lineage can be useful when trying to join a new coven. However, for the solitary practitioner or hedge witch who works alone, a self-dedication to the Old Gods may suffice. Most witches would agree that all paths lead to the same place, and that the route taken to get there is a matter of personal choice and what "feels" right.

THE MAGICK CIRCLE

Witches generally cast a magick circle in which they perform rituals, worship the Old Gods and work magick. Although a circle isn't always necessary or practical, it does create a sacred space which, if cast correctly, will protect those within and act as a container of built-up energies.

A traditional circle is 2.75 metres (9 feet) in diameter, but any size will do. A circle can be cast anywhere – in a bedroom, a garden or on top of a mountain – the possibilities really are limitless. Of course, anywhere naturally associated with magick is a good place to start – a sacred stone circle, a faery mound or near a waterfall can work well.

There are several steps that witches take in order to cast the circle before using it. The first is the cleansing of the space. It is necessary to do this to ensure that no stray energies or spirits are present inside the area where the circle will be cast. The cleansing can be done in several ways, but the most popular are sweeping the perimeter with a besom while visualizing any negativity being swept away; censing the area with a burning Thurible and a space-clearing incense such as sage; or sprinkling with spring water that has been blessed in the name of the Old Gods. The cleansing, or space clearing, is always done widdershins, as it is an act of banishing. Some witches will use one or more of these techniques, while an adept might simply perform a cleansing by standing in the centre of the space and banishing any energy with his or her mind.

The second step is to actually cast the circle itself. Again, this can be done in several ways, but it is usually done with either a wand, athame or magick sword. The witch will usually begin at the north end and walk the perimeter of the circle deosil while pointing his or her chosen tool at the ground, visualizing potent magickal energy of blue fire pouring out of the tool and leaving a trail in its wake. Once the witch has made one full circle, he or she may walk around again, but this time having moved the tool to medium height in mid-air. A third circumnavigation, this time holding the tool above the head, makes a stronger circle. Once the third circle is complete, a spiral of three circles of energy at different heights is created. The circle is now cast.

It is unwise for anyone to walk across the threshold of the circle as they may damage it. If access is required by other witches, or if the witch needs to leave the space temporarily, he or she will "cut" a doorway in the west using the same tool used to cast the circle. The doorway will be closed by repeating the "cutting", but in a reverse action.

The magick circle represents a number of different elements: the circle and spiral energy represent life, Mother Earth, the Wheel of the Year and the Horned God's birth, death and rebirth. The circle is cast three times because the magickal number "three" is venerated in witchcraft as the number of the Triple Goddess: Maiden, Mother and Crone. The Law of Three is invoked.

Witches believe that the circle is a sacred place where time and reality as we experience it day by day are temporarily suspended. It becomes a space between worlds, a place where magick, meditation and ritual can take place in the presence of the Old Gods and other magickal beings and forces. It is a sacred space that must be treated with respect; only those who are trusted by the witch or coven are ever invited to enter.

Inside the circle, many witches will raise the "Cone of Power". This is raw energy that, when given focus in magick, is released from the circle to fulfil its intent. The power might be raised by ritual dance, chanting, singing or playing a musical instrument such as a drum.

Witches believe that during magickal practice any energies invoked, such as God or Goddess energies, spirits or preternatural beings cannot enter the circle unless invited, and thereby the space inside is safe while the area outside the circle may not be. For this reason you will not find a witch invoking energies that may harm people while there are any spectators present outside of the sacred space. (The presence of spectators would be unusual, however, as magick and worship are usually carried out in privacy or even secrecy.)

THE CARDINAL DIRECTIONS

Within witchcraft the cardinal directions – north, east, south and west – are important. Each direction corresponds to different elements, and each has its own magickal elemental guardians. The concept for these guardians was first recorded by Paracelsus, an alchemist from the 16th century. He named the directions and their guardians as follows:

North – "Gnomus", derived from the Greek word "*gnoma*", which means "knowledge", thus "the knowing ones" – now known as Gnomes.

East – "Sylvestris", derived from the Latin word "*silphe*", which means "butterfly", thus "the winged ones" – now known as Sylphs.

South – "Vulcanus", derived from the Greek word "*salambe*", which means "fireplace", thus "the creatures of the fire" – now known as Salamanders.

West – "Undina", derived from the Latin word "*unda*", which means "wave", thus "the creatures of the waves" – now known as Undines.

Belief in preternatural magickal beings and creatures is generally accepted by witches. They believe that these forces exist in the realm between worlds, and can be experienced by witches through magickal practise, divination and meditation.

The altar is always set up inside the circle in the northern quarter. The implements and tools are laid out according to the correspondences with the elements, with each piece of equipment being ruled by an elemental guardian.

The Northern Quarter – Earth

The northern quarter corresponds to the element of earth. This element is represented on a witches' altar by a stone, crystal, or a dish of fresh soil. The primary elemental guardians associated with earth are called Gnomes – not the kind you find in your garden, but rather a preternatural form of spirit creature that lives within the earth itself. Gnomes are generally perceived as being small, short in stature and of stocky build. They can be visualized within the roots of trees and plants, in mossy dells and in deep caverns beneath the surface of Gaia. Their prime energy has a masculine focus, and they rule the emotions of stability, strength, growth, wisdom and prosperity. Secondary elemental creatures associated with earth include Satyrs, house spirits named Brownies and tree spirits called Dryads. The colour symbolically associated with Gnomes is green.

The Eastern Quarter – Air

The eastern quarter corresponds to the element of air. This element is represented on a witches' altar by the smoke of burning incense or a smudging feather. The primary elemental guardians associated with air are called Sylphs. They are generally perceived as winged creatures, and can be visualized in snowflakes, storm clouds, winds and rushing leaves. Their prime energy has a female focus, and they rule the emotions of creativity, thought, travel, freedom and inspiration. Secondary elemental creatures associated with air include faeries. The colour symbolically associated with Sylphs is yellow.

The Southern Quarter – Fire

The southern quarter corresponds to the element of fire. This element is represented on a witches' altar by the flame of a burning candle. The primary elemental guardians associated with fire are called Salamanders, and are generally perceived as lizard-like creatures; they can be visualized in burning fires, candles and lanterns. Their prime energy has a male focus, and they rule the emotions of passion, energy, dynamism, sexuality, enthusiasm, willpower, energy, purification, motivation, impatience and anger. Secondary elemental creatures associated with fire include Firedrakes, which have the appearance of serpent-like dragons, and Acthnici, which appear as balls of flame. The colour symbolically associated with Salamanders is red.

The Western Quarter – Water

The western quarter corresponds to the element of water. This element is represented on a witches' altar by a chalice or cauldron filled with liquid. The primary elemental guardians associated with water are called Undines. They are generally perceived as graceful mermaid-like creatures, and can be visualized in oceans, rushing rivers, waterfalls, rain and lakes. Their prime energy has a female focus, and they are the most emotional of all elementals, ruling love, psychic matters, healing, friendship and unity. Secondary elemental creatures associated with water include mermaids, Naiads, Selkies and water nymphs. The colour symbolically associated with Undines is blue.

The Fifth Element

Witches believe in a fifth element known as "Ether", or "Spirit". This element is not ruled by a cardinal direction, but rather is represented by the uppermost point on the pentacle. Within the magick circle it is omnipresent, and is represented by the sum of everything else. The Goddess, Horned God and ancestral spirits are all associated with the fifth element.

Calling the Quarters

In traditions of witchcraft that utilize the magick circle, once the area has been cleansed and the circle itself has been created, the next step is to summon the Elementals to guard and watch over the proceedings. The high priestess or priest will usually perform this ceremony, which is known as "Calling the Quarters". In turn, the caller will visit each cardinal direction of the circle and call aloud a magickal invocation to summon and stir the forces to guard the circle and those within it.

The presence of the Elementals is also required if anything is to be done "in their presence" and they are usually summoned first, before the Lords of the Watchtowers (*see below*) or any deities in the shape of the Goddess or Horned God.

THE LORDS OF THE WATCHTOWERS

You will often hear mention of the "Watchtowers" within the newer traditions of witchcraft. These have their origin in the distant past, and are ruled by the "Lords", whose names originate in the stars. Referred to as the "Watchers" in ancient scriptures, they were sent to watch over man by the Old Gods, and take their names from the four royal stars that shine in the skies in the cardinal directions over which they preside.

Some witches will call forth the Lords of the Watchtowers to stand guard over the circle, much akin to the Elementals. Also known as the "Grigori", a word that means "those who watch and never sleep", they are described as spiritually and physically enormous. The perception of the Grigori as "towers" comes from the notion that the Lords stand atop four towers that are magickally invoked at each cardinal point around the magick circle, guarding the witches within.

The Watchtower of the North

The guardian of the Watchtower of the North is named Formalhaut, and the star from which it derives can be found in the constellation of Pisces. It marks the winter solstice – Yule.

The Watchtower of the East

The guardian of the Watchtower of the East is named Aldebaran, and the star from which it derives can be found in the constellation of Taurus. It marks the spring equinox – Ostara.

The Watchtower of the South

The guardian of the Watchtower of the South is named Regulus, and the star from which it derives can be found in the constellation of Leo. It marks the summer solstice – Litha.

The Watchtower of the West

The guardian of the Watchtower of the West is named Antares, and the star from which it derives can be found in the constellation of Scorpio. It marks the autumn equinox – Mabon.

INVOKING DEITIES

Once a magick circle has been constructed and the presence of the Elementals, Watchtowers, or both, has been invoked, it is time to ask the Goddess and her consort, the Horned God, to bless the space with their divine presence.

The high priestess or priest will usually perform the invocation of deity by reciting a written invocation such as "The Charge of the Goddess" or "The Charge of the God", both by

Doreen Valiente. Some witches will invoke deity with a special ceremony called "Drawing down the Moon", in which the Goddess is believed to manifest through the body of the high priestess. However, most covens will use chanting to invoke the Old Gods – the change may be from a book written by other witches, or it may be specially written.

Often one will hear witches talking about different gods and goddesses. In essence, these are all part of the same "one", but manifest different energies through a variety of mythical deities from many sources. There are literally hundreds of gods and goddesses ranging from Celtic, Egyptian, Greek and more. Witches usually choose those deities to which they feel drawn as they learn about The Craft, and these become central to their magickal practice.

CLOSING THE MAGICK CIRCLE

At the end of the ritual or celebration, the Magick Circle, which has been constructed and now "exists" between the magickal realm and our everyday world, must be closed. It is important that it is not simply abandoned as the energy it exudes will interfere with the local genius loci.

To close the circle, the same person who originally cast it will begin at north and walk widdershins around the circle three times. Beginning overhead, they will use the same tool as for casting, and will visualize the energy they "saw" pouring out of the tool, being reclaimed into it. After making three circumferences of the area, the circle is banished and the space is returned to everyday use. A faint energy memory of the presence of the magick circle may be felt by those with strong psychic sensitivity even after the witches have long gone. If the same area is used repeatedly, it will, over time, become infused with magickal power and its general "feel" will change. This might make the magickally uneducated feel uneasy, but a witch will always feel "at home" where the arts magickal have taken place.

THE MAGICKAL WINDS

In magickal belief the wind deities are known as the "Anemoi". Anemoi is a collective word that describes the four greater wind gods and the four tempest winds that derive from Greek mythology (there are similar versions in old Roman beliefs). Although the names of the tempest winds derive from ancient demons, they are not all malign, with a variety of correspondences associated with them. Each of the tempests rules a cross-quarterly direction.

Each of the eight winds was given a direction to rule over, and over time each became associated with different seasons and weather conditions. Witches might summon the wind gods for magickal ritual or spellcraft.

The four cardinal, greater wind gods are Boreas (the leader), Eurus, Notus and Zephyrus.

Boreas – The North Wind

His name means "devouring one", and he is the chief god of winds. Associated with horses and perceived as an old man with a shaggy beard, wearing a billowing cloak and carrying a conch shell, his temper is violent – as is the north wind. Boreas is the bringer of winter in Greek myth. The Roman equivalent god of the northern wind is known as Aquilon.

Eurus – The East Wind

Eurus, the wind of the east, brings warmth and rain, but is associated with bad luck. The Roman equivalent god of the eastern wind is known as Vulturnus.

Notus – The South Wind

Notus is the bringer of storms in late summer and autumn, and strikes fear into farmers' hearts as he is the destroyer of crops. The Roman equivalent god of the southern wind is known as Auster.

Zephyrus – The West Wind

The gentlest wind and messenger of spring, Zephyrus is the bringer of warm breezes. The Roman equivalent god of the western wind is known as Favonius.

The four lesser Anemoi, known as the tempest winds, are Kaikias, Apeliotes, Livos and Skeiron.

Kaikias – The Tempest of the North East

This bad-tempered wind is perceived in deity form as an old man wielding a shield of hail stones. His name derives from the ancient Greek "kakia", meaning "evil". The Roman equivalent lesser wind deity is Caecius.

Apeliotes – The Tempest of the South East

A friendly deity who brings refreshing rains to crops and is depicted with a benign smile and long flowing hair. He brings fruit, flowers and grain. The Roman equivalent lesser wind deity is Subsolanus.

Livos – The Tempest of the South West

Livos is the friend of seafaring folk and is often depicted holding the stern of a ship. The Roman equivalent lesser wind deity is Africus.

Skeiron – The Tempest of the North West

The last of the tempests is Skeiron, depicted as an old man holding a mighty cauldron; he holds it at a tilt. This tempest represents the onset of winter. The equivalent Roman lesser wind deity is Corus.

MAKING MAGICK

Magick is the process of using focused thought, natural energies, spoken words and ritual to create change – whether for good or bad. In witchcraft, it is the inner power of the witch, focused with concentrated intent, that creates the change. Because in magickal belief all things are linked, it is possible to change all things with magickal practice.

The use of correspondences, ingredients and rituals, whether learned or self-created, adds to the focus of the energy which, when released, affects change in the mortal and spirit realms.

White Magick

One will often hear people using the term "white witch", or "white magick". This is in fact an oversimplification of a complex subject that has a less frightening sense when it is used. In reality, there is no such thing as white or black magick. All magick could be considered grey, as it is the intent in the witch's mind that "colours" the magick.

What is perceived as good to one person is not necessarily good to another. In this way, the witch is responsible for his or her own magickal actions and, in modern witchcraft, will act within the Law of Threefold Return (*see page 55*).

Timing of Magick

It is important to perform magick at the correct time. The phases of the moon are relevant as they reflect the type of magick that should be performed at any given time.

The results of magick may be seen immediately, or they may take some time to manifest. Once the magick ritual or spell has been performed it is important not to focus on it. The witch will put it out of his or her mind and forget about it, and it will never be discussed.

Spellcasting

The casting of spells is a major part of the witch's life. A spell is a spoken or written magickal invocation that might include a ritual in which correspondences and timing is important.

The energy required to give the spell its power will be drawn from within the witch either by focusing his or her mind, chanting or dancing. When the energy has built up it will be released into the universe.

In some spells repetition, rhyme and rhythm are important. A witch might repeat an invocation over and over again, building its energy and intent, or he or she may rhythmically stroke a poppet to banish an illness. Repetition and rhythm allow the energy to build up slowly, and allow for the intention of the witch to become clear.

Abracadabra

Commonly used as a word of magical conjuration for amusement and theatrical stage effect, the word "Abracadabra" actually has its roots in the arcane magick of the middle centuries.

In its earliest known form, the word was widely used and was thought to be a powerful charm against illness, fever and even the plague. A witch or sorcerer would inscribe the word on a piece of paper or amulet that would be worn about the inflicted. Scribed in an ever decreasing triangle cone, it was believed that just as the word itself diminished, so too would the illness.

ABRACADABRA
ABRACADABR
ABRACADAB
ABRACADA
ABRACAD
ABRACA
ABRAC
ABRA
ABR
AB
A

The incantation's heritage can be traced back to the 2nd century BCE. It was originally published as part of a poem called "De Medicina Praecepta", written by Quintus Serenus Sammonicus, physician to the Roman emperor, Caracalla, who prescribed the charm to cure the sick (although some say that he merely borrowed the word and that it was already in magickal use).

The origin and original meaning of the word has been lost in time, but there are several interesting theories, the first of which states that the word derived from an Aramaic phrase "abhadda kedhabra", which meant "disappear like this word". Another school of thought says the word comes from the Hebrew phrases "abreq ad habra", which translates to "hurl your thunderbolt even unto death" or "avar k'davar" which roughly means "it will be according to what is said".

The Gnostic god Abraxas is also thought to be a possible source for the word, as his image is sometimes found on charms and amulets warding off the evil eye that date from the 2nd century, the time when "Abracadabra" was first seen published. It is also thought to be a possible name for an ancient demon, long lost in the grimoires of ancient thought.

Aleister Crowley, the magician and occultist who made a name for himself as "The Beast" and studied arcane scriptures for decades, thought that the word's true form should be "abrahadabra", and that it held potent magickal power.

Modern witches sometimes use the word to seal spellcraft, thereby using it as an end to the magick – "it will be according to what is said" – and it is also used in charming and banishing magick.

Weaving Magick

There are a few basic warnings and rules to which witches adhere when planning magickal rituals and spells. The first rule is: do persist! Magick *does* work, but it sometimes needs strong persistence if the focus or energy is weak.

Secondly, be extremely precise in what you ask for. For example, if a witch were to ask for a large sum of money, he or she may find that his or her favourite aunt drops dead and leaves them the money they asked for. Think about what you are asking for and be precise in how it will come to you and what the effects of that will be. Be magickally responsible.

Thirdly, remember the all-important Law of Threefold Return. This relatively modern concept is accepted by many witches, and states that what you give out will come back to you three times.

TYPES OF MAGICK

There are several different types of magick: Glamour (*see below*), Warding (*see below*), Binding (*see page 63*), Blasting (*see page 63*), Banishing (*see page 63*), Constructing (*see page 63*), Hexing (*see page 64*) and Charming (*see page 64*).

Glamour

Magick that affects the way something appears or is perceived is called glamour magick. For example, a spell of invisibility or to change the perceived colour of someone's eyes would be called "glamour". Likewise, if a witch casts a spell to become attractive to someone who does not find her so, thereby altering the way she is otherwise perceived, this is also glamour; so too are beauty spells.

Warding

Magick or spells that are cast for protection or safety are known as "warding magick". Such magick might include spells for the protection of a new home, or for a safe journey.

Witch Balls

A witch ball is a brightly coloured orb of glass that is believed to act as a protective charm against evil magick and ill fortune. Thought to be a corruption of "watch ball" – which "watched" over the house – a witch ball is hung in a dark corner where stray energies may gather or spirits may hide. It absorbs evil and entraps negative energies.

Witch balls were commonplace in the 18th century, when cottages across the land hung them in their windows to ward away evil. They were particularly common in seafaring towns, where they were eventually substituted with glass fishing floats, these being more common and easily obtained.

Purpose-made witch balls are traditionally coloured green or blue and are hollow. Their attractive colours and shiny surfaces act as a beacon for evil spirits, which become enchanted by the beauty of the orb and subsequently trapped inside it. Alternatively, the spirits flee in terror after catching a glimpse of their own reflection in the shiny surface.

By the 19th century the practice of hanging charmed balls in the home had reached America, and these soon became a decorative feature on Christmas trees. We now know them as baubles, but they once hung atop branches to ward away disruptive spirits.

In the Ozark Mountains of America, the term "witch ball" was also used to describe a hex in the form of a small, hard ball made from black hair and beeswax which, when thrown at a victim, brought death.

Witch Bottles

These pot-bellied bottles, filled with a mixture of herbs and human bodily fluids, were made by Cunning Men and Women and hidden in chimney stacks and inside walls during the witch hysteria of the Middle Ages. With the rise of so-called "witches", an abundance of remedies in the form of counter-magick against their malign powers entered society. The witch bottle was perhaps the most well known.

For several hundred years the production of witch bottles was widespread. England's most famous maker of witch bottles was a Cunning Man named James Murrell, who used iron to forge his versions. The traditional type was constructed of a "Bellarmine" bottle; these were manufactured widely in Germany and were made from stone. The base resembled the pot-belly of a fat Catholic inquisitor named Robert Bellarmine. This, combined with the grim bearded face (also sported by Bellarmine) that also adorned the bottles led to them becoming known as "Bellarmine" bottles, although they were also called "Greybeard's" and "Bartmann's" bottles. The face and shape were not intended to replicate the features of the inquisitor – the connection was a satirical cultural statement. The face, which was actually intended to scare away evil, was later interpreted as that of the Devil, though it was in fact meant to scare "him" off! Bellarmine bottles were also manufactured in Holland and Belgium, but were not introduced to British manufacture until after 1660.

Into the bottle were placed a selection of ingredients which, when mixed together, were thought to create a powerful antidote against black magick. This included bent iron nails – iron was believed to be in itself a charm against magick – needles, thorns, fabric hearts, hair, nail clippings and urine. The ingredients were supposed to deflect and destroy curses that might have been cast upon the household or its inhabitants. The bottle would be sealed with wax and hidden away in the chimney, under the floor of the threshold or plastered inside the walls of the home to work its counter-sorcery.

The inclusion of human elements was supposed to confuse any curse that might be sent from an ill wisher. The power of the curse would come across the bottle first and misinterpret it as the target of the magick, thus protecting the real intended recipient from harm. The thorns, needles and other sharp ingredients would impale the magick, rendering the curse unsuccessful and in some cases reflecting it back to the original sender, causing them to experience the pain and agony they had wished upon the owner of the bottle. The spell of the witch bottle would continue unless it was broken in pieces. In some anecdotal tales, the ill wisher is reported to have pleaded with the owner of the witch bottle to destroy it, suffering badly from its counter-curse that had been returned to the sender. In other accounts it was said that if the bottle had "caught" a witch's curse, it could be thrown into a fire where, as it exploded, the ill wisher would die and the spell would be broken.

The successful hiding of the witch bottle was an extremely important element of the curse, and many were not discovered until the building was torn down. They were often found beneath the fireplace itself. The chimney was a particularly vulnerable port of entry for malign influence (and even for the witch herself), and therefore it was a favourite place to hide the magick bottle.

In contemporary witchcraft the construction of witch bottles continues, albeit with a slightly different intent. Rather than return unwanted energies to the sender, modern-day witch bottles are usually bewitched to capture negative influences and destroy them. They might include blades and thorns to cut the curse in pieces, protective herbs such as rosemary and garlic and pieces of broken mirror to deflect evil away. Other objects and ingredients might include red wine, to drown ill-sent wishes; crystals with protective properties; and a tangled thread to bind the curse. Salt, which is used in a variety of magickal practices as a powerful force of exorcism, is likely to be the key ingredient while the human essence might be hair, nail clippings, urine, menstrual blood or semen. Other possible ingredients used both now and in the past include feathers, sand, vinegar, shells, glass, wood, bones, coins, ashes, flowers and knotted string. The ingredients, which are charged upon a witch's altar before being placed into the bottle, are sealed inside with black or red wax. The ritual of construction is done during a waning moon or on the eve of the dark moon, as the magick is that of warding and binding.

In January 2004 a witch bottle, which had actually been constructed in a green glass candlestick, not in a bottle, was discovered in an old farmhouse in Navenby, Lincolnshire, during building work. There are records of glass phials and bottles having been used in place of Bellarmines to create witch bottles, although they were generally less popular with Cunning Folk. The candlestick charm had been struck with a pickaxe before being noticed, and thus its contents were released. It contained pins, hair and was bound with a leather strap. It was dated from 1830, which is much more recent than most other witch bottles that have been discovered, and is now on display at the Museum of Lincolnshire Life in Lincoln.

The most recently unearthed bottle, this time made of a traditional Bellarmine, was uncovered in Greenwich, London, in February 2007. Dated from the 17th century, it is unique in that it remains sealed and is the first of its type on record that has been found with the contents intact. It was examined by Dr Alan Massey, a noted expert in the field, who claims that you can feel that there is liquid inside when you hold it in your hands.

There are around 200 historic witch bottles on record, of which 130 were constructed of Bellarmines. Examples of witch bottles can be viewed in a number of different museums, including the Pitt Rivers Museum, in Oxford, and the Museum of Witchcraft in Boscastle, Cornwall (*see Chapter 1, pages 38–39*).

Witch Posts

The term "witch post" is a relatively modern one, used to describe curious wooden timbers that were carved with arcane symbols and incorporated into the construction of old timber-framed buildings around the Yorkshire Moors in the 17th century.

In many cases the witch posts have been incorporated into the construction of the chimney, with the carvings facing out into the room. In other examples, the posts have been near doorways, again facing into the room. It is suggested that their magickal power was to ward away evil from the household, and that their positioning is testimony to this. The chimney or doorway were both seen as being vulnerable parts of the home where malign forces might try and enter.

With only one exception, the witch posts on record were found exclusively in longhouses in and around the North Yorkshire Moors. (The exception is one found in an old cottage in Rawtenstall, Lancashire.) Just how many witch posts might have been destroyed during modernization of older buildings is unknown – they may have been much more widespread than is thought. The examples on record come from Glaisdale, Danby, Scarborough, Rosedale, Farndale, Egton, Gillamoor, Goathland and Lealholm; some have been removed while others are still in place.

The intricate carvings that decorate the witch posts incorporate many common designs, including primarily an "X" and several vertical hollows into which coins or pins might be placed as offerings to a house spirit, or to placate the energies in the building. Other common shapes include a pricked heart – an ancient symbol of sympathetic protection magick and the phases of the moon – deeply associated with witchcraft. Although no one knows for sure, it is likely that these posts were created to expel evil forces and act as counter-magick against any hex sent upon the household.

One theory relating to witch posts is that they were not created by Cunning Men and Women as magickal deterrents at all, but that they were in fact a ward created by a priest named Nicholas Postgate, who is known to have travelled in the North Yorkshire area at the times when witch posts were created. After visiting a building and dispelling any witchcraft that had been placed upon it, he would carve the cross into the wood to act as a barrier against further magickal intrusion.

Whoever actually created the witch posts, one thing is certain: they were intended to keep evil magick at bay and were a powerful ward given pride of place by their owners. Steve Patterson, a contemporary Cornish Cunning Man who fashions witch posts among other things, says that they also acted as a kind of tribal totem, and was taken from place to place when a family moved, the post conferring common rights of freehold on the new home.

Many of the witch posts were created in oak, but the one found in a Danby shoemaker's shop was fashioned from rowan. Rowan, also known as "witchwood", is believed to have powerful magickal properties of protection, further proof that these posts were indeed formed as protection devices. Several other posts are thought to have been made from the wood of this protective tree.

The best examples of the witch posts can now be seen in the collection of Augustus Pitt Rivers, an eminent 18th-century ethnologist and archaeologist, who amassed an amazing collection of ancient magickal items from all over the world. These are now part of his legacy in the museum bearing his name in Oxford. Other examples can be seen at the Ryedale Folk Museum in Hutton-le-Hole, Yorkshire.

In 2006 I was lucky enough to be involved in some interesting research concerning a curious find at an old 16th-century manor house in Lancashire called Mains Hall. The intriguing find was hidden inside a wattle and daub wall, and was discovered during renovations. It is thought to be a derivative witch post or charm of warding.

The "witch post" as it has become known, had, at first glance, been thought of by its owner as an ancient form of "tally stick", but after I was shown the stick and asked for my opinion, a more magickal use was pondered.

Along with the stick's owner, a research strategy was planned, and our first port of call was Graham King, of the Museum of Witchcraft in Cornwall (*see Chapter 1, pages 38–39*). The museum is the centre of occult studies in the United Kingdom, and has amassed an enormous amount of ancient documents pertaining to magickal practices all over the world. This collection includes a large amount of material on English folk magick, which we thought might provide clues as to the identification of the stick.

After taking a look at the photographs of the stick that had been supplied by the owner, Graham and his assistant, Hannah Fox, decided to check against records of alchemical and runic alphabets to see if the symbols matched. In some cases they were very close, but they did not tally exactly. Largely based on the fact that the artefact was discovered inside a wall, over a doorway entrance to the Hall, the museum decided to file the documents under "witch post", as this was the most likely identification of the object.

Graham was quick to point out that traditional witch posts are usually on show inside the building, rather than being "hidden" – they are typically carved into a doorway, fireplace or newel post. The symbols on such witch posts grant the household magickal protection against malign influences, including witches with ill intent towards the building or its inhabitants.

In order to conduct further investigations, Graham and Hannah suggested we contact Brian Hoggard, an expert in folk magick. After contacting Brian at *Apotropaios* – his online folk magick resource – he agreed to offer his expert opinion. He concluded that the artefact had been highly prized by its owner, as it had been repaired (it has a break at one end) and concealed. He also suggested that it may have some connection with family lineage or descent, but admitted that this was a hunch and was not based on any concrete evidence.

Next we contacted Ian Evans, who conducts research into magickal protection of houses. Ian told me: "Your staff, at least when it went into the wall, certainly had a ritual purpose and its placement above the door (front or back: it doesn't matter) was significant. It was, I believe, intended to deter witches and/or evil spirits from entering the house. The symbols were perhaps a warning that this was a household that should not be taken lightly." He went on to say that in some cases, practitioners of folk magick would use a variety of symbols from different sources, and therefore not all the symbols may come from the same arcane alphabets. He also suggested that we contact Dr Owen Davies at the University of Hertfordshire, who has written several books on traditional English magick.

Dr Davies told us: "I am sometimes sceptical of some of the claims made regarding timber marks and their magical significance – some are merely carpenter's marks made for practical purposes of assembly. However, I am certain that this stick had a magical purpose, not only because of the symbols but also because of its location over an entrance. I presume it served the same purpose as written charms that were secreted over doorways – i.e. protection from evil spirits and witches.

"I've been comparing the carvings on the stick with charms and magical symbols from medieval and 16th-century charms and books of magic. The semicircle is likely to be a quartered circle, which crops up in magic charms, as do vertical lines intersected by two horizontal lines. The significance of the crosses is obvious. As a group of symbols they don't make any particular sense together, and I would speculate that it was a simple concoction of symbols created by a Cunning Man or Woman that was meant to have the appearance of occult significance."

The stick is now back in its rightful place after having made a whistle-stop tour of the entire country! I hope that its magick will continue to protect those that live at Mains Hall.

Spirit Houses

The spirit house is an ancient form of folk magick and serves a similar purpose to a witch ball. Fashioned from the fallen twigs of sacred trees, which are woven together to create a globelike cage structure, the spirit house is hung in the home to provide a haven for an otherwise troublesome or mischievous spirit.

Magickal herbs, feathers and sometimes stones are placed around or inside the spirit house to attract the spiritual energies. Once entered, it is believed the spirit cannot escape and is trapped inside the cage, where it can do no harm to the members of the household.

I have used a spirit house for many years. It was originally made by a Dartmoor witch, and has coloured ribbons and stones attached to it. Rather than keeping house spirits inside against their will, mine is charged to allow them entry and exit as they please. Instead of acting as a prison, it is a defined space that they can call their own.

Sprite Trap

Similar to the spirit house, but used to catch unwanted preternatural beings that might be troubling the household, the sprite trap is a form of magick that catches sprites at night.

Formed from a blackthorn stave and copper wire, a web of red threads is bound to the wood. The magickal Dagaz rune is carved into the wood to empower it and the trap is loaded with an enticement in the form of a lit candle that is thought to attract the faery beings, much akin to a moth being drawn to a flame.

At nightfall the trap is placed wherever the spiritual disturbances have been taking place and it is left until dawn. After the trap has caught the sprite, it is removed from the location and the thread web is cut from the stave with a white hilted knife. The thread web, which is believed to contain the sprite, is placed into a bottle that is corked and sealed with red wax. It is then buried and forgotten about. If the bottle is ever discovered and the seal broken, the sprite would be released. Although it may be angry about being imprisoned, it would be disorientated by the fact that it was buried away from the location where it was caught. It would, therefore, be unable to take revenge upon those who captured it.

Cat Protection Magick

Prior to the 18th century it was common practice to place the body of a dried cat and mouse into the roof space, wall or beneath the floor of a house in order to bring protection from rats and other vermin. The cat and mouse would be posed in a lifelike posture before being sealed up to work their magick. It has been suggested that the "hunting" pose will ward off the spirits of trespassing witches' familiars in the form of spirit cats that may try and enter the building, so this charm is thought to work on both a practical and spiritual level.

There are over a hundred examples of mummified cats on record being found in England.

A particularly good example can be seen at The Red Cat Hotel, near King's Lynn, in Norfolk, which takes its name from the feline found hidden in the building.

The Cunning Shoe

Concealed shoes – that is, shoes intentionally hidden in wall cavities, chimneys and beneath floorboards in old buildings – are relatively common throughout England. Indeed over 1,200 examples of this early form of sympathetic magick have been recorded to date, according to Brian Hoggard.

It is important to note that in times past, shoes were a valuable commodity as they were among the most expensive items an average family would have to buy. It is therefore clear that by discarding them in magickal practice, belief in their effectiveness as a charm of protection must have run very deep.

The local village Cunning Man or Woman would advise householders to conceal a single shoe in the fabric of a house with the intention that it would act as a magickal decoy and that any evil spirit or ill intent sent upon the family would be caught in the shoe and dispersed. This belief harkens back to the end of the 13th century when the rector of North Marston in Buckinghamshire is reputed to have cast the Devil into a boot. Many of the examples discovered in England date back centuries, but there are more modern examples dating from the beginning of the 20th century as well.

The most recent discovery of Cunning shoes was made at The Aspinall Arms inn in Mitton, Lancashire. A pair of ancient children's shoes, faded by the centuries and measuring only 7.5 centimetres (3 inches) in length, were found concealed beneath floorboards in the building in July 2007. They had lain undisturbed for 300 years according to a local historian who examined them, and were only found because the building was undergoing renovation. The landlord stated in the local press that he would return the shoes to their hiding place, where they would continue their warding magick. It is suggested that perhaps they were a charm against the "witches" at nearby Pendle Hill (*see Chapter 1, pages 20-23*). Although they are not unique, pairs of shoes found together are much rarer than the more common single ones.

In her book, *The Apocraphya* (Walking Stick Press, 2003), Gilly Sergiev states that Cunning shoes were also buried at sacred sites by women who wanted to place magickal protection upon their husbands and lovers. After placing ingredients, including rose petals, dried nettle leaves and garlic, into the toe of the shoe, along with the "essence" of their loved one in the form of a strand of hair or nail clippings, the shoe and contents would be taken to a sacred site of the Goddess, such as a fairy mound, sacred spring or standing stone, and offered to her for protection. The shoe would then be left under the watchful eye of the Goddess, from where she would bestow her protection upon its owner.

While attending a witches' Sabbat at Long Meg Stone Circle in Cumbria in February 2007,

I discovered a tree bedecked with ribbons, money and handwritten spells. At its centre a woman's shoe had been placed between the branches. Without doubt, a modern Cunning Shoe under the protection of Long Meg.

Pierced Heart

A heart pierced with pins or thorns is an ancient form of folk magick. In order to protect the home from evil magick, the heart of an animal, such as a sheep, would be pricked and placed in the chimney to dry out. As it shrivelled up, so would the magick that had been sent to bring harm upon the household.

In itself the shape of a heart is a powerful magickal amulet denoting love and life. Modern witches use a pin cushion made of red fabric and shaped as a heart to cast spells. The magickal intention is written on the cushion with letters or symbols made of pins and placed upon the altar to charge.

Binding

Magick that is cast to stop something that is in the midst of happening is called "binding". For example, a binding spell might silence a gossiper, stop a bully or put an end to a love affair. Binding magick is always performed with clear intent, ensuring that personal hatred and anger are not involved.

Blasting

In medieval times, a witch would "blast" the crops of a farmer if he had upset her. Blasting is the act of making something infertile. In a modern context, this mean rendering an actual person infertile, or it could mean that a situation that would be rendered infertile and lose abundance. A witch would traditionally use a thorny blackthorn staff to point at her subject when blasting them.

Banishing

In banishing magick a witch will cast away something he or she wishes to be rid of. This is different to binding in that instead of simply stopping something, it is banished, sent away never to return. Examples of this type of magick might include a witch banishing someone who has wronged them.

Constructing

Magick that asks for something that does not already exist to be created or constructed is known as Constructing magick. An example might be for a new job to come into someone's life, a new relationship or a new direction.

Hexing

Hexing in its basic form is magick that intends to send harm upon something, whether this be a person, a group of people, a family or even a place. Also known as cursing, once cast, a hex must be dispelled and banished before its effects will stop. A hex might be placed upon an enemy or upon someone who has treated another badly.

Charming

Charming is a cross-cultural form of folk magick, examples of which can be seen in the history of magick around the world. It incorporates the making of amulets, talismans and ritual objects to bring about magickal change in their presence. Also known as sympathetic magick, charms can be created for good or bad purposes.

The Hand of Glory

The "hand of glory" dates from the late 16th century. It is made from the right hand of an executed murderer, which must be cut off while the body is still hanging from the gallows.

After the blood is squeezed from the flesh, it must be embalmed in a shroud and steeped in "saltpetre" or "salt and peppers" for 14 nights. The hand is then dried either in the sun or wrapped in vervain (a herbaceous plant that is believed to repel demons) and slowly baked in an oven.

Once dried and preserved, a "dead man's candle", fashioned from the fat of the same murderer, fresh wax, sesame and with his hair as a wick, is fixed between the fingers of the hand. In an alternative recipe, the entire hand may be dipped in the mixture so that the fingers themselves may be lit as candles.

Once fashioned and lit, the hand of glory casts a powerful magick over those that see it, for it renders them motionless and speechless. It is widely featured in anecdotal tales of thievery, whereby the burglar would use the hand of glory to ensure that the occupants of the house would remain in a deep sleep while he robbed them. If the candle refused to light, this was taken as an indication that a member of the household was awake and could not be charmed.

According to one account, a young servant maid observed a thief in her master's house and tried to dowse the flames so that the household might wake and catch him, but she could not put out the flame with water nor beer. After throwing fresh milk on the grisly charm, its hypnotic flame finally went out, releasing the occupants of the building from the spell and waking the entire family.

A counter-spell can be prepared in preparation for deflecting the magick of the hand of glory. The fat of a white hen, blood of a screech owl and bile of a black cat would be mixed and smeared across thresholds, chimney stacks and window frames. Wherever the ointment had been placed, the hand of glory would have no effect.

An example of this charm can be found in the Whitby Museum, in Yorkshire, where, according to its website, it is the most popular exhibit!

Mole Foot Charm

In order to avert toothache and cramps an old folk charm directs you to collect moles' feet. Dry them out and place them into a small bag before wearing it around your neck!

The Magickal Mistletoe Pouch

Mistletoe is a plant sacred to the Druids and renowned for its powers of fertility and protection. At Yule, mistletoe must be gathered, dried and crushed and placed in a pouch made of green fabric. When securely fastened, the pouch can be hung over a doorway to promote harmony in the home and offers a warm welcome to visitors throughout the year. If you kiss a lover beneath the mistletoe pouch, or indeed any sprig of the plant, your love will deepen. Hung over the bed, the mistletoe pouch can induce restful sleep and peaceful dreams.

Lemon Charm

To bring happiness and prosperity to a friend, a witch would take a fresh lemon at midnight, the "witching hour", and stick brightly coloured pins into it. The colours chosen would reflect happiness and health and by pricking the lemon the pins would destroy its bitterness and subsequently any negativity around the subject of the charm.

Horseshoe Charm

An upturned horseshoe hung over a doorway brings good fortune to the building, but care must be taken to make sure it is mounted with both ends pointing up into the sky, otherwise the "luck" may fall out of it.

Rowan Tree Charm

A simple charm for protection can be made from two sprigs of the rowan tree. Tied together with red ribbon or thread in the shape of a cross and inscribed with the Ogham symbol of the rowan tree, the charm brings protection to the home or, if worn on the body, the wearer.

Another powerful form of rowan-tree charming is made by threading dried berries on to a cord and hanging it on the back of the front door to deter unwanted intruders and enemies. This form of protection can also be utilized as a personal talisman of protection by wearing the string around the neck.

Chilli Pepper Charm

In the grip of winter when the winds are bitter cold, the witches of old were challenged to bring warmth into the house. They would bind together hot chilli peppers and hang them over the fireplace to bring extra warmth.

Garlic and Ribbon Charm
In order to silence a noisy spirit, a witch would bind together a string of garlic bulbs with red, blue, green and white ribbons before hanging it where the disturbance was taking place. The colours of the ribbons represent the four elements – earth, air, fire and water – and the garlic performs the exorcism of the spirit.

Snail Shell Charm
Forms of fertility magick can be found throughout history. One powerful charm to encourage pregnancy was the snail shell charm.

Associated with sexual prowess, snails' shells would be bound together with a red cord before being hung around the home. The red colour signifies passion and love, and the shells encourage fertility.

Three Bee Charm
An old Cornish witchcraft charm to ensure a happy life. By placing three dead bumble bees in a blue pouch and hanging it in a sunny spot of the home, the charmer will attract health, happiness and good fortune to the sun-blessed spot. An example of a three bee charm can be seen in the Museum of Witchcraft in Cornwall (*see Chapter 1, page 38*).

Orange Charm
In olden times, to ensure a lifelong happy union, two oranges would be stuffed with cloves, before being joined together with a stick. This sweet-smelling charm would then be fastened to the underside of the couple's bed, or attached, unseen, behind the bedhead.

Hag Stones
Naturally holed stones are known as "hag stones" or "holey stones". They are created over hundreds of years by the forces of water, and are considered valuable talismans by witches. Like most magickal items, it is believed that they should not be bought for money; rather, they should be sought out in rivers, streams and beaches to ensure that their magickal power is not jeopardized.

Hung over the main entrance to a house, the stones ward away evil and fend off wandering spirits, while placing them near to the bed will ensure peaceful sleep as a bad dream will be dissolved by the stone, after passing through the hole to reach you. Worn around the neck on a red cord, the stones give protection to the wearer; they can also be hung on a string and used as a pendulum if they are small enough.

Sometimes you will hear people refer to these stones as "fairy stones", as they can also be used as a "key" to the Faery Realms. If you peer through the centre of the stone, you might catch a glimpse of a faery being.

In other uses, a hag stone strung on a long cord and hurled around in the air was thought in times past to dispel bad weather, storms and rain clouds.

I have found two hag stones in my lifetime – one on a beautiful beach in Branscombe, Devon, and another on Hayling Island, off the coast of Hampshire. If you spend a little time searching, you might be lucky enough to find one yourself. It's a fun way to spend your time at the seaside and a valuable magickal tool for you to use in your Craft work.

MAGICKAL METHODS

There are many ways of performing the various types of magic we have explored. Below is a sampling of some of the more popular methods witches use to practise their magic.

Witch's Ladder

Making a witch's ladder is an effective magickal practice, during which an intent is tied into a piece of cord or rope while the desired outcome is focused in the mind of the witch. The colour of the cord should correspond with the desired outcome of the magick, and the length should be divisible by three (as previously mentioned, the number three represents the Triple Goddess, and is considered a powerful magickal number).

To make a witch's ladder, first tie a knot at each end of the cord, then tie one in the middle, then tie one in the middle of each space that is left until you have tied nine knots. As you tie each knot the following incantation should be said aloud:

By knot of one the spell's begun,
By knot of two the spell is true,
By knot of three so mote it be,
By knot of four the open door,
By knot of five the spell's alive,
By knot of six the spell I fix,
By knot of seven the gates of heaven,
By knot of eight the hand of fate,
By knot of nine the spell is mine.

Both solitary practitioners and covens use the witch's ladder to perform magick. If working as part of a group, the cord can be passed around the circle with each covenor tying one knot and chanting the appropriate magickal words before passing it on to the next.

In some records, the completed ladder should be buried and forgotten about, while in others it should be kept in case the magick needs to be undone later. To reverse the effect, the knots can be undone to release the magick tied into them and the cord burned.

In another variation of the witch's ladder, human hair or nail clippings would be tied into the knots to bind someone to the witch's will. The bound cord would be stored in a box until the offender was no longer a threat and the knots could be untied, dispelling the magick.

Sea Witchery

Centuries ago, without the ability to accurately predict weather patterns, sailors would employ the services of a witch before they went to sea. After paying the required fee, the witch would "whistle up the wind" in a cord or handkerchief and give it to the sailor.

Working near the sea, where the Elementals of air and water would aid the witch in her work, the first knot would be charged by the witch to contain a gentle breeze, the second a strong wind, and the third a tempest. As the witch tied the knots they would whistle and the strength and length of the whistling would be replicated in the strength of the winds she tied into the cord. When the gust was insufficient to drive the boat, a knot would be undone on the cord, thereby releasing the required wind into the sails and ensuring a swift and safe journey for those aboard.

Wort Cunning

In many traditions of witchcraft, especially Celtic traditions, herbs and trees are believed to have magickal properties and sacred uses. Herbs have long been used in healing and magick, though the herbalists of the past might have been called witches for possessing arcane knowledge. Herbs have many uses, including in cookery, burning as incense and healing the sick. The traits and significance of each plant vary from culture to culture, and their attributed magickal properties have developed over many centuries of witchdom.

In centuries past, trees provided fuel for warmth and cooking, shelter as building materials and defence as weaponry, so it is easy to understand why the tree played such a vital role in the daily lives of many. By touching a tree a witch might sense its "spirit"; indeed, many believe that preternatural spirit creatures known as Dryads live within trees.

I was once forced to fell a willow tree in the garden of a former home to make way for an extension, and a fellow witch showed me a ritual to entice the Dryad to leave its home and move into a small branch. It was simply a case of placing my hands on to the trunk of the tree and explaining that it would soon be felled, and that in order to survive, the tree spirit, or Dryad, should move into the selected branch where it would be safe. I then cut the branch from the tree and have kept it safely ever since.

III

SEASONS OF THE WITCH

IN THIS CHAPTER WE EXPLORE THE WHEEL OF THE YEAR,
a fundamental part of the witch's lifestyle. The ever-changing seasons of
life, death and rebirth are echoed in the philosophy of the witch.
Called "The Sabbats", they are the nights of magickal forces, celebration
and ritual that unite the worlds of humankind and magick at eight
special times of the year.

"The Wheel is never still; as the witch learns,
like a mill, it turns and turns."

ou will often find witches using the abbreviations "BCE" or "CE" when describing particular years in an era. These stand for "Before Common Era" and "Common Era", and are used in place of the widely adopted Christianized versions "BC" and "AD", standing for "Before Christ" and "Anno Domini", meaning "In the year of our Lord". This latter method of labelling eras dates back to 525 CE, and was adopted throughout Western Europe during the 8th century. The terms derive from a traditionally accepted year of the birth of Christ, and thus derive from Christianity. For this reason, many Pagans and witches prefer to use alternative terminology that is not associated with the religion that persecuted their ancestors.

THE MAGICKAL YEAR

Witches observe a yearly calendar of "Sabbats" (from the word "Sabbath") that occur eight times a year. These hearken back to old agricultural celebrations and the solstices and equinoxes. The calendar begins on the first day of November, and the first Sabbat of the year is Yule. The eight Sabbats are known collectively as the Wheel of the Year. As the year progresses the wheel turns, making one complete revolution every 365 days.

In times past, witches were thought to fly upon their besoms to the Sabbat to meet with the Devil and copulate with him after enjoying a feast of unbaptized babies! This was an untruth popularized during The Burning Times, when witchcraft was illegal and witches were classed as heretics. In reality, the Sabbat is a day of celebration and ritual during which food and drink is shared and ritual magick performed. Through one revolution of the Wheel of the Year, the story of the Triple Goddess beginning as Maiden and evolving to Mother and finally Crone, unfold. So too the story of the God, who is born at Yule and grows to his most powerful at Litha before being cut down at the first harvest and descending into the afterworld, only to be reborn once again at Yule. Witches consider this cyclic tale to be very important as it reflects all that we see in the world around us as the Wheel of the Year turns.

THE SABBATS

There are eight Sabbats in one turn of the Wheel of the Year. The four Greater Sabbats – Samhain, Imbolc, Beltane and Lughnasadh, and the four Lesser Sabbats – Yule, Ostara, Litha and Mabon. The Greater Sabbats are always celebrated on the same dates, while the Lesser Sabbats are celebrated on or around the dates given; this varies year by year dependent on the position of the earth in relation to the celestial forces above.

YULE
Lesser Sabbat
On or around 21 December – Winter Solstice

The word Yule is pronounced "yool", and comes from the Anglo Saxon word "yula", meaning "wheel" (as in "of the year"). It is sometimes called Yuletide, while the Druids called it Alban Arthan, meaning "Light of Winter". The Roman version was Saturnalia, while to Christians it is, of course, Christmas.

The consistent theme of Yule is rebirth. In the darkest time of the year, when the world is frozen and in stasis, witches celebrate the return of the light and the sun, personified in the world of witchcraft as the Horned God who is born of the Goddess at Yule. Through the recurrent theme of birth, death and rebirth, which manifests through the Wheel of the Year, the God is reborn at Yule, bringing hope and light back to the dark world.

Yule is celebrated on the winter solstice, the shortest day of the year. From here on the days become longer as the God grows, represented by the sun's power, which grows daily after the solstice. As the Horned God is also the father of the reborn God, he is seen as reincarnating.

The similarity between this ancient theme of rebirth in the twilight of the year and the story of the Christ child being born at Christmas is no accident. Yule, like many other Pagan celebrations, was Christianized by the Church in an attempt to stamp out the Old Gods and replace

CHRISTMAS TREES

The bringing in of a green tree at Christmas is of Pagan origin. It symbolized the welcoming in of the Old God to the home, in the hope he would bless those that lived there. The symbol of green life against the dead world would have been particularly inspiring to the ancients and by bringing him into the home, they would be asking the God to return, in the form of the sun. The acts of hanging baubles and lighting the tree with candles have their origins in witch balls (*see Chapter 2, pages 55–56*) and in bringing light into the home to encourage the growth of the sun as the God.

the age-old beliefs with new ones, hence the story of Christ being born on 25 December was created. In fact, the date of 25 December for the alleged birth of Jesus Christ is debatable. Shepherds were "watching their flocks in the fields around Bethlehem" when the child was supposedly born, yet between November and March sheep would not be in the fields; they would have been brought undercover for the winter months. It was simply convenient for the Church to adapt the existing popular Pagan celebration, with its theme of rebirth, into its own version of the birth of Christ.

The Yule log (now represented as a chocolate pudding) is of ancient Pagan origin. The log would be carefully chosen from the branches of a sacred tree before being ceremonially welcomed across the threshold of the home on Yule Eve. After being carried three times around the house it would be decorated with ivy, ribbons and colourful decorations before being ritually set alight on the fire hearth, the heart of the home. As the Yule log burned it would bring the God into the home in the form of the light it created. After the log had burned out, a small piece of the remnants would be reclaimed as a lucky charm that would be kept in the hearth until next Yule, when it would be used as kindling to light the Yule log. In this way the God was ever present in the home, and the kindling lighting the new log each year would be symbolic of his reincarnation.

Wreaths of greenery, which are often placed upon doors and in our homes around Christmas time, represent the Wheel of the Year. The green colour symbolizes regrowth and the Green Man (*see Chapter 4, page 89*). The hanging of mistletoe in the home is a Druid ceremony; the white beads represent the seed of the God, under which couples kiss and ask for their union to be blessed by him. Mistletoe would be hung above the main door where it would bless all who entered through the year, until Yule, when it would be cast into the fire and replaced with a new sprig. This was another ceremony of reincarnation.

Furthering the reincarnation theme at Yule, the Holly King (who reigns between Litha and Yule) and the Oak King (who reigns between Yule and Litha) fight a duel. The Holly King dies and the Oak King prevails. The lighter half of the year now begins – days grow longer and oak prospers in spring and summer, as does the God as the Green Man.

Modern witches celebrate all of these age-old traditions at Yule. They bring greenery into the home in the form of holly, ivy and evergreen trees; they also light candles and burn the Yule log.

IMBOLC
Greater Sabbat
2 February

The witches' Festival of Light, as it is often called, is known as Imbolc, pronounced "imolk". Also known as "Oimelc", the name of this Sabbat means literally "in the belly" or "milk of ewes", and its theme is the return of life in the abundance that is stirring at this time of year. Lambs are born in the fields and nature begins to come back to life: animals emerge from their winter hideaways. Although the air is still cold and the world is in the grip of winter, the fire festival of Imbolc is a celebration that the light is returning to the world and growing fast. The God, who was reborn at Yule as the sun, is now a young man and manifests as Robin Goodfellow.

The Celtic Triple Goddess, Brigid, is closely associated with Imbolc. She is a goddess of spring and her flower, which has poked its head through the icy ground frost at Imbolc, is the snowdrop. The Goddess is the Maiden aspect of the Triple Goddess concept during Imbolc – young and carefree.

It is traditional for Pagan and magickal folk to welcome Brigid into the household by fashioning a corn dolly, or poppet, in her likeness from the harvest sheafs cut down the previous year. The doll would be dressed in white by the women folk and decorated with ribbons and jewellery. A soft, welcoming bed would be prepared for Brigid, near to the hearth of the home. After being "called in", the poppet would be placed in the bed and a wand placed next to her. The wand symbolized the phallus of the young God, who represented the fertility and abundance that would encourage prosperity for those working the magick. The act of creating the poppet and bed by the fire was seen as an invitation for Brigid to spend the night inside the home. The emphasis was on making the bed seem attractive, and offerings would be placed around it, such as food and drink.

The ashes in the hearth would be examined the following morning for signs that Brigid had visited, leaving either footsteps in the ash, or having used the wand to draw signs that must be interpreted for their meanings.

Another activity honoured at Imbolc is the making of sun crosses, or Brigid's Crosses as they are sometimes called. Fashioned from straw, corn sheafs or rushes, these are a solar symbol and a ritual of sympathetic folk magick to encourage the sun to increase, ensuring an abundant harvest. In modern times they are made and hung in the home as talismans of prosperity, protection and fertility. Any remnants of the Yuletide tree or greenery that had decorated the home were burned at Imbolc, to let go of the past and make way for the new. This is a practice that continues today.

The lighting of great hearth fires and many candles at Imbolc is central to its celebration – the light has penetrated the darkness of winter and is growing. To symbolize this, all lighting would be extinguished, including all hearth fires, plunging the households of each village into darkness. Then, from the fire of Brigid, a piece of kindling would be taken into the home and its hearth fire would be lit. Brigid had brought light into the home and the celebration of the return of life to the land had begun.

The Christianized version of Imbolc is known as Candlemas. Its theme of candles and light is borrowed from the older Pagan celebration. Again, the Church, unable to destroy this "heathen" celebration, twisted its original meaning and claimed it, misleadingly, as its own.

OSTARA
Lesser Sabbat
On or around 21 March – Spring Equinox

Ostara, pronounced "O' 'stara", is celebrated at the spring equinox – the first day of spring. It is also known as Alban Eilir by the Druids – meaning "light of the earth", Eostar in some Pagan traditions and Lady Day and Easter in the Christian calendar.

The Sabbat is named after the Teutonic goddess of spring, Eostre, who was connected with the Greek goddess, Astarte. It is claimed that the Christian word "Easter" is directly derived from Eostre, whose themes are celebrated at this time of year.

The symbols of eggs and the hare are at the centre of Ostara. The egg is the symbol of this feast day for a variety of reasons – including the fact that it is a universal symbol of renewal and new life, bringing with it hope and promise of the future. The egg was associated with Ostara because it was the time of year when hens would begin laying eggs – bringing food and sustenance. Hens only lay eggs during times of the year when at least 12 hours of sun hits the retina of their eyes, and thus eggs were laid only between the spring and autumn equinoxes.

BELTANE
Greater Sabbat
1 May

The great fire festival of the Pagan god Bel and Celtic god of the sun, Beltane, which literally means "bright fire" in Old Irish, is the most joyous of the witches' Sabbats. Also known as May Day, Beltene and Bealtaine, Beltane is pronounced "Bel tain". At Ostara, witches celebrate the

THE TALE OF THE HARE AND EOSTRE

The significance of the hare, which later became the "Easter Bunny", is of Pagan origin. The tradition of the hare hiding eggs that are searched for and then found has its roots in this ancient story:

All animals in the woodland loved Eostre, and at the spring equinox they would gather gifts to offer to her. One of her devotees was a young hare who wished to find a special gift for Eostre, but knowing her to be powerful and able to obtain anything she wished for, he was confused about what he could possibly give that would be of any value to her.

One day he came across a beautiful, fresh egg while foraging in the vegetation, and he was just about to break it open when he thought of Eostre. Perhaps this would make a perfect gift for her? He soon realized, however, that she probably had all the eggs she could ever need and so, wrapping the egg carefully under his arm, he returned home.

Later that evening he wondered how he might make the egg special so that it would reflect the beauty that Eostre brought to the world each spring. He began decorating the shell with colourful paints made from the flowers in the forest and drew symbols of Eostre all over the egg. When he had finished he bounded through the forest in search of the goddess and presented her with his decorated gift. Eostre was so pleased that she wanted all children, themselves representative of new life, throughout the world to enjoy the same treat. Thus the tale of the Easter Bunny delivering decorated eggs was born.

The tale of course has been largely forgotten, and the careful decoration replaced with gaudy silver foils and mass-made chocolate sweets, but the principle is the same. The egg-decorating custom came originally from the Teutonic traditions in which Eostre was first worshipped, and now witches and Pagans continue the tradition by using natural dyes made from plant and herb extracts to colour eggs before drawing symbols, pictures and words that represent their wishes upon them, and burying them in the ground as "seeds" that will come to fruition over the summer months.

fertility of nature, while at Beltane it is human fertility that is celebrated with wild frenzy and playful abandon.

As the sun grows stronger day by day in the sky, the God has reached manhood. Together with the Goddess, the pair consummate their sexual union. The marriage of the gods is also a theme with couples on earth, with handfasting being traditionally undertaken at Beltane. At

PERFORMING THE MAYPOLE DANCE

1   Place the maypole firmly in the ground and attach an even number of streamers of your chosen colours to the top with nails. They should be one a half times the height of the pole in length.

2   Each dancer holds the end of a streamer taut and every other dancer faces deosil. The remaining dancers should face widdershins.

3   When the music begins, the dancers should weave in and out of each other, alternating between passing the person coming towards them on the left and then on the right.

Beltane the union is said to hold particular value, as it is also the time of the union between God and Goddess; male and female. In a special ceremony, the couple will be joined together in magickal union and their hands will be bound together to symbolize their love for each other. Pagan handfastings can be undertaken for a year, a lifetime or forever. Once tied together the couple will jump over a besom, which symbolizes them entering a new stage of life as a couple, leaving behind their lives as single people.

In the natural world, everything would have been blooming and the undergrowth would have been lush and green at this time. The green leaves that appeared on the trees represented the growth of the Green Man as the God, who was born at Yule. Great hill fires, known as balefires, were lit and farmer's cattle would be driven through them, the act magickally purifying them from disease, poisons and illness.

The maypole was at the centre of Beltane celebrations. Traditionally felled from a hawthorn tree, the pole would be erected on the village green and crowned with foliage. Colourful streamers or ribbons would be attached to the top of the pole, and Pagans would dance around it, weaving the ribbon around the trunk in an organized frenzy of fun and laughter (*see above box*).

The pole itself represents the phallus of the God, while the act of encircling and eventually engulfing it with the streamers symbolizes the mating ritual of the God and Goddess. This ritual would magickally grant plentiful blessings upon the land and the lives of those who took part.

Inhibition is put aside during the themes of Beltane, and singing, dancing and feasting is actively enjoyed. It is the first day of the Celtic summer, when life is good, crops are growing and the sun God, now balanced and equal with the Goddess, shines brightly down on the mortal realm.

LITHA
Lesser Sabbat
On or around 21 June – Summer Solstice

The word "solstice" literally means "sun stands still", and Midsummer, called "Litha" by modern Pagans and witches, is a celebration of the longest day, when the power of the sun, represented as the male aspect of deity, is at his strongest. Pronounced "Lee tha", the name of this Sabbat derives from a Saxon word that literally means "the opposite of Yule" – Litha lies on the opposite side of the Wheel of the Year in the witch's calendar. Druids know this celebration as Alban Hefin (*hefin* means summer in Welsh), and it is also referred to simply as "Midsummer" in some witchcraft circles.

On Midsummer's Eve, the preternatural creatures of the Faery Realm are said to be abroad in the land of the living, and care must be taken to avoid upsetting them. This is also a time for harvesting herbs for magickal use and a potent time for spellcasting. Magickal plants are cut using the sacred white hilted knife of Boline, and care must be taken to ensure that they do not drop onto the ground after harvesting, lest their magickal energies drain away into the earth.

At Litha, the Goddess is to be blessed by the Sun God; harvest would soon come and a plentiful crop would be asked for. The Goddess is also the bountiful Mother aspect of the Triple Goddess concept at Litha. She has mated with the God at Beltane, and her blooming can be seen in flowers, birds and animals. The God as the Green Man, is manifest as wild abundance in the forests and woods; at Litha he is king, and at the zenith of his strength. After Litha, the God begins to change, slowly beginning to turn towards the dark half of the year as trees, plants and life slowly begin to wane and die. Without death there can be no life, just as without darkness there can be no light.

SUN WHEEL

One tradition at Litha is to make a sun wheel out of thin tree branches and decorate it with the colours of the Sun God. When it is complete, it is hung in the branches of a tree or some wild place as a reminder of the God's power and to ask for his protection. In an old European tradition, a huge sun wheel would be fashioned and would be set alight before being rolled down a hill across fields to be blessed by the Sun God. Harvest would soon come and a plentiful crop would be asked for.

The position of the standing stones, or monoliths, at Stonehenge are perfectly aligned so that they mark the position of the rising sun at the Midsummer solstice. As the sun rises over the heel stone it casts a long, phallic shadow into the heart of the circle itself, representing the joining of the Sun God (male) and Earth Mother (female).

As takes place at Yule, at Litha the Oak King (who reigns between Yule and Litha) and the Holly King (who reigns between Litha and Yule) fight a duel. This time, the Oak King dies and the Holly King prevails. The Holly King prospers in autumn and winter, as does the God as Lord of the Wild Hunt.

The themes of Litha are fulfilment and change. That which was planned at Yule and set in motion by burying eggs at Ostara will now have reached fruition. But change is also upon us. The dark half of the year beckons in the shadows and awaits us on the following day, when the sun begins to die and the days become shorter.

LUGHNASADH
Greater Sabbat
1 August

The first harvest (there are two) is the Sabbat of Lughnasadh. Pronounced "loo nasa", the name means Lugh's assembly and refers to the Celtic god of the same name. It is also known as Lammas in the Christian calendar, which relates to Loaf Mass – the time when bread is baked as wheat crops are harvested.

Lammas is a celebration of harvest. In times past this "harvest" would have been agricultural, but in a modern context it can be an appreciation of what has been obtained in terms of receiving that which was requested earlier in the Wheel of the Year from the Gods.

As the crops are harvested in the fields, the God too is harvested. Cut down with the wheat, he is manifest as John Barleycorn and symbolically dies, beginning his journey into the underworld.

Sacrifice is the main theme of Lughnasadh. In past times a loaf in the shape of Lugh, the God, would be made from the first flour ground from the harvest and offered on the altar as thanks to the God and Goddess for the bounty received. When the loaf is eaten, it symbolizes the God offering himself as a sacrifice – providing nourishment, but dying in the act, only to be reborn again at Yule.

The last sheaf of grain would not be cut; rather, it would be carefully plucked from the ground and fashioned into a corn dolly before being given pride of place in the home, where it would grant blessings upon those who lived there over the dark winter months to come. (The same corn dolly might be used at Imbolc as the Brigid poppet, or a new one would be made.)

Fruits and grains would be collected and stored in preparation for the coming dark months, when food is scarce and abundance gone. The first harvest of Lughnasadh might be plentiful, but the underlying theme of the oncoming death of the land should not be forgotten. Modern witches celebrate this festival with harvesting, cooking and feasting – a time for enjoying the fruits of one's labour. Witches give thanks for what they have and prepare for what is to come.

MABON
Lesser Sabbat
On or around 21 September – Autumn Equinox

The autumn equinox is known in contemporary witchcraft circles as Mabon. Pronounced "mah bon", the name derives from a Welsh god figure of the same name, and was penned as a witchcraft name for the autumn equinox by Aidan Kelly in the 1970s. The term is most commonly used in the United States, where the rise in popularity of Paganism, witchcraft and alternative faith systems has lead to a boom in published books on the topics, thereby spreading the use of the term. In England, many pagans and witches refuse to use the name, calling the festival simply the autumn equinox or the Druidic name Aban Efed. The Sabbat is also known as Harvest Home, and as Michaelmas to Christians.

Mabon is the second of the two harvest festivals in the Wheel of the Year, and is the Feast of Ingathering and Witches' Thanksgiving. Many believe it is a modern-day creation by the contemporary Pagan movement in the United States, although some references in Anglo Saxon history do indicate that a sacred festival took place at this time of the year.

The word "equinox" comes form the Latin word "*aequinoctium*", meaning "equal night", and on the autumn equinox balance is a central theme to the festival. At this time of year days and nights are the same length. It is a season of abundant harvest and thanksgiving.

Traditionally at Mabon, the Eleusian Mysteries, which relate to the afterlife, are observed in rituals and sacred dramas, while feasts of ripe fruit, nuts and vegetables are enjoyed. The cornucopia is a prevalent theme at this time, and represents the Horned God giving forth his generous abundance.

SAMHAIN
The Great Sabbat
31 October

Samhain, meaning "summers end", is the Great Sabbat of the witches, and is over 6,000 years old, dating back to 350 BCE. It is the last day in the cycle of the Wheel of the Year and in the Celtic calendar. Pronounced "sow een", it is also known as Samhuinn, Saven, Mischief Night,

PUMPKIN CARVING

The hollowing out of pumpkins is an Americanization of an ancient magickal ritual in which the flesh was scooped out of turnips and a demonic face carved in the remaining carcass. After placing a candle inside, the turnip would be positioned in a window to scare away any evil spirits that might be intent on bringing harm or trouble to the home. The use of pumpkins instead of turnips became favoured when the custom migrated to America, where they are known as Jack O' Lanterns.

Last Harvest, Blood Harvest and Hallowmass.

The commonly used name today, "Halloween", derives from the earlier names of "All Hallows Eve" or "All Hallow Even", both Christianized versions of the original Celtic witches' Sabbat that was demonized by the Church. By naming 1 November All Hallows Day and 2 November All Souls Day, the Christian church attempted to blot out the ancient customs, believing them to be a form of devilment. (In actual fact Pagans do not believe in the Devil; the Devil is a concept that was created by the Christian Church.)

At Samhain, as the mists of autumn gather around the bare trees in the twilight and the rusty leaves fall onto the ground, it is easy to see why this time of year is particularly associated with fear and uncertainty. Winter is coming and centuries ago that meant troubled times ahead. Would the supplies of food last through the cold and dark times that were fast approaching at this time of year? Would the weak and infirm make it through the winter?

As the sun sets on Samhain the rift between the mortal realm and the spirit world is at its weakest. The Celts believed that the night of Samhain existed "outside of time" and therefore could be used to view any other moment in time. Its primary themes therefore are the return of the dead and magickal divination. It is a time when mischievous sprites might cause trouble for the living, and this is the theme of the most well-loved Halloween tradition: the making of ghoulish glowing pumpkins with frightening smiles (*see above box*).

The theme of returning ancestors was both acknowledged and given the greatest respect at Samhain. Food and drink would be laid out to appease any visiting spectres that might return for one night to the places and buildings they had known in life. This was the origin of the "treat" in "trick or treat" as we know it today. If the spirit was not given a treat in the form of an offering, it might play a trick on the inhabitants of the household. Altars with black and orange candles, the central colours of Samhain, are erected in memoriam of those in the Summerland, and pictures of deceased ancestors and items they had owned are displayed alongside offerings of their favourite foods or drinks as hospitality for the visiting spirits.

The ceremony of the Dumb Supper is traditionally enacted at Samhain. During this supper, chairs and plates of food are set for the visiting spirits alongside those for the living guests. The feast is eaten in silence, the living remembering those that have gone and perhaps receiving a psychic message from the spirits present at the table.

Because of its strong association with the dead, Samhain is sometimes called "The Festival of the Dead", and most of the traditions revolve around this central theme. Communicating with spirits at Samhain is easier than at any other time of the year. A divination tool such as a dark mirror, scrying bowl, spirit board or the tarot may be employed in order to receive guidance from beyond.

At Samhain unmarried females might play a game at the stroke of midnight by staring intently at their own eyes in a mirror by the light of a single candle. It is said that in the gloom of the mirror a vision of their "husband to be" will manifest. Another traditional game is bobbing for apples, using only your teeth, in a pail of water. This too may originally have been a magickal divinatory custom.

The Goddess has become the withered Crone at Samhain, a wise woman whose deep knowledge and secrets are there to behold for those with the ability to access them. She carries within her womb the unborn God who will be reborn at Yule. The God has descended into the afterworld, and is manifest as Lord of the Wild Hunt, the Horned God who, although sacrificed at Lughnasadh, has survived in the shadows of the afterworld.

As Samhain draws to a close and midnight passes, so another turn of the Wheel of the Year passes, an ever revolving cycle of birth, death and rebirth.

BONE FIRES

The term "bonfire", originally known as a "bone fire", derives from a ritual that took place on Halloween night. On this night it was customary to light enormous fires and throw upon them the bones of perished cattle.

THE MAGICKAL MOON

In witchcraft the moon, which represents the female Triple Goddess (the sun represents the male Horned God) is considered sacred and is of great importance. As the moon directly affects tides on earth, the monthly menstrual cycle of women and the moods of all men (the word "lunatic" derives from strange lunar behaviour at the full moon), it is important that different types of magick are performed during the correct lunar phase of the moon.

Dark Moon

The "dark of the moon" – that is, when the moon cannot be seen and is black in the sky – is the time when banishing or dark magick might be undertaken. It is also the time for hexing and cursing – but always remember the "threefold law" (*see page 55*).

New Moon

As the new moon appears in the sky above, witches perform construction magick (*see page 63*) for new projects and goals. It is also a time when lengthy rituals associated with the moon will be instigated, there being many days of waxing to follow.

Waxing Moon

As the moon "waxes" – that is, gains in strength – this is the time for performing magick and rituals that ask for construction or invoking (*see page 63*). This may be a new job, a new home, a better relationship or increased intuition. It is a time of positive magick.

Waning Moon

As the moon "wanes" – that is, decreases in strength – this is the time for performing magick and rituals that ask for banishing and destruction (*see page 63*). This may involve casting away a disease, getting rid of a person who is taking advantage of you or bringing an end to a troublesome situation.

ENGLISH MEDIEVAL FULL MOON ESBAT NAMES

January – Wolf Moon
February – Storm Moon
March – Chaste Moon
April – Seed Moon
May – Hare Moon
June – Dyan Moon
July – Mead Moon
August – Corn Moon
September – Barley Moon
October – Blood Moon
November – Snow Moon
December – Oak Moon

Full Moon

Nights of the full moon are important to witches as they are particularly potent for making magick and honouring deity. They are called Esbats, the name deriving from the old French word "*s'esbattre*", which means "to frolic". Most covens and solitary witches observe the Esbat rites at every full moon.

While they are generally regarded as secondary to the Sabbats, Esbats are still important to those who follow the path of the witch. Midnight during a full moon is considered the most potent time of all, and is commonly known as the "witching hour".

While the names of the monthly full moons differ from culture to culture, I have always favoured the English medieval names (*see box, left*).

There are different themes that relate to each full moon throughout the year. A learned witch might use these individual themes to celebrate the Esbats, but for the novice it is enough to observe these special nights and to simply use them for making magick.

Blue Moon

On the rare occasions when two full moons occur in the same calendar month, the second full moon is known in witchcraft as a blue moon. This happens infrequently – about once every 2.5 years – hence the saying "once in a blue moon". In witchcraft the occurrence of a blue moon is thought to be a time of heightened communication between the witch and the Goddess (as the Moon).

IV

AS ABOVE, SO BELOW

THE CONCEPT OF THE GREAT MOTHER GODDESS AND HER
consort, lover and child, the Horned God, is a central belief in most
witchcraft traditions. While many witches need no further names to
understand these deities, others need stories, titles and histories to develop a
relationship with them. In this chapter we will look at a wide and varied
selection of gods, goddesses and other beings that are considered aspects of
the Goddess and Horned God. While some witches believe that all gods
and goddesses are part of the same universal omnipotent force, others see
each deity as having its own existence, separate from the others. Although
there are literally hundreds of deities called upon, venerated and
worshipped in different traditions of The Craft, this chapter is a good
starting point of introduction to the better known gods and goddesses.

"Divine deities, the witches greet,
many in number; now we meet."

English Gods

HERNE
Spirit God of Forests and Hunting

he mystical spirit god of nature and the "Wild Hunt", Herne's exact origins are lost in the mists of time. Either of Anglo Saxon or Celtic descent, he is equated with the great Celtic Horned God, Cernunnos. The shortened version "Cerne" has been changed in some examples to "Herne". It is also suggested that the name may derive simply from the English word, "horn", another stark connection with the generic concept of the witches' Horned God deity.

The traditional appearance of Herne, atop a flying steed and galloping through the skies collecting lost souls, relates to the "Wild Hunt", variations of which can be found in many cultures and in the history of witchcraft. The Wild Hunt is a procession of spirit animals and huntsmen who roam the countryside at night collecting souls of the dead. This image of Herne as a ghostly spirit god, as opposed to a deity, has connections with one of the more well-known stories of his origin.

Legend has it that Herne was a young huntsman who, while out hunting one day with King Richard II (reign 1377–1399) in Windsor Great Forest in Berkshire, saved the King from mortal death by standing in the path of a stag who was about to charge at him. Although Herne survived, his body was mysteriously found later hanging from an old oak tree, swathed in deerskin and with the head of a stag mounted upon his own. The tree became known as "Herne's Oak", and became associated with his spirit form thanks in part to the playwright William Shakespeare, who described the ghost in his story, *The Merry Wives of Windsor*. The tree fell of old age on 31 August 1863, but it was replaced soon afterwards by the young Queen Victoria, with a new oak tree planted on the same spot. This also died, but another "Herne's Oak" was planted in 1906.

Whether a spirit from the time of King Richard or a manifestation of the Celtic Horned God Cernunnos, Herne is an enduring image of the witches' God with his antlered head, shamanistic deerskin cloak and dwelling in the forests of old England, where he is said to appear at times of national crisis.

THE GREEN MAN
Spirit God of the Green

The Green Man is ancient; well over a thousand years have passed since the concept of this archaic nature deity began. Although I have placed this "god", if you can call him that at all, in the English section of this chapter, he is such a powerful universal symbol that examples of his presence have been found all over the world. Primarily noted for featuring in the architecture of old buildings and furniture, Green Men or "foliate heads/masks", as they are often called, have been found on Roman columns in Turkey that date back to the 2nd century; on 8th-century temples in Rajasthan, in India; and across Germany, France, Italy and Holland. They can also be found in abundance in Britain, with England, Scotland, Wales and Ireland all having their fair share. One notable building is Rosslyn Chapel, in Midlothian, Scotland, which features many examples.

What is interesting is that Green Men feature more heavily in areas where rich forests covered the land – the West Country, Yorkshire and Nottingham, for example – and it is typically in these ancient woodlands that the Green Man speaks to those who seek him, through trees, grass and bushes.

The appearance of the Green Man, most often carved in stone or wood, is that of the face of a man peering out from leafy undergrowth. In some cases, the greenery surrounds the face, while in others the foliage spews forth from his mouth or morphs with aspects of the face; an indication that the life of man and that of nature are strongly intertwined.

The term "Green Man" was first penned in 1939, when Lady Raglan used it in an article she was writing for *The Folklore Journal*, and it has been used ever since. Green Men can be found in churches and cathedrals the length and breadth of the country. The suggestion is that they were incorporated into Christian architecture to encourage followers of the old Pagan faiths to come to church. Whatever the reason, he lives and dies with the trees and plants in an enigmatic cycle of birth, death and rebirth, which features heavily in many Pagan religions and especially witchcraft.

As a Pagan fertility figure, nature spirit and archetype of the Horned God, the Green Man represents a witch's oneness with the earth. He is a celebration of the "green" that is "life", and a reminder that despite death, life will come again. In essence, the Green Man is an enduring reminder of the abundant green life force that surrounds and supports us all.

Greek Gods and Goddesses

PAN
God of the Wild

Pan, whose name means simply "all", is one of the oldest Greek gods. Possibly pre-Olympian, his origin may be as an ancient nature deity. He is very much connected with witchcraft for his obvious semblance with other horned deities who represent the Horned God.

Pan was the son of Hermes who, after being tricked, fornicated with a nymph resulting in the birth of the goat-footed god on Mount Lycaeum in Arcadia, a mountain district in ancient southern Greece. He is depicted with the head, arms and upper torso of a muscular man and the dark hairy legs and cloven hoofs of a goat. Atop his head are two small pointed horns, which jut out from his curly hair. He is often shown sporting a goatee beard and with piercing eyes.

The god of nature, lust and raw sexuality, Pan was worshipped in Arcadia from the 6th century BCE. He is King of the Satyrs, a race of panlike nature spirits who might be encountered in wild places and dark woodlands (fauns are the Roman equivalent). It is from Pan that the word "panic" derives, the haunting sound of his pan-pipes striking fear into travellers in lonely places where he ruled. He is the protector of shepherds and flocks and is lord of meadows, forests and wild places.

Pan was a sexual adventurer, and is recognized as a god of lusty indulgence. His time was often spent chasing wood nymphs, dancing and revelling in his woodland paradise. He is also a god of wild abandon, indulgence and pleasure.

In one legend Pan desired a nymph named Echo. She was a dancer and singer who scorned male attention. After ignoring Pan's attempts to seduce her, his followers tracked and killed her. Echo's body was cast in pieces across the world, the sounds of her last words are repeated over and over again.

In another story, a nymph named Pitys turned herself into a pine tree in order to escape Pan's advances. Similarly, a third nymph, named Syrinx, beloved by all woodland creatures, scorned Pan's affections. After pursuing her to a river, a water nymph turned her into a bunch of reeds. A breeze then blew through the leaves, creating hypnotic music, whereupon Pan picked the leaves and fashioned them into a pipe. He then blew into the pipe, creating a pan-pipe, also known as a "Syrinx".

The presence of Pan can arouse a variety of intense passions – temporary madness, fear, inspiration and unbridled male sexuality. Indeed, Pan's sexual adventures did not stop at wood nymphs; they also included mortal women and men. In a well-known Greek tale, Pan seduces a handsome young hero named Daphnis, from the island of Sicily. Daphnis had been abandoned at birth by his mother, and so Hera (the wife and older sister of Zeus) took pity on him and ensured that he would be found by the Arcadian shepherds. It is said that Pan taught Daphnis to play the pan-pipes.

The Roman equivalent god to Pan is called Faunus. Both gods are commonly associated with the star sign Capricorn.

POSEIDON
God of the Seas and Rivers

The brother of the Greek god, Zeus, Poseidon chose the deep oceans and violent seas as his mortal realm when the gods split the heavens and earth into separate kingdoms. He is the son of Kronos, the god of time, and Rhea, earth goddess. He can be equated with Neptune, the Roman god of the sea.

Poseidon has been called the "supreme lord of the inner and outer seas", ruling freshwater rivers and lakes as well as the mightier waterworlds. All creatures of the waters are his servants; mermaids and mermen, undines and water nymphs and the terrible sea monsters of the deep can all be summoned to do his bidding.

Depicted as a muscular man with a flowing grey beard and wearing a crown, Poseidon's symbol is the three-speared trident, with which he prods the clouds to bring rain storms to earth. He rides a chariot pulled by *hippocampi* – magickal creatures of the sea with the front body of a horse and the tail of a fish. Poseidon is responsible for earthquakes and tidal waves, and he is able to stir the seas with his trident, with which he is able to summon tempests and whirlpools.

With his mortal wife, Cleito, Poseidon fathered several children who later ruled Atlantis. He also copulated with Medusa on the floor of the Temple of Athena.

Poseidon is known as a creative god, having formed the creatures of the depths, and is the guardian of ships and all seafaring folk.

APOLLO
God of Music and the Arts

Apollo, twin brother of Artemis (although a day younger), is the son of Zeus and Leto. He is the Greek god of music, arts and all intellectual pursuits. Depicted as a handsome young man with flowing locks of golden hair, he is also the god of truth, and is unable to speak a lie. As god of music he plays the lyre for all to hear; he also taught man the principles of medicine and healing.

As a god of light, he is known by the titles "Phoebus" meaning "brilliant"; "Xanthus", meaning "the fair"; and "Chrysocomes", meaning "of the golden locks". After being fed ambrosia and nectar he attained great strength, and after slaying the serpent of Mount Pernassus, he dispatched the female "Pythonesses" to the neighbouring mountain town of Delphi and replaced them with male priests, who took over the running of the famous Oracle. Through this connection, he also became a god of prophecy.

The symbols of Apollo are the lyre, his bow and silver arrows, the laurel tree, the crow and the dolphin. He is often depicted riding his sky chariot pulled by four horses, his golden hair flowing in the wind.

PRIAPUS
God of Virility, Fertility, Lust and the Penis

As the god of male genitalia, Priapus is always depicted with a humungous phallus, which is often erect. He is the protector of sheep, fruit, bees, vines and the garden.

The son of Aphrodite, his paternal origin is disputed, although Dionysus is a likely candidate. At birth he was deemed so ugly that he was sent to earth and dismissed from the realm of the gods. He grew up among the wild things, counting shepherds and wood spirits as his friends. This lead to an introduction to the satyrs and to their supreme deity, Pan.

The followers of Pan, noted for their unashamed sexual exhibitionism and carnal behaviour, were unable to include Priapus as he couldn't achieve sexual excitement – until one day, when his penis suddenly grew to an enormous size and stood mighty and erect before them.

This disablement struck fear into those who might lie with him, and to anyone who came across him. Indeed, Pan sent Priapus to stand at the entrance to the wild forest, where he was to guard the path from invaders, displaying his terrifyingly mighty manhood to any who might challenge him. This was a warning that in simple terms meant "no trespassing or you will be violently raped". Subsequently, statues of Priapus with an erect phallus were often displayed at doors and gateways as protectors of the household. It is from this state of permanent erection that the modern medical term "priapism" derives.

Later, the use of priapic statuary changed, migrating to the fields where, carved from fig-tree wood, the idol would encourage flourishing crops, its presence bringing fertility.

The Romans later adopted this same ritual, but the emphasis was more on Priapus's ability to scare away thieves than to promote plant growth.

HELIOS
God of the Sun

Son of the Titans Hyperion and Theia, and brother of Selene (Goddess of the Moon) and Eos (Goddess of the Dawn), Helios is the bright young Sun God of ancient Greece. A handsome god crowned with a shining aureole, he flies a chariot across the sky each day from east to west, creating the passage of the Sun. Helios is also the god of victory, riches and enlightenment; his gift to the world is light. This rich depiction of Helios is prevalent throughout the art, poetry and myth of the ancient Greek world.

In the most enduring tale of Helios, his son, Phaethon, after discovering who his father was, wanted to prove himself as a worthy son. To this end he attempted to ride his father's chariot, but its horses were so powerful that he was unable to control it, and he set the Earth on fire as he crashed awkwardly through the skies. Zeus, seeing the destruction that Phaethon was causing, sent a thunderbolt across the heavens, which killed Phaethon instantly; his body fell into the Eridanus River, where his weeping sisters mourned him evermore. The sisters eventually transformed into trees, and their tears turned into amber.

DIONYSUS
God of the Vine

The popular image of Dionysus enticing his followers to abandon tactful temperament and immerse themselves in lustfulness and exuberance is a popular one; indeed, he is the god of vegetation, fertility and wine, and the "Maenads" who worshipped him with song and orgiastic frenzy offered sacrifice to him in the form of their bodies.

Noted as having introduced viniculture to a variety of countries, Dionysus was also called "The Lawgiver" because he carried stone tablets upon which the laws of the land were engraved. He rode a great panther and carried a thyrus (staff), with which he could turn water into wine with a mere touch.

Dionysus is also the androgynous God of theatre and drama, and took lovers of both sexes. His unashamed celebration of intoxication, ectasy and sensuality ensured that when the Romans created their own gods, Dionysus was not left out, and was given a "Romanized" name: Bacchus.

HERA
The First Greek Goddess

Queen of Olympus and the first goddess of Greek mythology, Hera, which means "lady", was a vision of insurmountable beauty who wed her brother Zeus, the king of the Greek gods. She was the eldest daughter of Kronos, god of time, and Rhea, the goddess of the earth, and the sister of Demeter. She was born on the Isle of Samos on the banks of a flowing river.

The marriage of Hera and Zeus took place in the Garden of Hesperides, where Gaia, Mother Nature, gave Hera golden apples as a gift. Hera was Zeus's third wife, the first two being Metis and Themis.

A rapturous young beauty, Hera is often regarded as a vindictive and angry goddess, filled with vengeance and jealousy. This perception derives from Zeus's constant inability to remain monogamous to her, resulting in the numerous offspring that Hera despised. Hera thus became a protector of marriage and monogamous relationships.

After discovering that she could conceive immaculately in the Garden of Flora, Hera gave birth to Ares, Typhon, Hephaestus and Hebe. They are collectively known as "the monstrous children of Hera" as they were conceived without united love.

The feathers of a peacock are associated with Hera, and so too is the month of June, the most popular time of the year for weddings. June takes its name from the goddess Juno, the Roman equivalent of Hera.

ARTEMIS
Goddess of the Wilderness

Artemis, daughter of Zeus and Leto, was born at Ortygia, and she helped her mother to deliver her twin brother, Apollo, after they crossed the straits to the island of Delos. She is associated with many other goddesses: her stepmother, Hera, her cousin, Hecate, and the moon goddess, Selene.

Depicted as a huntress, Artemis is the protector of the wild. Armed with a bow and silver arrows, which cause no pain, she watches over animals and all of Mother Nature's creations. She is also a powerful defender of women during childbirth and a protector of young children. Despite this characteristic, she never married or bore any children of her own, despising the concept of marriage, which would put an end to the freedom she so enjoyed.

Greek art that features Artemis shows her as an athletic, vivacious young woman who roams the forests and wild places with her female companions. As a shape shifter and magick maker, she can turn herself into a young doe to explore the forest unobserved.

In contrast to her strong protective qualities, she is a force to be reckoned with. In one of her most enduring tales, she is watched by a young mortal hunter named Actaeon while bathing in a secret pool. When Artemis sees him she transforms him into a stag, and his hunting hounds, unable to identify the animal as their master, savagely attack and kill him.

It is believed that the Roman goddess Diana was modelled on the legends of Artemis. The name "Diana" was favoured by Pagans because in Celtic "Diana" means "divine" and "brilliant". It is after this goddess that the contemporary tradition of Dianic Witchcraft takes its name.

DEMETER
Goddess of Agriculture

Sister of Poseidon, Zeus and Hades; and daughter of Kronos, the god of time, and Rhea, the earth goddess, Demeter is the Greek goddess of corn and the harvest, whose power is reflected in the changing seasons and themes of rebirth.

The most generous of all Olympian goddesses, Demeter spent much time with man showing him how to sow, cultivate and reap good harvests. With her brother Zeus she bore a child, Persephone, with whom Hades, god of the underworld, fell in love.

Hades entombed Persephone in the afterworld and made her his wife, an act that had been sanctioned by her father, Zeus. Betrayed, Demeter took refuge in the city of Eleusis, commanding that the land go barren and the crops fail until her daughter was returned to her. Eventually Zeus sent Hermes to the afterworld to command Hades to release Persephone so that she could rejoin her mother and the land would be restored. As she left the afterworld, Hades gave her a gift of a pomegranate to eat. Persephone had not eaten while beneath the ground, and hungrily she ate the seeds, thereby magickally ensuring that she would have to return to Hades for four months of the year.

This story is reflected in nature. Just as Persephone makes her annual compulsory pilgrimage to Hades in the afterworld, so Demeter withdraws her gift of fertility from the land, creating winter, until springtime, when with Persephone's return, the land comes back to life once more under Demeter's command.

Demeter remained in her temple at Eleusis, where she taught the Eleusian Mysteries to her followers. Bound in secrecy, their exact rites remain a mystery, but were considered important for many centuries. It is thought that during these rites, Demeter taught her followers how to live joyfully and how to die without fear.

Depicted holding a cornucopia of plenty and with a wheat crown, Demeter is often shown wearing a blue robe and holding a sceptre, a symbol of her great power over the land.

GAIA
Earth Mother Goddess

Gaia, which means "grandmother earth", is the primordial deity goddess of Greek mythology. From Gaia, the earth and all forms of life that inhabit it came. Existing long before time began (Kronos, the god of time, was born of her), Gaia was herself born of a great void in which chaos reigned supreme.

After creating the earth, the seas and the underworld that lie hidden beneath, Gaia made herself a husband and mate – Uranus, or the skies – with whom she gave birth to the Titans.

In modern goddess worship, Gaia is revered as the embodiment of Mother Nature, the Earth and all its inhabitants. She is the goddess supreme, from whom all other gods and goddesses came.

As witches connect strongly with the earth and nature, Gaia is a deity of ultimate power, who is often included in rituals and magick. In Roman myth her equivalent goddess is Terra.

HECATE
Goddess of the Night

Although commonly thought of as a Greek deity, Hecate, goddess of the darkness, crossroads and witchery, is a pre-Olympian goddess of Thracian origin. She is very much a part of modern witchcraft practice, as Hecate is associated with the dark of the moon, the Crone aspect of the Goddess. She is a triple goddess, depicted in ancient art with three heads – those of a dog, a horse and a serpent; the oldest such image dates from the 5th century. The Roman equivalent of Hecate is Trivia, but there is nothing trivial about this powerful goddess of sorcery.

Often depicted in contemporary literature as a hunchbacked hag, this modern image is not a true representation of Hecate of the ancient Greek culture. This is an example of demonization by the Christian faith, which disliked her association with magick and sorcery, and her ubiquitous title, "queen of the witches" (this title is also attributed to Aradia, the Italian daughter of the goddess Diana).

The Ancient Greeks would place a totem of Hecate at crossroads where, with her three heads, she would guard three directions simultaneously. They would also place offerings at her image on nights of the dark moon. Later, the same practice evolved to protect private dwellings, where statues of Hecate, if placated, would guard doorways and see off evil spirits.

Hecate navigates easily between the worlds of man and spirit, sending torment to those who displease her and granting the wishes of those who bravely face her. She is queen of the night and protector of witches.

In the Greek legend of Persephone, Hecate becomes her ward, accompanying her in her annual return to Hades in the underworld. With a blazing torch, her primary symbol, she lights the way for Persephone through the darkness, past Thanatos, the god of death; Hypnos, the god of sleep; and Morpheus, the god of dreams, and into the inner sanctum of Hades. Just as her torch brought illumination to Persephone, so Hecate brings hidden wisdom to those who seek it.

A triple goddess with dual aspects of good and evil, Hecate is a powerful force in witchcraft, both ancient and modern. She can instigate change for better or worse, reveal inner secrets and light the way in darkness. She is the true protector of magickal folk and the dark mother of the world of witchcraft.

Celtic Gods and Goddesses

CERNUNNOS
God of Animals and the Wildwood

The witches' Horned God has many aspects, forms and names. One of its strongest manifestations is in the Celtic nature god, Cernunnos. The name probably derives from the Latin word "*cornu*", meaning "*horned*", and depictions of this deity date back to megalithic times when our ancestors drew his body and stag-horned head on the walls of caves by the light of a flickering fire. The Druids knew him as "Hu Gadarn".

The most notable image of Cernunnos was found on the Gundestrup Cauldron, in a peat bog in Denmark, and is now housed in the National Museum of Denmark, in Copenhagen. Here he can be seen with an antlered head sitting cross-legged holding a torc – a Celtic symbol of nobility – in his right hand and a serpent – a symbol of regeneration – in his left.

He is a primeval horned deity of part human, part animal appearance. With the horns of a stag and swathed in animal fur, he is lord of the Wild Hunt – the leaf-covered Green Man, the lusty goat god Pan and Herne the hunter epitomized as one deity. Lord of all animals, he has the ability to shape-shift from god to animal to tree, his horns becoming the lofty branches of the oldest oak in an instant.

In the ancient past, man covered himself in animal skins and bones and mounted horns upon his head in a shamanic attempt to commune with Cernunnos. Such exhibitions, although magnificent, are not needed, for he can be found in any wild place where the leaves whip around in the wind and wild nature spirits dwell.

The great Mother Goddess gave Cernunnos existence, and together with her he brings perfect balance, male and female. He is the first father of life, son of the Goddess and wild spirit. As the Wheel of the Year turns to harvest, he sacrifices himself, manifests as John Barleycorn and descends into the darkness of the shadowy afterworld, where he comforts the spirits of the dead until he is resurrected once more. Strong, fertile and powerful, he rests in the knowledge that he will go on never ending, for he is the lord of the dance of life.

CERRIDWEN
Triple Goddess

The great Celtic mother goddess Cerridwen is a classic triple goddess with maiden, mother and crone aspects, although it is the haggard crone that is widely depicted in Cerridwen imagery. In a well-known story, she lived on an island in the middle of a lake with her husband, Tegid, and their two children – Creirwy, the most beautiful girl in the world, and Avagdu, the ugliest boy in the world. As a consolation for Avagdu's unfortunate looks, Cerridwen mixed a secret spell of six herbs in her bubbling cauldron for a year and a day. (This period correlates directly with the traditional witch's apprenticeship period prior to initiation.) She was aided by a young assistant named Gwion, with a plan to make Avagdu the most brilliant, knowledgeable and inspired boy in the land.

One day, while stirring the potion – called "greal", which may be linked to the "holy grail" – Gwion accidentally splashed three drops of the magickal liquid on to his hand. He was instantly granted the secret knowledge of the worlds within and without. Knowing that Cerridwen would be angry that he had acquired the gift intended for Avagdu, he shape shifted into a hare and ran away.

Cerridwen transformed herself into a greyhound and pursued him, so he changed into a fish and dived into the river. Cerridwen then changed herself into an otter to continue her chase, so Gwion shape-shifted himself into a bird and took to the skies. Cerridwen transformed into a hawk and soared above him, whereupon he transformed into a grain of corn. Cerridwen became a hen and hurriedly gobbled him up in her beak.

Nine months later, after resuming her usual form, Cerridwen gave birth to a second son, Gwion, who had been growing in her womb after she had eaten him as the corn grain. Disgusted, she contemplated killing him, but instead threw him into the raging sea where he was rescued by a Celtic prince named Elffin. He grew up to become Taliesin, the greatest bard in Celtic history, serving in the court of Prince Elffin.

The themes of change, rebirth and transformation are key to Cerridwen. Through her cauldron of inspiration, the wisdom of ages can be found. It is a symbol of the womb of the Goddess, from which all life is born, and an important magickal symbol in witchcraft.

The image of Cerridwen stirring her magick cauldron is perhaps where the stereotypical image of an old hag mixing a fateful brew at Halloween derives: Cerridwen as the Crone, mixing the magick of transformation in her cauldron of inexhaustible plenty.

ARIANRHOD
Welsh Celtic Moon Goddess

A major mother goddess in Welsh lore, Arianrhod, whose name means "silver wheel", is a goddess of the moon. Her home, "Caer Arianrhod", or Castle of Arianrhod, lies in the starry sky and the Aurora Borealis. She is worshipped in moonlight, especially on nights when the moon is full, and manifests as a beautiful sorceress with a shining wheel. It is upon this wheel that she spins the souls of the dead off to the Summerland.

Arianrhod is the goddess of karma, time, beauty and reincarnation. She is the mother aspect of the triple goddess of the witches in Welsh Celtic lore. She led a life of declared chastity, until it was discovered by a magician named Math that she had secretly conceived twins – Dylan and Fetus. As a shape-shifter she transforms herself into an owl to fly in the night skies. Symbolizing wisdom, initiation and inevitable death, she peers into the souls of mortal men through the beady eyes of the owl.

BRIGID
Triple Goddess of Fire

Brigid is one of witchcraft's most important mothers. As a classic triple goddess with three aspects, she relates directly to the witchcraft principle of deity. Born of The Dagda, the good god of the Tuatha, her main centre of worship was in Kildare, Ireland, although her influence was widespread across England too, where she was known as "Brigantia". As a goddess of fire and light, her name means "bright one" and her festival is Imbolc (*see Chapter 3, page 75*), when she brings light back to the world at the end of winter, thawing the frozen ground and bringing snowdrops back to life. Until relatively modern times an undying fire was tended by 19 virgins at Brigid's sacred shrine in Kildare. Every twentieth day Brigid herself would tend the flames, unseen by her followers.

A triple aspect goddess, Brigid is many things at once. Unlike other triple deities, Brigid is strong and ageless in each aspect. She is a master blacksmith, keeper of the fiery forge and hearth, where she transforms one thing into another. She is also the nurturing midwife who is both healer and protector, and the poetess, bringer of wisdom, guidance and prophecy.

Although Irish in origin, the influence of Brigid spread throughout England, where even today she exerts her presence through a variety of place names: Bride Cross, Bride Stones Moor, Bridestow Hill and Bridekirk, all in northern England; Bridestow, Bridford and Bridport in the south west and even Bridewell in London, to name just a few. In the home, Brigid's Cross, a four-pronged symbol, is often hung to ask for her protection.

LUGH
Irish Celtic Sun God of Light and Harvest

The Celtic sun god, Lugh, is depicted as a handsome, youthful man, full of vitality and with boundless energy. His name means "the shining one". His feast day is 1 August, when witches celebrate the Sabbat of Lughnasadh, the assembly of Lugh, the first harvest (*see Chapter 3, page 80*). His associated animals are the white stag and the raven.

As master of many crafts, legend tells us that when trying to gain entry to the feast of King Nuada in Tara, he was turned away until he listed his many talents – smith, champion, harper, hero, poet, historian, sorcerer and craftsman – after which he was welcomed in. In some records his calling is given as Lugh Samlioldanach, the latter half meaning, "of many arts".

Italian Goddesses

ARADIA
Daughter of the Goddess Diana & Queen of the Witches

The Italian daughter of the moon goddess Diana, Aradia, highly regarded as queen of the witches by contemporary magickal folk, was sent to the mortal realm by her mother to be "a teacher unto women and men". As a gift to the mortal realm, Aradia gave the power of magick to the oppressed followers of her mother, Diana, granting them the ability to act against a corrupt state and Church, and to gain their freedom. The name "Aradia" means "altar of Diana" in Italian, and she is the primary deity of Stregheria, Italian witchcraft.

The origin of the story of Aradia lies primarily in a book written in 1899 by Charles Godfrey Leland entitled *Aradia – Gospel of the Witches*. Therein the author describes the parentage of Aradia – she was the creation of a union between Diana, the moon goddess, and Lucifer, the god of light and the sun. The book is a collection of fragmentary oral and written traditions and magick spells presented in an entertainingly mystical fashion.

Raven Grimassi, a prolific contemporary author on Stregheria, describes Aradia as both the name of an ancient goddess from the 14th century and the name adopted by a mortal named Aradia di Toscano, who was born in 1313 and was the founder of the Stregheria tradition of The Craft.

In some contemporary traditions of witchcraft, Aradia is worshipped as a lunar goddess and is given high regard as the daughter of the Goddess herself.

EGYPTIAN GODS AND GODDESSES

RA
Supreme Egyptian God of the Sun

In Egyptian history, Ra was the supreme god of the sun and the most well-known solar god in the entire Egyptian pantheon. His original name, "Ra"; his adopted name "Re"; and his later name, "Amun-Ra", all literally mean "the sun". As the sun brought forth warmth, light and growth in the world, he was perceived as the grand creator of all things and a giver of life.

Depicted bedecked in gold and with a sun disk encircled by a serpent above his head, Ra was also sometimes shown with a falcon's head and holding an Ankh, the Egyptian symbol of life. The sun itself was known as "the eye of Ra", through which he could see all.

By the fourth dynasty of Egypt, the followers of Ra had become so widespread that the pharaohs were thought of as mortal sons of the god himself and were named "sons of Ra", literally meaning "his sons on earth". The pharaohs began erecting solar temples, obelisks and pyramids in his name and aligned them with the sun's movements.

By the fifth dynasty Ra was the primary god of Egypt. The centre of his cult following was a city named Heliopolis, meaning "city of the sun". According to some scholars he was the one god of Egypt, and all other deities were simply an aspect unto him.

Another deity, Amun, meaning "what is hidden", was also gaining popularity during this time. A patron of the city of Thebes, Amun was a god of the winds who brought life through his breath and represented creation. The state decided to merge the two popular gods in an attempt to unify the cults and the people, and thus Amun-Ra was born. Together, the themes of creation and hidden secrets make Amun-Ra one of the best known Egyptian gods. He is still worshipped today in eclectic and Egyptian traditions as an aspect of the life-giving god of light.

ISIS
Goddess of Motherhood, Magick and Life

The great Egyptian goddess Isis was born of the earth god Geb and the sky goddess Nut. She was sister to three brothers – Osiris, Seth and Horus (the elder). The first records of Isis worship date back to the fifth dynasty of Egypt, but it wasn't until much later that it became widespread. In Greco-Roman times she was worshipped by followers who formed cults, and were known as the "*pastophori*", which meant "servants of Isis". (It is from this name that the modern word "pastor" originates; Christianity being young at the time.)

Temples of Isis were erected in Iraq, Greece, Rome and even in England, where the remains of a Temple of Isis was found at Hadrian's Wall. The modern-day Fellowship of Isis has a worldwide following, lead by Lady Olivia Durdin-Robertson; its headquarters are based at Clonegal Castle, in Enniscorthy, Ireland.

Isis's reputation as a feminine goddess of rebirth, magick and protection originates from the legend of her time in the mortal realm. Unlike other gods and goddesses, Isis walked happily among man, teaching skills such as weaving flax and grinding corn to make bread.

It was usual in the Egyptian dynasties for brothers and sisters to marry, thus keeping the blood line pure, and this was echoed in the realm of the gods. Isis married her brother Osiris, but their jealous brother Seth murdered him and secreted his body in a coffin that was swept away down the Nile. When Isis recovered the body, she discovered that the phallus had been lost and set about learning the magickal arts so that she could restore it. After creating a new penis in wax and gold, she transformed herself into a sparrow hawk and flew into the air where, with her new found magickal powers, she fanned life back into Osiris with her wings.

After Osiris had recovered, Isis bore him a son, Horus, the sun god. Isis later became the most powerful goddess in Egypt after she tricked Ra (*see page 101*) into revealing the secrets of his omnipotent powers and, together with her son Horus, they created and sustained all life.

Depictions of Isis often portray her with outstretched wings that confer protection on those that worship her. She is an archetypal goddess of motherhood, relationships and magick. Her name literally means "queen of the throne".

Phoenician Goddesses

ASTARTE
Goddess of Fertility and War

Astarte, which means "she of the womb", is a goddess of fertility and war who was worshipped in ancient Phoenicia, a country on the shores of the eastern Mediterranean that corresponds to modern Lebanon and the coastal plains of Syria.

A goddess of opposing natures, she is both the fighter robed in flames, carrying a quiver of arrows, and a goddess of desire who by night retreats to the underworld to her lover.

She is often depicted upon the back of a great lioness, standing naked and holding a mirror and lotus flower in one hand and two snakes in the other. At other times, to represent her fierce nature, she is depicted with the head of a lion.

She is the goddess of first-born children and the first fruits of the harvest.

Hindi Goddesses

KALI
Goddess of War and Destruction

A much misunderstood goddess, Kali is the "great black mother" who is a contradictory deity, acting as both creator and destroyer of the world around her. She is a powerful force of creativity who was creator, mother and wife of Shiva, the supreme Hindi god.

Depicted as a huge, dark-skinned woman, often naked and with many arms, her tongue protrudes from her face, adding to her already disconcerting appearance. In her hands she holds weapons and symbols of her authority as well as the severed head of Raktavija, the demon chief. Around her neck she wears a necklace of skulls into which are engraved the letters of the Sanskrit alphabet, which she created.

Kali is the goddess of destruction and death, much feared and misunderstood. To those who face her and learn her hidden secrets, she becomes the ultimate mother figure, both comforting and supporting. She is often called "Mother Time", for she both creates life and destroys it, as the path of time always leads to an inevitable end.

Norse Gods and Goddesses

ODIN
Father God of War and Magick

Odin is the father of the Nordic gods and the husband of Freya (*see page 104*), with whom he had seven children: Balder, Bali, Bragi, Hoder, Thor, Tyr and Vidar. He is the son of Thor, whom he later succeeded as father of the gods, and the giantess Bestla.

After hanging from the branches of the World Tree, Yggdrasil, for nine days and nights, Odin acquired deep magickal knowledge and became the most powerful god of magick in Norse legend. He is a god of testing, and rewards only those that have made sacrifices such as he did on the World Tree.

From his home in Valhalla he sent forth his two ravens, Munir and Hugin, to the realm of man to keep watch over mortals and report back to him. To aid him in his magick he used a bewitched ring called Drawpnir and a magickal spear called Gungnir.

Associated with horses and ravens, Odin was killed and consumed by the great wolf Fenris, son of Loki, his blood brother (*see page 104*), and the giantess Angurboda.

LOKI
The Trickster God

Loki is a god with many faces, and a god whose energy might either help or hinder. He is the god of trickery, with a quick wit and deceitful demeanour. He has been called "the shape changer" because of his ability to transform himself into any shape, including that of a mortal. He is also called "the father of lies" because he achieves his ends not by force, but by trickery and cunning.

As a blood brother of Odin, Loki is a primary god of the Nordic people, but one that cannot be trusted, for he brings earthquakes, fire, death and destruction.

After taking Siguna as his wife, Loki bore Hel, goddess of death, together with the giantess Angurboda, and boasted openly of his bisexual lecherous antics with other gods and goddesses. He is father of Fenris, the great wolf and enemy of the gods, and also of Sleipnir, the eight-legged steed of Odin.

In witchcraft, Loki is a paramour of dark magick and is possessed of an energy that should not be taken lightly.

FREYA
Moon Goddess of Fertility, Love, Sexuality, War and Death

Originally one goddess, Freya is now sometimes regarded as two separate deities: Frigga and Freyja. Strongly associated with war and death, she fights alongside her husband, Odin, in battle. She was the leader of the valkyries, her priestesses, and ripped through the storm-ridden skies in her chariot drawn by flying cats, wearing a flowing cloak of feathers and an amber necklace (amber is strongly associated with witchcraft).

At the end of summer Freya departs the mortal realm, causing the leaves to fall and the world to be cloaked in snow. She returns again in spring, bringing abundance and fertility to the world.

Freya was responsible for bringing magick to the northern peoples, and Friday ("Freya's day") was named after this Scandinavian goddess.

Together with Odin, Freya mothered Baldu, god of light. She is a noted protector of marriages, but she has a promiscuous reputation nonetheless and took several lovers, including Loki, the trickster, blood brother of Odin (see page 103). Her brother was Frey, the Teutonic god of fertility.

BAPHOMET
Androgynous Deity of The Knight's Templar

Known as the "ram god of Mendes", Baphomet is usually depicted along the lines of Eliphas Levi's famous 19th-century drawing of the deity. In it Baphomet is portrayed with a goat's head and horns between which the "flame of intelligence" shines; a pentacle upon its forehead; androgynous arms that point up to the moon of Chesed and down to the black moon of Geburah; bare female breasts; a human torso covered in scales, a caduceus between its legs in place of a phallus; wings and cloven hoofs. (Baphomet is often misrepresented as a symbol of Satanism because of its frightening appearance.) The image encompasses all aspects of life and death, with animal, mortal and esoteric influences, and is described as "a divine androgyne", encompassing all of life and death in one image.

The name "Baphomet" is of unknown origin, but it is suggested that it derives from the Greek words "*baphe*" and "*metis*", which together mean "absorption of wisdom". It is alleged that Baphomet was worshipped by the secretive order of Knights Templar as a bringer of fertility and abundance. Jacques de Molay, the leader of the order, was burned at the stake in 1314 after being accused of worshipping the Devil in the form of Baphomet.

V

TOOLS AND SIGILS OF THE CRAFT

DO WITCHES REALLY STIR GHASTLY BREWS IN BUBBLING
cauldrons? Well, not exactly, but as you will see in this chapter, the
cauldron, broomstick and traditional pointed hat all have their rightful
place in a witch's life. As popular culture has twisted and morphed the true
origins of these elements, I will take you back to the roots of the imagery
associated with witches. I will also share some of the secret sigils utilized in
magick. These arcane symbols, whether written or inscribed, lend their
powers to the magickal intent of the witch.

"In the circle the Witches dance;
with knives aloft, and brooms they advance."

itches usually have a personal altar or shrine set up permanently in their home. It is a place where they can commune with the Old Gods, present offerings, "charge" magickal items and generally connect with their spirituality.

Home altars can be simple or elaborate, and are usually staged in a quiet corner or room out of the way of the hustle and bustle of everyday life. If possible, the altar should be in the north, but this cannot always be achieved.

In a magick circle (*see Chapter 2, page 46*) a witch will set up an altar in the northern quarter, upon which the ritual tools and various implements and symbols of The Craft will be placed. The altar might be on a table, a slab of stone, a tree stump or simply on a piece of cloth laid on the ground. In addition to these items, offerings and decorations appropriate to the season, Sabbat or planned workings may also be included, such as flowers, crystals, herbs, nuts, seasonal foods, fruit and drinks.

CONSECRATION

Many witches fashion their own tools, but you can buy them from witchcraft suppliers around the world. Whether they are homemade or bought for the purpose, it is necessary to consecrate them for magickal use.

Until a tool has been consecrated it is said not to be a magickal item; the act of consecrating it in a ritual in which it is blessed by the Goddess and God and cleansed by the Elementals unlocks its magickal potential. It is typical for a witch to inscribe magickal sigils, runes and symbols on to their tools in order to personalize and imbue them with additional powers.

THE ALTAR LAYOUT

IN THE NORTH (EARTH)
Goddess image (on the left)
Horned God image (on the right)
Silver Goddess candle
Gold Horned God candle
Pentacle
Stang
Sea salt
Stone
Runes
Ogham staves
Crystal ball

IN THE EAST (AIR)
Drum
Bell
Censer
Pendulum
Smudging feather
Wind roarer
Dark mirror
Tarot cards
Athame
Magick sword
White hilted knife
Boline

IN THE SOUTH (FIRE)
Candle
Wand
Priapic wand
Burin

IN THE WEST (WATER)
Scrying bowl
Asperger
Drinking horn
Chalice
Teacup

IN THE CENTRE OF THE ALTAR
Book of Shadows

IN THE CENTRE OF THE MAGICK CIRCLE OR EITHER SIDE OF THE ALTAR
Cauldron
Besom

Following consecration, many witches keep their tools as close to their body as possible, even sleeping with them for a spell. The act of keeping the tools in the aura of the witch's body is said to imbue the tool with the personal power of the witch, and make it an extension of the physical body.

Once consecrated for magickal use, the witch's tools are stored carefully when not in use, never lent to anyone else and rarely even held by anyone other than the witch, of whom they have become part.

TOOLS OF THE CRAFT

The tools are split into three categories: ritual tools (*see below*), which are used in most magickal rituals; magickal tools (*see pages 115–117*), which are used to perform some kinds of magick and divinatory tools (*see pages 117–123*), which are used in scrying and divination.

Ritual Tools

SILVER GODDESS CANDLE

A silver candle is lit to the left of the altar pentacle to signify the presence of the Goddess. The colour represents the feminine moon and the light welcomes her divine presence.

GOLD HORNED GOD CANDLE

A gold candle is lit to the right of the altar pentacle to signify the presence of the Horned God. The colour represents the masculine sun and the light welcomes his divine presence.

PENTACLE

The pentacle is the most powerful symbol of witchcraft and adorns the altar in the northern quarter, where it is ruled by earth. Altar pentacles might be carved from wood, silver or copper, or painted or engraved on stone. As a sigil the pentacle can dispel evil; as a paten it can be used to share consecrated foods. It is also a tool of magickal invocation and meditation.

STANG

The stang is a forked staff made of sacred wood that represents the horns of the God. It can be used as an altar by being pushed into the ground, and should always be shod with iron at each end to ensure the magick contained within the tool does not leak out.

According to Cecil Williamson (*see Chapter 1, pages 38–39*), forked staffs were sometimes used as "talking sticks" in the past. He explained, "...to use them, dig the end into the earth. Then angle the stick so that each branch of the forked end goes either side of the bridge of your nose to gently rest against your closed eyelids. Then concentrate on the earth pulse. Soon you will sense the beat. This rhythm then leads to the opening of your third eye – the one that sees things past, present and yet to come".

SEA SALT

A dish of sea salt is placed upon the witch's altar for its power to ward against and destroy evil. Its colour is pure and its ability to preserve is contrary to the destructive nature of evil. Ruled by earth, it is used to purify and exorcise in ritual and in magick.

STONE

Some witches will incorporate a stone in the northern quarter of the altar. This represents the earth in its basic form, and is also sacred to the Goddess as it is part of Mother Nature herself. The stone might be engraved with magickal sigils, such as the triskelion or labyrinth, or it might be a crystal of a favoured colour.

DRUM

Sacred drumming has its roots in tribal shamanism, but the same technique is utilized in witch-craft. The sound of the drum awakens the spirit, accompanies chanting or dancing and its hyp-notic rhythm can help to induce the trance-like state required for weaving magick.

BELL

A bell is used to "call the quarters" by many witches. It is believed that the sound vibration can be heard not only on the physical plane, but also in the magickal realms. The sound of a bell can dispel evil and by ringing one during potent points in magickal ritual, the sound is said to augment the power raised.

CENSER

The censer is used to waft purifying incense around the sacred space before the circle is cast. It is also used to offer libations, in the form of herbs and resins, up to the Old Gods; the smoke that rises from the censer is carried up to the realms where the gods dwell. Some witches use a thurible instead of a censer. This is a similar tool, but is hung from three chains, allowing it to swing around easily. Burning dried herbs on charcoal in a censer is an activity that many witches enjoy.

SMUDGING FEATHER

The use of a feather to sweep away harmful energies is prevalent in witchcraft. Feathers are ruled by air and are particularly powerful when used to waft around incense smoke – the tools combined being more potent.

"Smudge" is a special kind of smoke that has the power to cleanse and dispel evil. It is created by burning dried sage together with sweet grass leaves. Shamans and healers often use feathers to "comb out" a person's aura, the natural design of the feather being very similar to that of a comb.

CANDLE

The candle is ruled by fire and is placed lit in the southern quarter of the altar. Many witches use a red pillar candle as standard, as the colour increases its association with the Elementals of fire. If candle magick is to be performed, then a different colour, related to the intention of the magick, will be used.

WAND

A witch's wand can direct and focus magickal energy. It is ruled by fire, and can be used for the conjuration of spirits and the invocation of the Old Gods. The wand is associated with fire because the ancients believed the power of the flame lay dormant in all wood, waiting to leap free as fire.

The traditional woods for fashioning a wand are hazel, ash, rowan and willow, but any sacred wood will make a wand with a specific purpose or power. The wood should be cut from the tree with its permission when the moon is waxing or full to ensure its magickal power. The wand is sometimes used to cast the magick circle.

PRIAPIC WAND

Also known as a "thyrus", a priapic wand, shaped to represent the male phallus, is a powerful fertility tool used to focus male energies. It gets its name from Priapus, the ancient Greek god of fertility, who is depicted with a huge or erect phallus. Modern witches sometimes fashion a priapic wand from a pine cone and stave of sacred wood.

According to Nic Davidson in *New Witch* magazine, issue 15, the female devotees of Dionysus, who were known as "Maenads", which means "crazed", met on mountainsides dressed in animal skins and wielding pine cone-tipped wands.

At Imbolc, a priapic wand may be placed with a poppet representing Brigid, the Celtic triple goddess, in a specially prepared bed as a form of fertility magick with the intention of bringing the world back to life in abundant form (*see Chapter 3, page 75*).

ATHAME

Perhaps the most controversial tool of witchcraft, the athame is a ritual blade, but it is never used for cutting. It has the power to summon the Elementals, cast a magick circle and destroy unwanted forces. The athame dates from the Middle Ages, when the first records of its use in magick have been found. The magickal knife is also used to "draw" magickal sigils in the air during rituals and summonings.

The athame is traditionally made of steel or iron, is double bladed and mounted in a black hilt. Traditional witchcraft, which forbids the use of metals, dictates that the athame must be made from a blade of flint or slate.

During the symbolic "Great Rite", the athame is plunged into the chalice to represent the sexual union of the God entering the Goddess. The athame is the phallus and the chalice, the womb of the Goddess.

MAGICK SWORD

Some witches use a magick sword instead of an athame to cast the magick circle. The sword holds more authority, and is often possessed by the male high priest of a coven. It is particularly potent in defending against malign forces that may try to enter the scared space.

WHITE HILTED KNIFE

In contemporary witchcraft a white hilted knife is used for magickal cutting. Never used for mundane work, the white hilted knife can be used to gather herbs, plants and flowers, prepare incense, slice ritual foods, inscribe or cut candles and make charms.

BOLINE

The boline is a sickle-shaped knife used by Druids for harvesting plants for magical use. Some witches include a boline in their working tools, while for others the white hilted knife serves the same purpose. The crescent shape of the blade can be seen as symbolizing the moon, while traditionally the hilt is white.

BURIN

A burin is a small pointed tool used for inscribing magickal symbols into wax or wood. Many witches do not see the need for the burin, as the white hilted knife can be used for the same purpose.

ASPERGER

The asperger is used to sprinkle consecrated salt water around the ritual space in an act of cleansing and purifying. It may be a bunch of herbs tied together, a pine cone-tipped rod or a metal wand with a holed sphere at one end.

DRINKING HORN

Representing the Horned God, the drinking horn is used to share ritually blessed wine or some other drink in the name of the God. After being filled with liquid, it will be passed in turn around the circle. Used with the chalice, which represents the Goddess, the drinking horn can bring balance to a ritual. Because it is filled with liquid, it is ruled by water.

CHALICE

The chalice is the cup of the Goddess, which holds pure water or delicious wines that are consecrated and shared during magickal rituals. It is a female symbol ruled by water, which is held within it, much like the womb of a mother. A witch's chalice may be pewter, wooden, glass or made of pottery.

Along with the athame, the chalice is used by witches to symbolically enact the "Great Rite", and it also relates to the mysterious Holy Grail.

BOOK OF SHADOWS

The Book of Shadows is a handwritten magickal record book in which a witch records traditions, practices and beliefs. The name is contemporary, with older magickal records being known as "Grimoires".

The book might include lists of correspondences concerning crystals, herbs, colours, numbers, magickal words and incantations, moon phases and records of spells cast, with results noted. Rather than a textbook of practice, the Book of Shadows is a reflection of the witch's personal experience and learning. Traditionally, a newly initiated witch will copy the Book of Shadows of their teacher and initiator, and upon their death the book will be burned.

The name "Book of Shadows" refers to the fact that what is written in the book is a mere shadow of the underlying magickal truth the words record.

CAULDRON

The cauldron is an archetypal image associated with witchcraft. In it, a witch will mix magickal ingredients and burn sacred woods. The traditional pot-bellied shape is representative of the womb of the abundant Mother Goddess. By writing wishes and casting them into a burning cauldron, they are thought to be sent directly to her. She will then instigate their transformation or change. Associated with the Crone aspect of the Goddess, the cauldron is also thought to be a direct link to the afterworld, a portal through which spirits and energies may pass. The cauldron is ruled by water.

BESOM

The besom, or broomstick as it is more commonly known, is an ancient symbol associated with witches. The image of a witch soaring through a storm-swept sky astride a broomstick with her black cat familiar while cackling at the moon prevails into the 21st century.

The idea of witches flying on broomsticks dates back to the Middle Ages, when an ancient

Pagan fertility rite was performed by men and women in fields of corn. In order to encourage the crops to grow higher they would leap into the air while astride a broomstick or pitchfork. The latter is the origin of later tales concerning male witches atop flying pitchforks.

Imagery dating from the end of the 17th century shows witches flying with the brush section of the besom in front of them. The brush supports a candle that lights their way, but it is the older image, with the brush behind the witch sweeping her tracks from the skies as she flies, which endures.

Records of witches "flying to the Sabbat" that were written during The Burning Times have their origin in a special hallucinogenic ointment that would be smeared all over the stale (handle) of the besom before the "flight" began. In reality, this was a shamanistic spirit journey in which the witch would imagine she was flying.

In modern Craft rituals, the besom is used to sweep away evil energies from the sacred space before a magick circle is cast. It is also used in the handfasting witches' wedding ceremony, when the newly conjoined couple jump across the broomstick into a new life together. Modern-day witches often decorate their besoms with brightly coloured ribbons that represent the seasons of the year.

A witch's besom is traditionally made from broom, but in contemporary witchcraft different woods are used. The stale symbolizes the phallus of the God and the brush represents the womb of the Goddess. Together, they symbolize the life-giving union of God and Goddess.

Magickal Tools

WILLOW WITCHING BRANCH

In the witch's tool kit you may find a sprig of willow in the shape of a forked "Y". This is an ancient dowsing tool used for "willow witching". Dowsers and witches (who are not one in the same!) use a willow branch to find water deep beneath the ground. This was useful to farmers in times past when agricultural communities flourished or failed depending on the success of their crops.

In modern times, witches still use the same method for divining, but the targets have changed. Instead of just water, witches who divine may be able to find lost objects, pets or even people. Some also claim that they can identify areas of spiritual disturbance by the use of the willow branch.

By using maps instead of trudging around farmers' fields and by simply moving around a house to search for a target, willow witching has arrived in the 21st century.

WIND ROARER

This little-known tool was, according to Cecil Williamson (*see Chapter 1, pages 38–39*), used by

HOW TO USE A WITCH'S PENDULUM

To start with, you will need to decide which type of swing movement denotes a "yes" answer, which is a "no" and which is a refusal to answer. Usually, a circular motion is taken as a "yes", a side to side swing means "no" and a backwards and forwards swing indicates a refusal to answer.

To begin, you should ensure that you are relaxed and still, holding the pendulum in either hand and asking aloud if there are spirits present. Some people prefer to ask by sending out thoughts rather than speaking aloud. In this author's experience both work equally well.

After a little while the pendulum will begin to move, slowly at first, but then stronger, until an answer can be deciphered by the direction of movement. At this point it is wise to try and ascertain whether the movement is being created by an outside force, which you can ask to identify itself using the alphabet. To do this, you need to ask the energy to give a positive swing when the letter of its calling name is said aloud. By going through the letters of the alphabet it is possible to identify the energy this way. Once you know what is communicating with you, other questions may be posed.

Some witches believe that you should keep your pendulum near to your body at all times, so that your auric field permeates it and it "becomes one" with you. If this is not practical, however, try sleeping with it under your pillow and keeping it in your pocket when you are out on your travels – you may be surprised how often you use it!

witches in the West Country to summon spirit forces when working in wild places.

In essence a flat slice of wood secured at one end by a cord, it is rotated in the air at great speed above the witch's head in order to create the sacred sound which, in many cultures – including the Maori, Aztec and Navajo – was thought to open the doorway between the land of the living and the dwelling place of the gods.

Australian Aborigines are given a wind roarer at special ceremonial occasions, where they are known as the "voice of God". Used in magickal rain-making dances and to display sacred symbols that are handcarved into the wood, the wind roarer makes a truly haunting and strange sound. Steve Patterson, a Cornish woodcarver who specializes in handmade ritual tools, and who is a researcher into the magick of the wind roarer, comments: "...it is little wonder that the spirits come flocking in to see what the ghastly noise is all about".

Pendulum

Witches often use a pendulum to dowse for answers to questions in all sorts of situations. From finding out the best time to cast a spell to seeing if a location is home to unseen forces, this tool has a home on every witch's altar. It is believed that by posing questions to the pendulum, a "yes" or "no" answer can be obtained from higher forces. Some people believe that the answer comes from within ourselves, a kind of psychic response shown in a practical way, while others believe the pendulum is activated by forces outside of the mind, body or spirit.

Pendulums can be homemade or bought, and samples made from crystal, glass, wood and stone are readily available. Although nice to have, effective results can be obtained just by using a ring tied on to a piece of cotton, or indeed anything else that weighs down the thread and allows equal movement in all directions.

Divinatory Tools

Runes

The word "rune" means "secret" or "mystery" in early English, and refers to an ancient alphabet of sigils that each have magickal and divinatory meanings, and have been in use since the 3rd century CE. Popular in Anglo Saxon times in England and throughout other parts of Europe, the runes can be engraved on stones, crystals or staves of wood, or simply written down. In magick they are used to add powers to spells, candle magick and talismans, while in divination each of the 24 letters has a different meaning and can be interpreted by the reader.

The querant will randomly select runes from a bag while concentrating on a particular question or situation in their life, and the answers or guidance will be determined by which runes they choose.

Ogham Staves

The Celtic tree alphabet is known as "Ogham" and is usually engraved upon separate pieces of wood of the type each sigil or letter represents. There are 25 symbols in the alphabet,

THE FOUR AICME OF OGHAM

Aicme of Beith
Birch, rowan, alder, willow, ash

Aicme of Huath
Hawthorn, oak, holly, hazel, apple

Aicme of Muin
Scot's pine, gorse, heather, white poplar, yew

Aicme of Eabhadh
Aspen, spindle, honeysuckle, gooseberry, beech

five sets of five letters, and each group is known as an "aicme". The original medieval Irish Ogham alphabet consisted of 20 symbols, but five more trees and corresponding symbols were added much later. Each sigil relates to a specific tree, and has specific divinatory and magickal correspondences. Ogham staves can be used in the same way as runes, either for magickal work or divination.

CRYSTAL BALL

A shiny reflective orb of crystal, or more commonly glass, is known as a crystal ball. Through the practice of scrying (from the Old English word "descry", which means "to reveal") it is possible to divine the past, present and future in the orb. The word "divination" comes from "divine", as it is believed that the gift of second sight is given to their acolytes, the witches, as a gift from the gods.

Some witches will use a clear orb in which they focus their attention, clearing their mind and allowing pictures, emotions and sensations to develop. Others might use a black sphere of obsidian or bright green cat's eye.

DARK MIRROR

The dark mirror, scrying mirror or magick mirror is one of the oldest magickal tools used by a witch. The magi of ancient Persia, Greeks and Romans all used mirrors for scrying purposes. The witches of Thessaly wrote their oracles in blood upon mirrors and taught the art of mirror scrying in the moonlight.

The dark mirror is made of a highly polished obsidian plate which, when stared at, defocuses the eye, so that the magickal "third eye" may peer into the shadow realms.

A dark mirror is traditionally made with secreted herbs that aid divination. Constructed only in moonlight, it must be protected from sunlight by wrapping it in a dark cloth when not in use. Although used mainly for scrying purposes, the dark mirror can also be utilized in magickal practice as a portal to the afterworld.

A noted obsidian scrying mirror that belonged to the famous Elizabethan magician, Dr John Dee, is now on display in the British Museum, London.

THE TAROT

There are many forms of divination practised by the accomplished witch, yet tarot reading remains one of the most popular methods of divination for many wishing to gain a deeper insight into the past, present and future.

There is no definitive moment in history when we can say for certain that the tarot first came to be used as a method of divination, and the origins of the cards are still shrouded in myth even today. Many theories on where they originated exist, and the places suggested range from Ancient Egypt to China and India. There is little doubt, however, that tarot cards were in use in some form in ancient times, yet the romantic notion that they were linked to such esoteric groups as the Knights Templar, the Rosicrucians, the Cathars or even Moses cannot be proved. What is certain is that a form of playing card similar to the tarot of today was in use in Renaissance Europe in the 14th or 15th century.

The traditional tarot deck consists of 78 cards. There are 22 cards, each illustrated with a specific set of symbols, that make up the "Major Arcana". (The word "arcana" means "mysteries" or "secrets".) In addition there are 14 cards in each of the four suits: wands (sometimes called rods), cups, swords and pentacles (sometimes called coins). These 56 cards are known as the "Minor Arcana".

Our modern playing card deck is descended from the Minor Arcana of the tarot, and can also be used in the divinatory practice of cartomancy. Today's clubs correspond to wands, hearts to cups, spades to swords and diamonds to pentacles. Somewhere along the way one of the court cards, the knight, was left behind, giving us 13 (a magickal number in witchcraft) instead of 14 cards in each suit.

Today there is a limitless assortment of tarot decks available, but by far the most popular for many tarot interpreters is the Rider-Waite deck. It is based on illustrations by Pamela Colman Smith and was commissioned and guided by Arthur Edward Waite, an English mystic and member of the Order of the Golden Dawn.

The tarot, in addition to being used as a system for divination, can also be used in meditation and magick. Many witches take one card from their favourite deck in the morning as a focus for the coming day or to see what the day has in store for them.

Here is a list of correspondences or themes that are magickally associated with each card.

The Major Arcana

THE FOOL	THE MAGICIAN	THE HIGH PRIESTESS	THE EMPRESS
Choice	Mental ability	Wisdom	Growth
Crossroads	Application	Sound judgement	Prosperity
Major decisions	Willpower	Foresight	Continuity
Naivety	Greater powers	Intuition	Contentment
Innocence	Manipulation	Perception	Abundance
	Creativity	Femininity	The Earth Mother
		Mystery	
		Secrets	
		Trade	
		Financial negotiation	

THE EMPEROR
Balance
Control
Structure
Reason
Authority
Knowledge
Experience
Respect
Self-determination

THE HIEROPHANT
Conformity
Tradition
Rules
Establishments
Institutes
Learning
Initiation
Ceremony
Ritual
Religion

THE LOVERS
Opposing directions
Moving forward
Physical and meta-
physical
Decisions
New love
Balanced relation-
ships

THE CHARIOT
Success
Winning
Achievement
Drive
Ambition
Control
Victory with effort
Urgency
Impatience

STRENGTH
Strength
Endurance
Chivalry
Strong Resolve
Calmness in
frustration
Acceptance
Inner strength
Compassion
Persuasiveness
Guiding

THE HERMIT
Introspection
Personal quest
New directions
Giving guidance
Being guided
Learning or teaching
Solitude
Stillness
Withdrawal

WHEEL OF FORTUNE
Fate
Destiny
Change
Fortune
Life
Expansion
Fame

JUSTICE
Justice
Law
Legal documents
Fairness
Karma
Cause and effect
Truth

THE HANGED MAN
Surrender
Sacrifice
Suspension
Patience

DEATH
Transformation
End
Change
Rebirth
New possibilities

TEMPERANCE
Patience
Moderation
Balance
Harmony
Equality
Calmness

THE DEVIL
Materialism
Indulgence
Addiction
Force
Temptation
Bondage
Lust
Sex

THE TOWER
Tumult
Inevitable change
Karma
Upheaval
Breakdown
Release
Suddenness

THE STAR
Hope
Attainment
Goals
Inspiration
Spirituality
Blessings

THE MOON
Dreams
Intuition
Psychic power
Emotion
Imagination
Fantasy
Illusion
Deception

THE SUN	JUDGEMENT	THE WORLD
Opportunities	Judgement	Freedom
Success	Absolution	Travel
Prosperity	Rebirth	Liberation
Happiness	Regeneration	Triumph
Energy	Enlightenment	Culmination
Vitality	Realization	Balance
Love		Happiness
Spontaneity		Fulfilment
Hope		Spiritual balance

The Minor Arcana

THE SUIT OF SWORDS
The suit of swords symbolizes the element of air and represents Aquarius, Libra and Gemini. It represents action, force, ambition, courage, challenges and movement. The cards are indicative of thought, intellect, wit and reason. Swords also represent power, and as the sword has a double edge, intelligence and power can be used for either good or bad.

THE SUIT OF WANDS
The suit of wands symbolizes the element of fire and represents Leo, Sagittarius, and Aries. It represents energy, personal growth, inspiration, strength, intuition, determination and creativity. The cards speak of our personalities, egos, enthusiasms, self-concepts and sources of personal fulfilment.

THE SUIT OF CUPS
The suit of cups symbolizes the element of water and represents Pisces, Cancer and Scorpio. It refers largely to issues of love, the emotions, feelings, sensitivity and families. The cards are associated with any aspects of our emotions, from marriage to personal partnerships to work.

THE SUIT OF PENTACLES
The suit of pentacles is associated with the element of earth and represents Taurus, Virgo and Capricorn. It links directly to material possessions, emotional and financial security, business, commerce and trade. Pentacles refers to "earthly pursuits", property, home and a love of nature.

Playing Cards

Many witches will keep a deck of standard playing cards as part of their magickal tool kit, in addition to a deck of tarot. "Cartomancy", divination by playing cards, originates from the Far East, where it is known as "*naibe*" meaning "to foretell".

Several magickal correspondences can be correlated between the deck and witchcraft: there are 52 cards in the deck and 52 weeks in a calendar year; there are four suits and four seasons and four primary elements; there are 13 cards in each suit and 13 lunar months in a year; and there are 12 court cards and 12 signs of the zodiac.

When using the cards in divination to foretell future events, hearts signify love, friendship and domestic matters; spades signify difficulties, sorrow, treachery and infidelity; diamonds signify career, money and travel and clubs signify business. The cards are selected at random and are interpreted by the reader in a similar way to tarot card interpretation.

Scrying Bowl

Witches skilled at the art of scrying may include a scrying bowl in their magickal Craft tools. Although any bowl will do, it is better to put one aside especially for the purpose of hydromancy, which is scrying by water.

It is possible to use a cauldron for this form of scrying, but if a bowl is available this may be easier to manoeuvre. The bowl must be of a dark colour, so that when it is filled with water the reflective surface becomes a sheen of blackness, where the eyes might stare into the land of spirits and bring messages forth to the scryer. Similarly to scrying by dark mirror (*see page 118*), use of a scrying bowl may put the scryer into a trancelike state, in which it will be easier to make magick.

Teacup

Tasseography, fortune telling by tea leaves, has a long heritage. Indeed, the early Greeks were known to have predicted future events from staring at wine sediments. The first mass-produced, purpose-made tasseography cups were made in the late Victorian era and many witches include one in their tools.

Although it is not necessary to have an elaborately decorated cup, it is best to put one aside for the sole activity of divination and not use it for mundane drinking purposes.

Spirit Board

Although not an ancient magickal tool, spirit boards have found their way into The Craft, and are now commonly used to speak to those who have passed to the Summerland.

During the late 19th century, amid the furore and excitement of the "new" spiritualism movement, news of the first spirit board appeared in an American newspaper. It was named the "Ouija" board by its designer, William Fuld. The name derived from "oui", meaning "yes" in French, and "ja", meaning "yes" in German. It became an instant hit. Marketed across the United States and quickly copied by others, the spirit board became *the* device to use to contact the other side.

Spirit boards have suffered from bad press over the years and tales of terrible consequences from using them have become a common contemporary urban myth. (These tales always seem to involve a friend of a friend or some other distant person that endured the "horrifying" experience, never someone you actually speak to!)

The original Ouija boards are still produced in America, although the patent is now owned by Parker Brothers, a subsidiary of children's toy giant Hasbro. You can pick one up in any toy store. Though Ouija boards have a recommended use age of five years plus, they are nonetheless seen as a board game with no malevolent undertone or inherent danger.

You don't have to buy a readymade spirit board – the same results can be obtained with one made yourself. To begin, simply write the letters of the alphabet clearly on small pieces of paper, along with the words "yes" and "no", and place these in a circle on to a smooth polished surface, such as a wooden table. Then, using an upturned wineglass, place your finger and the fingers of any other witches taking part, lightly on to the glass.

One witch should act as the speaker and simply ask aloud for any spirits to communicate by moving the glass. It may take some time, but in my experience, and with a little patience, the glass will indeed move. Once a link has been made with a discarnate energy, it is important to understand who you are communicating with, and personal questions should be addressed to the energy to correctly identify it. If it is unable to answer these, it does not mean you should instantly dismiss anything it says, but equally you should be cautious. In the same way that you would not open the door to your home and invite someone in without knowing who they are, here you have made a link with the spirit world and you need to know who, or what, you are dealing with.

THE WITCH'S WARDROBE

Robes

Most witches wear robes to perform rituals and work magick. These might be homemade, or they might be bought for the purpose. They are always kept clean, and are always given a degree of reverence by their owners.

By donning the robes, the witch begins the spiritual journey that will transport him or her from everyday life into the mystical realm, where magickal practice takes place. On a practical note, if using naked flames or bonfires in magick, great care needs to be taken that long sleeves and flowing robes to do not catch fire!

The Witch's Hat

The archetypal image of a black conical hat features prominently in images of witchcraft, and the shape dates back centuries. The famous artist Francisco de Goya, who painted many well-known masterpieces depicting the activities of witches in the 18th century (albeit in fantastical fashion) is partly responsible for the widespread connection between witches and pointed hats. His infamously titled *Black Paintings* (1819–1823) shows scenes of witchery and madness, in which heretics are shown wearing conical hats. It is thought that these heretic hats were the predecessors of the "dunce caps" that were placed on the heads of naughty schoolchildren in the past.

The witch Doreen Valiente suggested that the witch's hat is a symbol of power dating back to the Stone Age, when cave paintings showing people wearing pointed head-dresses were daubed on walls. The wearing of horns is widely considered to have been seen as a symbol of strength, and was connected to the Horned God of the witches.

Another theory of how witches became associated with pointed hats goes back to the Etruscan period, when a coin depicting the head of the goddess Diana – widely associated with witches – shows her with a pointed hat on. In Ancient Rome, Pagan priests known as "flamen" wore cone-shaped headwear and medieval woodcuts show witches with the same headgear.

Pointed hats became fashionable in the late 16th and early 17th centuries. After the fashion trickled down to the lowly country folk who gradually adopted styles outdated in the cities, the Pagan country dwellers became associated with the pointed hat. The village wisewoman or farmer's wife, whose knowledge of herbs and healing dubbed her a "witch", became the only person left wearing the pointed hat. After the Church began to associate its shape with the horns of Satan, its association with evil was set in stone.

By the Victorian era, depictions of witches in children's stories and fairy tales always included a black pointed hat. By then it had become an accepted element of witches' garb and a symbol of wickedness.

In a more magickal train of thought, the hat is thought to represent the cone of power that is raised by witches to perform magickal workings. It is suggested that the brim of the hat represents the covenors with joined hands raising the energy inside the circle they create. In traditions of witchcraft that venerate the three degree system, the symbol worn by one who has attained the third (and highest) degree wears a pentacle crowned with an upward-pointing triangle. This symbol represents the witches' hat on the pentacle. It is worn both symbolically and literally by the third-degree witch, showing that he or she has mastered the art of magickal practice.

Cloaks

A cloak is an essential part of the witch's wardrobe. Often, a modern-day witch will have several in different colours and made from a variety of fabrics suitable for summer and winter outdoor use.

In times past, and even today, many covens adopt black cloaks as a means of disappearing into the night at a moment's notice. If the threat of discovery presents itself, the witch will pull the hood over his or her head and make for the shadows, the colour of the floor-length cape and hood effectively making him or her "disappear" into the night.

You will often see witches at Pagan gatherings wearing cloaks as part of their daily outfits, or strutting down the high street in magickal places such as Glastonbury, in Somerset, or Boscastle, in Cornwall. Some witches have elaborately decorated capes that reflect their moods or the seasons. Whatever the colour or design, a cloak is fun to wear, along with being magickal and practical.

Magickal Jewellery

Many followers of The Craft wear jewellery that they keep especially for rituals and for wearing to Sabbats and gatherings. Traditions that utilize the degree system often reward those who have achieved a new degree with a specific symbol to wear:

First Degree: a pentacle. This represents the promise a first degree witch has made to the Old Gods and to themselves, and plants them firmly on the path of the wise.

Second Degree: an upturned pentacle. The upper point of the symbol points downwards, indicating that the second-degree witch has learned about the magickal world around him or her and is now focusing inward on the deeper mysteries.

Third Degree: a pentacle crowned with a triangle. This indicates that the third degree witch has mastery of the cone of power, represented by the extra triangle.

Magickal Cords

In some Craft traditions witches wear a magickal cord around their waist during rituals and magickal practices. The colour of the cord varies from coven to coven, but relates to the degree achieved by the wearer. Traditional colours are black, red and white, and they are 2.75 metres (9 feet) in length.

The first cord is given to the witch at the first degree ritual, while the second and third are acquired as the witch progresses through the degrees. When more than one cord has been awarded, they might be plaited. Knots in the cord indicate "the measure" of the witch, which is taken at the initiation ritual. The cord is also known as a cingulum, and can be used for performing cord magick.

Skyclad

Witches that work without robes or clothing are known as being "skyclad", in other words, clad only by the sky. There are many reasons given as to why working skyclad is beneficial to magick, but a lot of witches will not work nude.

Far from being sexual, as is often incorrectly stated, some covens that work skyclad believe that clothes hinder the flow of psychic powers that come from the body of the witch. Others say that being naked makes you more sensitive and therefore open to the subtleties of the magickal world. Casting aside clothing and everyday jewellery also renders everyone equal in the eyes of each other. The covenor in the designer suit and his colleague in a high street store T-shirt are on an equal footing!

MAGICKAL SIGNS AND SYMBOLS

Witches' Alphabet

As a way of ensuring secrecy, witches often write magickal formulas, records and spells in a secret script known as the "Witches' Alphabet". The alphabet is also known as the "Theban Script", the "Alphabet of Honorius" or the "Witches' Runes"; it was first published in 1518. Its exact origin is shrouded in the mists of time, but it is often attributed to Honorius of Thebes, hence its alternative name. The letters J, U and W were not represented in the original symbols, but they have been adapted for modern use.

Pentacle

The pentacle is the most important symbol of witchcraft and magick. It is a five-pointed star drawn in such a way that it has no beginning or end. When encircled, it represents the earth, Mother Nature. It signifies many different things, including the five elements – earth, air, fire, water and ether or spirit – and also the body of man standing with legs apart and with arms horizontal. When drawn or engraved, it is known as a pentagram. The pentacle is used in magick as a talis-  man against evil forces, and as a Craft tool in pride of place on the altar. It is ruled by the element of earth. The symbol is often worn by witches as a sign of their belief, either on jewellery or embroidered on to robes or clothing.

The pentacle is sometimes, incorrectly, connected with satanism. This association can be traced back to the 19th century, when Eliphas Levi described an inverted pentacle as representing "the goat of lust attacking the heavens with its horns". The inverted pentacle was adopted as its power sigil by the Church of Satan in 1966, so its negative reputation is contemporary and is often dismissed by witches as irrelevant. Despite this reality, however, the pentacle (inverted or not) is often thought of by the uneducated as a symbol of evil.

Septagram

The septagram is a seven-pointed star that is often used instead of, or in addition to, the sacred pentacle by witches who follow the Faery and Celtic-based traditions. It is also known as the "elven or faery" star. Like the pentacle, it is drawn continuously with one line joining the beginning at the end.

In faery magick the points of the septagram represent the sun, the moon, the forest, the sea, the wind, magick and spirit. In other traditions the points symbolize the seven planets, seven alchemical metals and seven days of the week.

Ankh

The Ankh is an ancient Egyptian symbol of life and immortality, sometimes referred to as the "key of life", and has been adopted by modern Pagans and witches for use in magickal practices. The exact origin of the symbol is unknown, but popular theory dictates that it represents the union of male and female – the upper part representing the female genitalia and the lower part representing the male. Together, the union of the two brings life into the world.

It is often depicted in Egyptian art, both ancient and contemporary, as an amulet carried by the gods, particularly relating to deities conferring everlasting life upon those who have entered the spirit world.

Hexagram

The encircled hexagram consists of two separate triangles placed over each other so as to create a six-pointed star. The triangle with its tip pointing north symbolizes love, truth and wisdom, while the triangle pointing downward represents the world, the flesh and the Devil. The first triangle symbolizes the spiritual world, while the second represents the material. The two combined form the whole.

The symbol also incorporates the alchemical symbols of the four elements – earth, air, fire and water – signifying a combination of opposing forces within one magickal sigil, which, as a group, represent the whole. The two triangles also represent the opposing sexes – the triangle pointing upwards, representing fire, is male; while the triangle pointing downwards, representing water, is female.

This sigil is also known as the Seal of Solomon because it was inscribed on a ring worn by the king, granting him the power to command and banish spirits. It was also carved upon Solomon's temple at Jerusalem. The symbol is not in fact Jewish, as is often claimed. Rather, it is actually a much older symbol that was adopted by the Jews because of its meaning. The Freemasons also adopted the symbol, and it adorns many of their buildings to this day.

| EARTH | AIR | FIRE | WATER |

Triskelion and Spiral

The triskelion is an early Celtic sign that consists of three conjoined spirals drawn with one continuous line, suggesting the movement of time. It symbolizes the sun (birth), afterlife and reincarnation, and can be found engraved in ancient stones and in pre-Christian Celtic art. It is directly related to the Goddess herself, the three spirals representing the Triple Goddess aspects of Maiden, Mother and Crone. It may also indi-

 cate the three journeys of initiation undertaken by witches, as the spiral in its single form is one of the oldest symbols of human spirituality, having been found engraved on tombs around the world dating back thousands of years. The lone spiral is also used as a symbol of witchcraft, denoting the inner journey that a witch must take in order to learn the hidden mysteries of magick, and also as a sacred symbol of the Goddess.

Triquetra

The triquetra was a pre-Christian Celtic symbol of the Goddess, and also of the Nordic father God, Odin, in northern Europe. It is commonly associated with contemporary Goddess worship as it lends itself to the Triple Goddess concept, yet it is unlikely that it represented this in centuries past. It is more likely that to the early Celtic peoples it symbolized the unity of earth, sea and sky, or mind, body and soul, as these were the spiritual philosophies of the early Celts.

Labyrinth

The labyrinth is an ancient symbol that can be found in many cultures, and has a deep significance relating to the spiritual journey. Examples of the symbol can be found in Neolithic art, Native American petroglyphs and at sacred sites, notably at Rocky Valley near Tintagel, in Cornwall. By tracing a labyrinth with your finger it is possible to enter a deep magickal trance, and it is also used in transformation magick to great effect. By entering the spiral-like labyrinth, it is impossible to get lost; the one-way path allows one to find the centre and exit.

Ancient Minoan labyrinths were sacred to the Mother Goddess, and were used in initiatory rituals. In medieval times they were carved into the floors of Christian cathedrals as a symbol of pilgrimage to God. Today, the symbol is popularly found in Pagan sites as a symbol of the journey to the inner self and enlightenment.

Sun Wheel and Sun Cross

The eight-spoked sun wheel derives from the four-spoked sun cross and represents the eight witches' Sabbats, which combined make up the Wheel of the Year, which symbolizes the witch's year and each of the important festivals.

The four-spoked sun cross, from which the sun wheel evolved, represents the four seasons.

Eye of Horus

The Egyptian Eye of Horus is a potent symbol of protection often carried as an amulet to ward against misfortune and the evil eye. Typically used in protection magick, it represents the eye of the falcon-headed god Horus, and is also sometimes called "The Eye of Ra" (Horus and Ra were both gods of the sun). The symbol is thus a solar, masculine sigil.

VI

WHICH WITCH
IS WHICH?

THROUGHOUT THE WORLD OF WITCHCRAFT THERE HAVE BEEN
numerous noted personalities associated with magick. Some of them are
well known and have been the subject of much discussion in a variety of
different media, while others prefer not to be in the limelight and to remain
in the shadows. In this chapter we will meet some well-known witches
who practise The Craft in the 21st century. I am indebted to them for their
agreeing to be interviewed for this book, and hope that the reader will take
an interest in "meeting" a varied cross-section of real practitioners of the
arts magickal. I have reproduced verbatim the questions that I set each cor-
respondent and their answers that follow.

"In 1951 the witch was made free.
They're out of the broom closet, as you will see."

MAXINE SANDERS
Priestess of the Goddess
✱✱✱✱✱✱✱✱✱✱✱✱✱✱✱✱✱✱✱✱✱✱✱✱✱✱✱

Maxine, you were not born into a family of witches, so how did you first discover witchcraft?

My first meeting with a witch was in 1946, when Alex Sanders, a friend of my mother's, was a regular visitor to our home. My father disliked Alex intensely, which obviously caused a problem in my mother's and Alex's friendship. Not long after my father's death, Alex accepted an invitation to one of my mother's soirées, where God and His mysteries were the topic of discussion. Alex brought other dimensions into the conversation: the Goddess and witchcraft. I was 14.

Alex led a very public and controversial life as "king of the witches". Where did this title originate?

Many thought it was a controversial life. Alex didn't – it was natural to him. The title "king of the witches" was not given as a sign of respect, but in recognition of The Craft being brought into the present. In the early 1960s, Alex was an initiated priest of the Goddess, and was proving to be a problem to The Craft. He was a catalyst and a showman who was attracting the attention of the media. Eventually, those who recognized the inevitability of The Craft's evolution believed Alex's actions would be enhanced by the restrictions the title "king of the witches" would impose upon him. This was regardless of those who, at that time, enjoyed making the occasional mysterious public appearance, and yet supported the few witches who wanted The Craft to stay hidden.

Widespread rumour dictates that Alex misinformed the public when he said that he had copied his Book of Shadows from his grandmother, who he claimed was a practising witch. Where do you believe his teachings originated?

Mrs Bibby, Alex's grandmother, was a wyrd woman who practised a form of witchcraft near Bethesda in north Wales. Alex, who had tuberculosis as a child, spent time with her while recovering. He learned some of the ways of magic from her and copied her recipe and spell book, although I think he had inherited a natural visceral understanding of magic as well.

Years later he received initiation from a Gardnerian witch called Pat. It was from her and others in The Craft that he copied the Book of Shadows. He believed that all information on magical matters, when proved workable, was worthy of being passed on. These days, there are many teachings, lectures, rituals etc., supposedly written by Alex Sanders, on sale. I have looked at some, but they have not been Alex's work.

Your coven often worked skyclad when it appeared in the media. What, in your opinion, is the benefit of being skyclad or robed during rituals?

We appeared skyclad when the media took photographs because witches worked naked in their circles. We also appeared robed for the same reason. No doubt, the photographs of us naked were enthusiastically circulated, possibly because we were a particularly good-looking coven! Being naked for the sake of it would be a bit of a bore; we were proud to be witches and wanted to live in a society where we could practise our religion, unafraid of the persecution that was ubiquitous at the time. The work of the circle dictates whether the priesthood is robed or not. Initiation, raising power with fire, intense dance and creating the ladder or necklace of the Goddess are the immediate practices that come to mind where nudity is practical, and therefore preferable. The conscious donning of robes enhances ceremonial practise of The Craft.

After becoming part of Alex's coven, you were later handfasted and legally married, but you separated in 1973. Did you remain in contact with Alex until his death in 1988?

Alex and I separated because of Alex's homosexuality. However, our love remained constant until Alex's death in 1988. We were often tempted to remarry, though; life and witchcraft made this a dream, something to do when we grew old.

You have now retired publicly from teaching others, stating that you feel this is better performed by a younger priesthood. Why do you say this?

Witchcraft works with fertility and rebirth as a basis for its rites. Elders of The Craft have earned respect because of their experience and knowledge, which they pass on willingly, however, time does not always bestow wisdom. The Craft is constantly evolving and while the basic truths are steadfast, methods of expressing and working those truths are continually changing, and so they must – otherwise they will surely die. Youth is ever curious and eager to experiment and practise in a way that is natural to this moment. Age is unremitting and makes the metaphorical jumping over the cauldron and riding of the broomstick a fond memory rather than effective magic.

You now practise magick alone in the mountains near your home. Do you think that solitary Craft practise is something all witches should experience?

For most of the cycle of the year, I practise the ways of magic and worship the God and Goddess in the mountains of Snowdonia in north Wales. I occasionally work with the coven that attends the stone circle of the "Temple of the Mother". This year it is my turn to host the gathering of the elders, when we meet to work, worship and enjoy the company of companions from all traditions of The Craft. All initiates follow an individual path.

Since taking a back seat from the media frenzy you once courted with Alex, how has your spiritual life changed?

Alex did not court the attention of the media, he just couldn't help attracting it. Eventually those who had a different ability (writers and musicians) took on the work of bringing The Craft into the moment. I continue to practise the disciplines of the priesthood and still endeavour to follow the path of the initiate. The Craft and magic are my spiritual vocation.

When you look at the ever-growing worldwide witchcraft community, how do you think The Craft will change or develop as we move further into the 21st century?

The change and development of witchcraft is the responsibility of The Craft priesthood. I hope that they will retain the beauty of The Craft's rituals and guard their sacredness.

LAVINA
High Priestess of The Craft
✳✳✳✳✳✳✳✳✳✳✳✳✳✳✳✳✳✳✳✳✳✳✳✳✳✳

Lavina, you are now a high priestess of witchcraft, but you were brought up in a Christian children's home and your first involvement with the spiritual world lead you to Satanism. How did this happen?

Being raised in a Christian children's home and having clairvoyant powers made people in the church believe I was possessed by the Devil! The church I was attending was Baptist, and during the service there would always be a moment of silence where people were allowed to speak aloud. I would psychically see things around people in graphic detail, and on one occasion, to everyone's shock and horror, I called out that the minister had been enjoying an illicit affair with one of the other churchgoers! This caused some problems!

It was decided that I was possessed by the Devil and that prayers and holy water were needed to cleanse me. This was undertaken in front of the entire congregation. I still thank the Goddess for giving me such a strong will and mind of my own because otherwise I could have been traumatized for life, and been scared away from any form of religion or spirituality forever.

During my teens I discovered Satanism; the whole occult way of living appealed strongly to me and I began to look around for a satanic group I could join. I was living in Amsterdam at the time and being an angry teen, and the negative side of magick was attractive to me. At that time I questioned nothing and accepted everything I was told.

What made you decide to turn your back on Satanism and explore other spiritualities?

I experienced a lot of unpleasant things during those years when I was a Satanist; many of which I am now ashamed of. Because I was such an angry young woman it was very easy for the Satanists to convince me that everything that I was doing was "right".

I can remember that one of the priests made other Satanists drink my blood on various occasions; they believed that my psychic ability would be passed on through the blood being ingested.

I became anaemic and very ill. This put a seed of doubt in my mind and I began to question what I was being taught. I decided to begin distancing myself from Satanism, but it is not simple to "walk away" from people like that; they were not prepared to let me go. After meeting a high priestess of The Craft, I found the strength to eradicate satan from my life once and for all.

I bumped into this amazing woman in the middle of the street and complimented her on her wonderful red flowing hair. Despite being in her fifties, she had the aura of a much younger woman and she positively "shone" with inner radiance. She thanked me for my compliment and commented on my long black hair and lace dress. She also asked why I was so thin and angry. She invited me to go for a coffee with her and I told her about my life. She told me how to protect myself and gave me the first steps toward my life as a witch. I recovered my health quickly under her advice, and the rest as they say, is history!

I believe that it was necessary for me to go through my "dark period" in order to walk the life path that has lead me to today. My experience with the darker elements of the magickal life has given me expertise in possessions and disturbed houses, which I now specialize in. Nothing scares me anymore!

Your father is Dutch and your mother is a Romany Gypsy, from where you believe your natural clairvoyant abilities originate. Did you have spiritual experiences as a child?

My second sight is definitely from my mother's side of the family. I started to realize that I could see more than others from a very early age. I would come out with things about other children in the home, for instance; predicting that something would break or someone's relatives would forget to visit. I also told the staff things about their personal lives that I couldn't possibly have known. I could also see auras and played with spirit friends. For me it was all "normal". I found it strange that other people could not see what I could!

You are a trained midwife, counsellor and veterinary assistant. These are all in the realm of "healing" in some form or another; do you consider yourself a "healer"?

That's a difficult one. I don't like to be called a healer because the healing that I perform is from spirit, not from me. My hands are tools for the spirit world and I have no control over how much help or healing the client experiences.

When it comes down to my knowledge of herbs, crystals, mixing potions and writing rituals, I call this witchcraft, not healing.

You have lived all over the world and studied different spiritual traditions, including Pow Wow magic in America. What is this?

Pow Wow is a magickal practice from the North American Indians, and has many similarities to The Craft when it comes to ritual and working with spirits. The biggest difference is that you learn not from a teacher, but from within yourself through long periods of solitude, soul-searching and fasting. The spiritual awakenings take place in a sweat lodge, or by being sent away alone into the wilderness to be at one with nature and the ancestral spirits; even by being buried in some cases. Through these techniques I faced a lot of demons and grew both as a spiritual person and a witch.

Working with animals is another important part of Pow Wow magick. I met my own power animal through a shamanistic spirit quest and learned that when animals cross your path in this world it is a message from the Great Spirit. Essentially, Pow Wow magick is very simple and that is why I love it.

Who has influenced your path to witchcraft?

I have been fortunate enough to have many teachers; notably my two Wicca mums: Hendrina from Holland, a very strict, old-fashioned witch, and Silver Ravenwolf from America, a lovely open-minded Pagan. The combination of the two influences set me on the path to form my first coven and the tradition of New Age Wicca. My version of The Craft caters very much for the modern-day witch. It incorporates as much as possible from the old religion, but re-packages it, making it more accessible for the 21st century. Although its roots are firmly in the past, not forgetting our brothers and sisters through the centuries, it is set firmly in the new millennium.

You were initiated through the degrees and became a third-degree high priestess in 1996. How did this change your spirituality?

I don't think it changed me that much. I have lived the spiritual life for such a long time, communing with my spirit guide Josef, seeing auras and the like. It is great to see how witches do blossom, though, as they gain more knowledge and experience. Initiation is an important part of The Craft for me.

You now teach others and have your own tradition of witchcraft. What is this called and how does it differ from other traditions?

It is called New Age Wicca, meaning witchcraft for the age we are living in. A lot of things that were done in the olden days are either not possible or not acceptable anymore. Rather then being confrontational and stubborn and sticking to the age-old traditions, I believe in making The Craft available to people from all walks of life, and in order to do so we have to have walked the same road.

As an example, many covens used to work naked, and some still do. Although I agree with the old teaching that we should not be ashamed of the bodies we have been given by the Goddess and God, some people have issues with their appearance and rather than force them to strip naked and feel ashamed or worried, which will affect the energies in the circle, I allow them to be robed if they wish. I have learned over the years to honour and respect every witch for who they are and not to force anything in the name of tradition. This does not mean that I never work naked; I often do, but usually I am on my own or with a select group of witches.

Another part of my practice that has been

adapted for modern times are the lotions and potions that I used to mix. Many years ago I can remember preparing a preparation for a sprained ankle that consisted of crushed white cabbage being applied to the ankle for several days. This would not be possible today – I don't think my client would be welcome in a restaurant, shop or at their place of work smelling of old cabbages! So instead, I would prepare something more appropriate for today's society.

When treating stress, I used to mix fresh lavender and add it to a hot bath, but today people are too busy and cannot be bothered to clear up the flowers from the plughole and around the bath – they prefer to use an oil instead. The raw magick is still the best though, including the cabbage!

The appearance of my coven has also changed; we no longer have the same robes and tools. I encourage individuality in the coven; it makes the world a wonderful varied and colourful place. I love to look around the circle and see the different ways people choose to express their beliefs in the robes they wear and the tools they use. Now it is not uncommon to see a Gothic witch dressed in a black lacy dress standing alongside a shaman dressed in feathers and an Indian head-dress. The lazy witch may have a simple throw over her shoulders, and the medieval role-playing witch might have something from her re-enactment society! The only rule I do impose is that we are naked beneath the robes; this is a nod to our ancestors, who always worshipped skyclad.

You have initiated witches who have gone off to create their own covens all over the world, but who turn to you in times of need. How do you cope with this responsibility?

Over and over again I have been told by the spirit that I am given what I can cope with, and as I begin to move towards my crone years I am understanding that more. I have learned to let things run their course and only interfere if I am asked for help.

When it comes to teaching, I let people develop in whatever way the Goddess wants. I cannot be there to hold everyone's hands all of the time, but I can be a one-stop shop in times of need. Thank the Gods for email! For those witches I have initiated, a bond is made that cannot be severed. They can call, contact or summon me any time, day or night.

In a nutshell, it can be tricky to balance Craft life with everyday life, but I get a lot of help from the spirit world and my reward is job satisfaction!

Your eclectic tradition draws on many different spiritual philosophies that you have encountered around the world. Do you consider Eclectic Witchcraft to be as valid as other traditions that follow a more structured foundation?

Most definitely, and I daresay that the eclectic tradition is more appropriate for the type of person who turns to witchcraft from a variety of walks of life and previous spiritual beliefs.

In times past I think witches had it easier than we do today. Each village had its own Cunning Man or herbalist, and they were accepted in the community. Today, if we are not careful, we are seen as weird or even dangerous. I believe it is our responsibility to work towards changing that perception. I always teach my witches not to announce their beliefs to the world, just to live by them.

Religion causes war and fuels hatred, but the individual gods of each religion – Allah, Jehovah, Buddha and the Goddess – do not advocate fighting. It is the way people twist their teachings that causes the rifts. Witches are no different in this respect: at the end of the day we are still people. Greed, anger and jealousy are not strangers to witchcraft, but I hope that with eclectic teachings, as opposed to rigid traditions, I can encourage open-mindedness and acceptance among the spiritual communities. In the first-degree promise my witches say that they will be there for other witches no matter what.

Your relationship with deity is a day-to-day one. How does the Goddess and God manifest in your life and how do you communicate with them?

They are with me all the time. I honour them at my altar and ask for daily guidance each morning and thank them each night before I go to sleep. As a clairvoyant I am shown a lot through my second sight but I also regularly use a dark mirror for insights. Meditation also connects me with deity.

I also see the God and Goddess in the people around me, because in every man there hides a God, and in every woman, a Goddess…

JANET FARRAR AND GAVIN BONE
Priestess and Priest, Authors and Lecturers
✳✳✳✳✳✳✳✳✳✳✳✳✳✳✳✳✳✳✳✳✳✳✳

Janet, you are well known in the witch-craft community as a leading figure in modern witchcraft and a celebrated figurehead. Please tell us how you were originally attracted to The Craft and when?

When I came into The Craft, it was 1970. I was 19 years old at the time. I'd grown up through the 1960s, I was a flower child, I was a hippie, I knew the Beatles, Eric Clapton and Brian Epstein. I was, at the same time, a Sunday-school teacher. I was a good Christian from a good Christian background. A friend of mine became very interested in witchcraft and I basically went to bail her out. I had heard all about witchcraft, I knew it was all about sex and drugs and rock 'n' roll!

Well, I went to dissuade her from being part of Alex Sanders's coven. Now Alex Sanders was the gentleman who called himself "king of the witches"; I hasten to add that he was not accepted generally as the "king of the witches". He was an old rogue and a brilliant showman, and yes, he was a very, very good ritual magician.

When I met him I was quite surprised, because I found that under the showmanship was a very genuine spirituality. He started talking about this deity called the "Goddess", and I had never heard of the "Goddess". She actually meant nothing to me at this stage, but I rather liked the idea of being involved in the healing aspect, because although I had never wanted to be a healer, it was the remnants of my "let me heal the whole world" attitude.

Gavin, please tell me how you were originally attracted to The Craft and how you met Janet and Stewart?

I have a much more eclectic background than Janet. I first became interested in witchcraft in the early 1980s. Initially I was going to the local Spiritualist temple in my home town of Portsmouth, and was interested in the healing practices there. I picked up my first book on Wicca about the same time. I had always been interested in occult subjects; I bought my first tarot pack when I was 16 years old and used to attend festivals on the unexplained. I had developed my own "system" of beliefs. The first book I read was Doreen Valiente's *ABC of Witchcraft*. Well, that's when I knew what I was

– a Wiccan. There in the book was all that I believed in.

I joined my first magical group in 1985. This was an eclectic group and its members consisted of a ceremonial ritual magician, a Norse shaman, a couple of traditional spiritualist mediums as a well as a Sufi practitioner. It worked from the back of an occult shop in Portsmouth called Fifth Dimension. The group practised a mixture of magical practices, including earth magic – the clearing of ley lines etc., and ceremonial rituals. It was from one of its members, the Norse shaman, that a Seax-Wicca coven was formed. I had been the youngest member of the eclectic group, and had started to become a focus for a group of younger people interested in Wicca in my home town, so in early 1986 these people were all brought together and we were formally initiated into the coven.

I should point out that although we based our initial coven work on Ray Buckland's book, *The Tree: The Complete Book of Anglo-Saxon Witchcraft*, we quickly went beyond it. It was a good base to start from, but we wanted more. We started to work more with the material from Janet and Stewart's books, and started to create our own rituals and system of working. Because of this, the group also became quite eclectic in its approach. None of us saw anything wrong with this as it worked.

Janet, you were initiated into the Alexandrian tradition in 1970, but you have since moved away from the rituals laid down by Alex Sanders. Why have you not stuck with those original teachings and how have you changed as a result?

Stewart (Farrar, my late husband) and I were never really encouraged to look beyond what was being taught within the Alexandrian tradition while we were members of Alex and Maxine's coven. I should point out that it wasn't that we were discouraged in any way, just that Alex's teachings at that time were purely based on high magic. Stewart and I wanted to go beyond that. Although it was one of the factors that made us leave the coven, it wasn't the primary one.

Stewart and I had already been given "permission" to form our own coven as second-degree witches. We started experimenting with other forms of magic, and began to naturally move away from Alex's teachings. In the end, Alex had no choice but to give us our third degrees and allow us to fully hive off.

Technically I am Alexandrian by lineage, if you believe in the concept, which I don't, and certainly not in practice. When we moved to Ireland in 1976 we fully broke from the Alexandrian tradition's teachings. They were just not appropriate to the "Celtic twilight" of Ireland; the mythology, the folklore and the landscape.

I like to call myself simply a "witch". My own and my coven's practices are eclectic, but then, if you know anything about the history of Wicca, so are all the other traditions. Stewart and I did keep the basic Alexandrian framework for many years, but we had already started to adapt it when Gavin came into our lives.

I have rejected many of the dogmas that are in the Alexandrian/Gardnerian forms of Wicca. As I mentioned previously, I do not agree with the concept of lineage, as it is based on the principle that you aren't a witch unless you can prove descent from a particular person, i.e. Alex Sanders or Gerald Gardner. This concept alienates many witches who have had genuine spiritual initiations. There is only one true initiator and that is your God or Goddess that initiates you, and I believe this strongly. It is for this reason that we both say that there is no such thing as "self-initiation"; if the God or Goddess is initiating you how can it be "self-initiation"?

Janet, do you think conforming to a pre-defined tradition is a good thing? Or can more be gained by moving away from structured traditions?

It's really "horses for courses", to use that old phrase. Some people thrive in traditional-style covens, such as Gardnerian or Alexandrian, while others don't. Traditional groups certainly give you a good grounding in the basics, so they are good for those who are just joining

The Craft; a structured approach is good for learning in. I have noticed over the years, though, a tendency for many who have come from such traditions to find their "own way" after leaving them. They simply outgrow the need for the structure because they find it too restrictive, but they probably wouldn't have necessarily been able to do that if they hadn't been through that learning experience first. So, to really answer your question, I think there are benefits to both approaches; neither is better than the other. It really is what suits the individual best.

Janet, you were married to Stewart Farrar for many years and together accomplished a great deal. Please tell us how you first met and developed your magickal and personal relationship.

How I met Stewart, well, this is actually quite a funny story. Alex Sanders asked me if I would be the "initiate" for a photo session for a book that was being written about him. Well, there I was, stark naked and tied up, when the photographer leant across and said in a very calm and gentlemanly voice, "you've got something stuck to the bottom of your foot"! The calming voice came from none other than Stewart Farrar, who then attempted to pick the mole off the sole of my foot to no avail! That was my first contact with Stewart and, of course, the photographs were being taken for *What Witches Do* and the LP, *A Witch Is Born*.

I was already married to my first husband, Victor, when I first joined The Craft; we had married quite young. Stewart became my working partner in The Craft with the encouragement of Alex and Maxine. We complemented each other. I was 19 years old and had youth and enthusiasm, and he was 53, with worldly experience and wisdom. This worked for us not just on the magical levels, but also on a personal level as well after I divorced my first husband. We moved to Ireland in 1976, but by then we were already writing our own rituals for the coven and continued to do so when we got to Ireland.

It was in Ireland that we really discovered that we could complement each other as writers. I would research and come up with ideas for rituals related to our practice in Ireland, and Stewart would take care of the details. Eventually we realized that many rituals were suitable for publication, and they became the foundation of *Eight Sabbats for Witches* and *The Witches' Way*, along with other material we researched specifically for the books.

Janet, your books, The Witches' Way, Eight Sabbats for Witches and The Witches' Bible, are now regarded as "textbooks" for modern-day followers of The Craft. Do you still follow the principles you set out in the books, or have they been replaced with new ideas and concepts?

Those books are now over 25 years old, and even though our ritual practices and our system of working may have changed, we still follow the basic principles and philosophies that Stewart and I wrote in the books: the belief in divinity manifest as the Goddesses and Gods, the system of ethics manifest as "The Rede", the cycle of solar and lunar festivals and the practice of magic and psychic abilities as healing art. It doesn't matter what tradition you come from within witchcraft, these remain the same for all of us; they are the core beliefs of the witch.

Our practices may be slightly different to the books now. We have a different attitude to the way initiation works and how we perceive the Gods and Goddesses. This has resulted in us making changes to the degree system and how we run our coven, but these are changes to our system of working, not to the core belief structure, which we wrote about in these books. It is these beliefs that make you a witch, not the practice of lineage or initiation into a specific tradition.

In 1976 you moved to Ireland and began your own coven. What was this experience like, and what advice would you give other witchcraft priestesses and priests?

Actually, Stewart and I were running a coven before we left England for Ireland. We set up our first coven after leaving the Sanders' coven in December 1970. I had only been a witch for a year, and Alex had taken me from neophyte to third degree in 12 months; that was far too fast. There I was, only 20 years old, and I was a high priestess for goodness sake! What life experience does a 20-year-old have? It was daunting, to say the least; luckily I had Stewart's wisdom – he was 34 years my senior – to fall back on.

Personally, I don't think anyone below his or her mid-twenties is really up to running a coven – I certainly wouldn't recommend it. Which really gets me to what advice I would give to other priestesses and priests. The first is listening, as I've heard Gavin say: "the Goddess gave us two ears and one mouth." Good leaders listen twice as much as they talk. I think that's why our first coven worked; we listened to the members as we'd all hived off together. The second is to realize that you're a servant of the coven; this means you're there not to put yourself up on a pedestal, but to serve the Gods and help the other coven members on their spiritual paths. Take what you do seriously, but don't take yourself too seriously. Be willing to laugh at yourself when you make mistakes. There's not enough humility in The Craft nowadays; everyone wants to be "grand high" something!

Gavin, along with Janet you have recently published Progressive Witchcraft. What exactly is "progressive witchcraft"?

The term "progressive" is used in a descriptive way. It is a way of looking at Wicca or witchcraft; an attitude towards it. Someone who might want to use the term is describing his or her belief that Wicca, or for that matter all spiritualities, are not static. They look to the future; they develop, change and evolve over time. Saying this, they will look back to the truths of the past, but discard those things that they feel are now irrelevant to their spiritual growth. A progressive witch is therefore someone who questions and challenges the dogmas and doctrine that they see in Wicca, and asks the question, "are they relevant to me in the 21st century?" They believe that witchcraft is a living, evolving tradition, which changes over time.

The major difference is that the progressive witch puts spirituality and therefore divinity at the centre of their practice. This means all else follows from this, including ethics, morality, magical practice and even their lifestyle. Connection with the divine as one of the many deities it manifests becomes the most important aspect of their practice and life. It is therefore a commitment, a vocation, to serve deity. This does mean that deity is seen very differently to traditional Wicca. The ideas of the Triple Goddess and Dual God, the standard archetypal way of viewing deity remains valid, but they are just seen as useful magical concepts. What is important is that emotional connection. This means that a progressive witch is likely to be polytheistic in their outlook, believing that every path is valid and not necessarily believing that theirs is better than anyone else's.

They are also likely to adopt techniques, which may not necessarily be seen as Western tradition. Progressive witchcraft therefore sticks to one of the oldest Craft axioms: if it works, use it!

Within your coven you have developed a new "degree" system of initiation. Please tell us why you felt the need to do this and how the new system differs from your original initiations into Alexandrian witchcraft.

We were very concerned that the degree system as we had been taught it was becoming hierarchical. You have to remember that its origins are not in any form of traditional European Pagan practice, but from ceremonial ritual magic and Freemasonry. Our experience was that the degree system had become more about how long you had been in the coven rather than how much you had learnt or how much spiritual connection you had made during that time.

First, we tried to do away with the degree system completely, going to a one-initiation system. We found though that this wasn't enough – it didn't fulfil the needs of the coven – so we introduced a dedication ritual and eventually a third level: an eldership. Well, we ended up not with three levels, but four! We began to look at why this was. It really gets down to human psychology and the need for all of us to achieve goals. If we don't have them, part of our own psyche sets them for us anyway, a process the psychologist Abraham

Maslow called "self-actualization".

Our "degree" system, if you can call it that, is very different to the one we were actually taught. It is based not just on the accumulation of knowledge and magical skill, but also on spiritual achievement. For us, initiation must be a spiritual experience, a spiritual "epiphany" so to speak. As Janet mentioned earlier, we strongly believe in the concept of "there is only one initiator" and that is the divine manifest as God or Goddess, not ourselves. This means that we believe that initiation can take place in the mundane life of the witch. In fact, we don't separate the mundane from the magical. All life is magical; therefore an experience that changes you spiritually can take place in any area of your life, not just in the magic circle. We try to reflect this in our initiation rites.

You were both handfasted; please give us a flavour of this experience for those who have never experienced a structured spiritual joining of two people.

We were actually handfasted on 5 May 2001 in the garden of a public house in Kells, our home town. We had originally planned to be handfasted on Tara Hill, the seat of the old high kings of Ireland, but the foot-and-mouth scare had made this impossible, as the hill was farmland and had been quarantined. We had friends and relatives there from Ireland, England and the United States. An altar with the traditional magical tools and decorated with flowers was positioned in the centre of the garden. The handfasting ritual was beautiful; it was written specifically for the occasion and afterwards everyone circle-danced around the garden, including some of the staff working at the pub!

For us this was a highly personal and spiritual experience. Making the spiritual commitment in the handfasting to each other was more important than a legal piece of paper that declared us married under the law. It was a highly emotionally charged experience for us as we declared our love for each other before our Gods and shared it with our friends and family.

Gavin, you live in a magically charged area of Ireland. Please tell us a little about it.

We live in the heart of one of the richest concentrations of ancient spiritual heritage in Ireland: Kells, County Meath. We are less than 40 minutes from Bru na Boinne, Newgrange, the largest chambered tomb in the world; less than 15 minutes from Tailtu, the home of the Lughnasadh Funery Games (the ancient Irish 'Olympics') and 20 minutes from Tlachta, the Hill of Ward, the home of the Samhain Festival. There is a strong tradition of magical folklore in our area, and there are also fairy sightings. You can still see hawthorn trees standing in the middle of fields, which the older farmers refuse to cut down because they don't want to risk the wrath of the sidhe!

Many covens in Ireland connect directly

to ancient sites, or with the myths of the Irish. This is true of our current coven, which is named "Coven na Callaighe", after the hill in the Loughcrew Range. This is a Neolithic cemetery stretching over three hills – Patrickstown, Carn Bane West and Carn Bane East – also known as Slieve na Callaighe. "Callaighe" can mean many different things in Irish, including "hag", "wise woman" and even "nun"! Its literal meaning is "veiled woman", and it is interpreted locally as "witch".

There are the remains of seven chambered tombs on top of Slieve na Callaighe, dating back over 4,000 years. The place has a mystical, Celtic twilight feel about it; it is common for a low-lying mist to sit on top of the hill, but even so, you are still able to see the 360-degree view over seven counties in Ireland.

Slieve na Callaighe is named after the myth of the hill. It is said that St Patrick came to the top of the Patrickstown Hill and tried to claim the area "for Christ". He was met by a red-haired giantess, the Callaighe, who said that the land was owned by her, not Christ. St Patrick challenged her that if she could pick up all the stones on the hill and jump across the other two hills and back without dropping any, he would accept her claim. But, if she could not, the land would belong to Christ. Well, the giantess picked up the stones in her pinafore and made the first jump to Carn Bane East, but as she did so, stones fell out of her apron. Then she jumped from there to the next hill, Carn Bane West, and again, stones fell out of her apron. Frustrated, she turned around and jumped back to Carn Bane East, at which point she fell and broke

her neck. It is said in common myth that the only intact chambered tomb on the hill, known to the archaeologists as Cairn "T", is where the local people buried her.

Of course, the mound is far older than the myth of St Patrick. Cairn "T" has been dated to 3500 BCE, and contains some of the most amazing Neolithic carvings in the world. These stone pictograms mark the rising of the sun on spring equinox; they are an agricultural calendar believed to indicate to the local Neolithic farmers when to plant their crops. Behind the Cairn on the north side is what is known as the "Hag's Chair". This is a large stone throne weighing several tons, which dates back to the same period. We noticed that if you were to sit on the "chair" at the time of the full moon, the moon would actually come up behind your head. We believe this to be intentional, and that it may have originally been used for a form of trance-prophesy similar to the practices of the Greco-Roman sibyls.

I can honestly say that we have learnt a lot from these ancient mystical sites. They are inspirational, and we are lucky to live in a land that has so much to teach.

How do you both experience deity? Do the God and Goddess manifest in your daily life? If so, how do you see them?

We jokingly named our cottage "the house of a 100 deities!" Actually, it's more than that now. We have statues of the Goddesses and

Gods around our home: Greek, Roman, Egyptian, Norse, Celtic, Minoan, Hindu, Buddhist, Voudon, Native American and more. We even have Christian concepts of divinity, including the Madonna and child.

The principle deity we work with is Freya. Both of us had the connection with her before we even met, and she is really how we met. She brought us together through past and current life links. We consider ourselves to be her priestess and priest in the true sense of the word. That doesn't mean we don't work with other deities, we do, but she is our "principal life guide" and directs our personal work. We talk with her, laugh and joke with her, get angry with her, but we don't bow down to her, grovel at her feet or do anything like that. She comes to us in our dreams and makes sure that in everyday life we know when she is around! It's a very personal one-to-one relationship. Not surprisingly, the main shrine in our living room is sacred to her.

We don't adhere to the concept originally taught in The Craft: that all gods are one God and all goddesses one Goddess anymore. For us, the gods are individual personalities, just as people are. Yes, you can see them as concepts, but you can't have a personal relationship with an archetype. We suppose you could say that we are unashamed polytheists!

As you have both been "modern-day" witches for many years, how has the witchcraft community changed over the past decade and the new millennium?

Things have changed very fast in the last decade, let alone since we both first came into The Craft. The new generation coming in know much more about The Craft before they find and join a coven than we did. For us, there were just a handful of books, if we could find them. Now there is information freely available to everyone on the Internet on witchcraft and the magical arts. This means the new generation have higher expectations of those teaching them, plus in many cases, they don't have to throw off the monotheistic baggage that we did. They've been brought up in a pluralist society, which makes them more open to concepts within Paganism.

Both of us had to search to find groups. Now there are contact networks, open meetings, organizations such as the Pagan Federation and in some countries, even Pagan and Wiccan churches. Now the witch has a choice; they can be solitary or they can join a coven to train. When we both came into The Craft we took what we could find, and you had to join a coven and be initiated before you were accepted as a witch. Now you can pick and choose what tradition or way of working you would like.

Where do you both see The Craft going in the next decade?

Very good question! If you had asked us this question a decade ago we could have given you an answer, but now things are moving so fast it is difficult to say. Certainly we believe that The Craft is going to survive to the end of this millennia; but whether it will it be recognizable to us is a different matter. It's evolving and changing fast; there are new traditions appearing all the time and the younger generation is incorporating new ideas. We do not believe this to be a bad thing – quite the reverse. It's part of the law of evolution.

We believe that some of the major changes that occur in The Craft in the next decade will be in the way it is practised. Certainly The Craft is moving away from ceremonial high magic towards a more shamanistic approach. We believe this will continue and result in a more spiritually orientated Wicca, with direct connection to the gods being the principle teaching. We have already moved this way ourselves, as have several other covens and individuals that we know. There will certainly be more emphasis on the mysteries being taught because of this directional change.

For someone who is beginning on the path of The Craft, what advice would you give them and how would you advise them to live magickally in the 21st century?

Shop around! The days of going with the first teacher you find are over. Find a group or individual to train with, but don't mould yourself to fit in with *their* requirements; find one that fits *your* requirements. Of course, you don't have to be a member of a coven or be taught by another to be a witch. Listen inside; the gods speak within us and if we listen they will guide us. Don't take yourself too seriously and respect those willing to teach you. To be a witch is to be a servant, not a master. This is a tradition of service to the gods. If you are not willing to do this then you should not be contemplating becoming a witch.

GRAHAM KING
Curator, Museum of Witchcraft
✷✷✷✷✷✷✷✷✷✷✷✷✷✷✷✷✷✷✷✷✷✷✷✷✷

Graham, you are well known as the curator of the world-famous Museum of Witchcraft in Boscastle and as an expert in witchcraft lore. Why were you first attracted to witchcraft? Do you class yourself as a witch?

I am not sure that I *am* known as an expert in witchcraft lore – I am always unsure of those who call themselves experts and would never class myself as one. We do, however, have an excellent library here, so I can usually find the answers to questions about witchcraft.

Years ago I was more conventionally employed as managing director of a small manufacturing company. On returning from a particularly stressful trade show in America, I took to the hills of Wiltshire to unwind. I have always found walking to be a great way of sorting out problems and getting rid of stress. I met a group of travellers on Tan Hill, who were celebrating Lammas, playing music, dancing and enjoying the lovely summer's day. Cutting a long story short, they made me welcome and I spent a few days with them. I will never forget the beautiful sight of people dancing naked as the sun set over the vale.

This experience made me think: who was doing the right thing? Who had the better way of life? The travellers, or me?

Within a few days I put my business, cottage, and Jaguar up for sale; I did not have any plans, but knew that I had to get out of the "rat race". A Pagan friend of mine showed me an article about Cecil Williamson and his museum. "Williamson could not find a buyer for his museum", it said. "It may have to relocate to America". My friend suggested that I buy the museum, and the rest is history.

I think that "witch" means different things to people – it is difficult to define. I also try to keep my personal beliefs to myself. So, no, I do not call myself a witch.

The museum has a chequered past. Could you give us a brief history from its inception to the present day?

The museum was started in the 1950s by Cecil Williamson, with Gerald Gardner's help. It was originally located on the Isle of Man. After a few years, Gerald and Cecil fell out, as business partners so often do. Cecil moved his collection to England and Gerald continued running the original museum (without many of Cecil's artefacts) until his death a few years later. Initially, Cecil relocated his museum to Windsor, but met with a hostile reception – it was made obvious that the Royal Family did not want a witchcraft museum as a neighbour. Consequently, the museum moved to Bourton-on-the-Water, where it was (unsuccessfully) fire-bombed and then, in 1960, to Boscastle. Trouble followed the museum around – "born again" Christians persistently campaign about the evils of the museum – but it has survived. Today there are fewer complainers; indeed, most of the locals realize what an important role The Museum of Witchcraft plays for the economy of Boscastle.

You were lucky enough to know Cecil Williamson. Can you describe what sort of man he was?

Yes, I was lucky enough to know Cecil for the last few years of his life. He was a character and a gentleman, and I am proud to have briefly known him. Cecil's posh upbringing stayed with him; he was an old-fashioned gentleman who loved to talk. It was often a job to get a word in!

In his later years, Cecil kept to himself and had few friends. His wife died some years before him, and his daughters both lived overseas. I liked Cecil, and when he finally ended up in a nursing home I visited him every week.

Cecil was a great storyteller; his stories were often unbelievable, but have so often turned out to be absolutely true. He would tell of Gerald's attempts to stab him with his athame, and of a visit he made with Gerald to meet an unwell Aleister Crowley. I remember the famous Plymouth artist, Robert Lenkiewicz, painting Cecil just before his 90th birthday; Cecil was very unwell and could barely speak, but he posed proudly and with dignity for the painter.

We are lucky to hold many letters from Cecil in our archive. They paint an amazingly accurate picture – he wrote the way he spoke. If you are feeling adventurous, you could spend some time peering into Cecil's scrying mirror – I am sure that he still visits the museum. His mirror seems to break down the barriers of time, past and future – that's where I go to meet Cecil!

You exchanged contracts with Cecil after walking away from your previous home in Hampshire to Boscastle to begin a new life at midnight on Samhain, 1996. Why did you choose that particular time and Sabbat, and why did you leave Hampshire?

This was an opportunity for me to start a new life, to leave the old one behind, and to walk seemed appropriate. The Boscastle tourist season ends around the end of October, so it seemed appropriate to choose Samhain. The deeds were signed at midnight!

Cecil faced several challenges from locals who were opposed to the museum when it was based in other parts of the country. Have you faced anything like this, and if so, how have you dealt with such challenges?

I have tried to lead by example. The museum team have tried to be courteous and polite. We have engaged with the locals and in local activities. We still occasionally get death threats in the mail – I sometimes put these on display in the museum. Maybe once a year a noisy "born again" Christian will start ranting outside the museum, but they can usually be persuaded to leave without too much fuss.

The museum contained the remains of a local witch whom you put to rest. Could you please tell us who she was, why she was in the museum and why you removed her?

You are referring to the remains of Joan Wytte, a Wise Woman who died in Bodmin Gaol. While I am not necessarily opposed to displaying human remains in museums, I am obviously aware that it is a contentious issue.

Generally I feel that it is possible to display the mortal (as opposed to the immortal) remains of a person or creature with dignity in a museum. Joan, however, was used as a medical specimen; this was apparently common for convicts who died in prison. Her bones were wired together, and she was hung in a display box from a bolt through her skull. Unhappy with this arrangement, we initially changed the display and laid Joan horizontally in her box, which we lined with soft fabric. We even gave her some dried flowers. We still felt uncomfortable about Joan, though, and sensed that she wanted her remains buried. We did this secretly but with dignity in Minster Woods. A headstone near the site reads: "Joan Wytte, born 1775, died 1813 in Bodmin Gaol, buried 1998, no longer abused."

The museum is filled with thousands of interesting artefacts. Which ones are your favourites, and why?

This changes day to day, but I am consistently drawn to Cecil Williamson's dark mirror – it seems to be alive with spirits! It is a truly magical object.

I also am touched by the little "Fums Up" dolls that were carried by soldiers going to fight in the First World War. These and the other lucky charms made in the trenches touch me – people turn to magic when they need it most.

My favourite is the museum itself; the fabric of the building, the display cases, the entire collection, the whole thing is special. So many magicians, witches and occultists have visited and left their thoughts or donated artefacts that the place has become a site of pilgrimage – almost a sacred site. So, yes, my favourite object is the museum itself!

Boscastle became famous around the world for the floods of 2004, during which the museum was severely damaged. How has the museum recovered, and has the newfound status of the village affected the museum for the better or worse?

We would never want to go through another disaster like the flood – it was terrifying and we are still recovering from all the after-effects. In the long term, once the flood alleviation measures are in place and the construction crew have taken their diggers and dumper trucks away, we may end up with a safer village and possibly have more visitors.

The flood did make people realize what an important role the museum plays in protecting and preserving our heritage. I think people will value it more now – at least I hope so.

Have you managed to recover all the artefacts that were washed away in the flood? Are there any anecdotal stories about returning pieces?

The yelps of joy when a volunteer, sifting through the sewage-ridden mud, found an intact exhibit is a wonderful memory. There wasn't much good news around at the time, but seeing the collection come back together from the stinking mud was amazing – almost unbelievable. In the end, thanks to the diligence of the "rescue crew", we did not lose many artefacts.

Above the museum you have a library of books, papers and artworks that you make available to interested parties. What does this contain and what are the most treasured archives?

The library and archive is a lesser known but important part of the museum and its work. We collect all books, magazines and archives that relate to witchcraft, magic and the occult. We have a few old and rare publications, including Glanvill's famous *Sadducimus Triumphatus* from 1681, *The Displaying of Witchcraft* from 1677, by Webster, and Bromhall's *Treatise of Spectres* from 1658. We also have some trial pamphlets that describe in detail the trials that led to the execution of witches. Reading contemporary accounts of these trials is quite moving and upsetting.

We hold around 4,000 modern books on the subject of witchcraft, and we have a good collection of letters and documents from many famous occultists. Researchers often gravitate towards the Gerald Gardner letters and towards Alex Sanders' documents, but there are plenty of other important collections in the archive.

I love the fact that the library does not exclude any books – it is not our job to filter out books or bias the collection towards our personal taste. Where else would you find *Teen Witch*, Aleister Crowley's *Magick in Theory and Practice*, *Pagan Dawn*, the complete *Golden Bough* and copies of Alex Sanders' Book of Shadows?

The museum attracts visitors from all over the world. Have you had any unusual visitors, or visitors whom you were not expecting? Any celebrities?

We get lots of well-known celebrities visiting us; regulars include Dawn French, Laurence Llewellyn Bowen and the famous Jason Karl! I am proud to have met Prince Charles in Boscastle a couple of times and have talked about the museum to him. I even got to meet his mother in Buckingham Palace – who'd have thought it?

All the well-known witches and occultists visit the museum from time to time. My problem is that I never remember who is who – I am absolutely useless at remembering faces. My only excuse is that we do get to meet an awful lot of people in a year!

The museum now publishes artwork and music connected with witchcraft and sells it. Can you tell us a bit about this commercial venture?

The museum itself is a commercial venture – the success of the business ensures the future preservation of the collections and our heritage. The museum is almost entirely dependent on the income it receives from its visitors and the goods it retails, so I have to be a hard-headed businessman and keep looking for opportunities to enhance our income. It is really quite simple – the more money we take, the more we can spend on the museum.

Our most recent project fulfils all of our objectives: *Songs of Witchcraft & Magic* is a CD and booklet containing a collection of British folk ballads. This is a wonderful resource for researchers, it is entertaining and it raises funds that support the museum – that can't be bad!

We have recently granted a licence to The Occult Art Company to print and sell high-quality facsimile prints of some of the Richel Collection. (This collection of some 2,000 original occult artworks is held in the museum archive.) I have always thought that we should try and make our collections accessible to as many people as possible. If we can raise some money at the same time it's a bonus, so yes, we will be doing more publishing – watch this space!

ANNA FRANKLIN
High Priestess of the Hearth of Arianrhod, Coranieid Clan
✳✳✳✳✳✳✳✳✳✳✳✳✳✳✳✳✳✳✳✳✳✳✳✳✳✳✳✳

Anna, you found witchcraft after spending your childhood in a convent school. What early experiences turned you away from Roman Catholicism and towards the Pagan gods?

Though I have always been conscious of nature spirits and have always been drawn to the Old Gods, I was not brought up as a Pagan. My adopted family was Roman Catholic, and they sent me to a convent school to be educated by nuns. I felt lonely and out of place, but I devoured the classical library, reading about the Greek and Roman gods and goddesses, and when I prayed, I prayed to golden Aphrodite or wise Athene. They seemed much more real and immediate to me than the jealous God I was supposed to believe in.

I saw creatures in the woodland that no one else could see, and found pleasure in lonely places with the wild creatures. My family said I was mad and the nuns said I was damned. Then, when I was 18 years old, I found other people who felt the same way as me – they were called "witches".

How did you first come into contact with other witches, and how did this change your life?

In the 1970s, covens were secret entities and did not advertise themselves as they do now. Instead, they would recruit suitable members through various spiritual and occult discussion groups, and this is how I first made contact with witches.

My first coven was run by a lovely woman whose Craft name was Julia Isobel Reed, and it was she who introduced me to our native Brythonic (British) Celtic deities. I was excited to be admitted to the seasonal rituals, to the Esbats and to other workings. I copied down my first Book of Shadows, making detailed lists of herbs and correspondences, crystals, tools and spells. I was in danger of being seduced by the belief that these were the most important part of Wicca, but Julia was careful to show me that spells and rituals were only methods of accessing magic and were not themselves the magic.

This fact was brought home to me when I had been involved with The Craft for about a year, and had attended various rituals in people's living rooms and temples and was getting very involved with the words and paraphernalia of the occult. I thought I was progressing very well when a single incident made me rethink everything I had learned.

I had an experience with a spirit badger one night, alone in the woods. Suddenly, I realized that everything had become very quiet, as though these sounds had been filtered out or had come to me through a barrier. The clearing seemed removed from the rest of the world – separate, apart. I felt that if I were to touch its edges it would be like putting my hand into liquid; I would feel the resistance and see the ripples moving from it. I was acutely aware of the aliveness of everything around me; I could feel the sap running through the tree root on which I sat, and a faint glow surrounded the leaves of the undergrowth, which pulsed slightly.

The silence seemed to reach a pitch of intensity, and then a badger came abruptly crashing out of the undergrowth. I'm not sure how long we stared at each other, but it seemed like a long time. Something passed between us, some acknowledgement or greeting. At last he turned and left the clearing and the sounds of the night broke in on me again – louder than before – and the veil that had shrouded the grove was suddenly gone.

Later, when I told Julia about the experience, she told me that I had taken my first step on the path, saying that all the rituals and exercises I had been doing were nothing in themselves – they existed only to open the consciousness to the magic that is to come. It was some years before I discovered that the ancient Picts called their Druids "Brokan", or "Broichan", which is Gaelic for "badger", perhaps because the Druid or witch must learn all the secrets the badger knows: the energy of each place, the essence of each plant, the ability of each animal and the power of the Earth. My meeting with the badger was no coincidence, but one of many otherworldly encounters that would shape my life.

You have lived a very artistic life, painting, writing and in the world of photography. Are creativity and witchcraft linked?

Yes, I think they are. Most Pagans are creative people who write, paint, make music and so on. I think maybe we are more open to our intuitive side and to right-brain thought.

You have been initiated into the third degree, and your path has taken you through Alexandrian and Gardnerian to Traditional witchcraft. What type of witch do you consider yourself to be, and why?

The Hearth of Arianrhod practises traditional witchcraft. In Britain, "traditional witchcraft" is a phrase used to denote the pre-Gardnerian Craft (unlike in the US, where it refers to Gardnerian and Alexandrian Wicca). However, witchcraft is an imprecise term that may encompass various folk magic and shamanic practices throughout the world.

Although Wicca is a useful word that was adopted by Gerald Gardner to describe modern Goddess-centered, coven-orientated witchcraft, it has become rather devalued and diluted in recent years. Now there are also covens working within Judeo-Christian mythology and Luciferian witches who also claim the term "traditional witchcraft". To distinguish ourselves from these types of witchcraft and from Wiccans, we have decided to adopt the term "Wicce", an Anglo-Saxon word that can denote either a male or female witch. Witches in the Wicce tradition have far more in common with the tribal shaman than with the ritual magician.

Wicce defines a specific set of British magical practices stemming from the folk culture of people who worked close to nature, people who were farmers, peasants, blacksmiths and shamans. The roots of Pagan witchcraft are not found via Gerald Gardner, but in the Cunning Men, Wise Women and working-class societies like the Horsemen and the Bonemen.

If we try to look for evidence of Pagan survival in the last thousand years, we can find only fragmentary evidence of a belief in classical deities. However, we can see a consistent concern with the multiplicity of spirits associated with place, vegetation and so on, and practices designed to encourage or placate them. This was unlike the intellectual approach of ritual magicians, whose work was based on the predominant religion, Judeo-Christianity, and who sought their mysticism in the Cabala, tales of the Watchers and so on, rather than in the much despised working-class beliefs of Britain.

The concepts and rituals of grass-roots Pagan practice has rarely been part of the state religion, whether Christian or Classical Pagan. People who work closely with nature have an instinctive knowledge that there is a consciousness within it; that there are spirits of vegetation that can be influenced, powers of blight and bane that can be appeased and powers of fertility and growth that can be appealed to.

Very little is known of the magical practices and rituals of ordinary people in the ancient world, though we have examples of festivals centered on the natural cycles of the year and spells for fertility, curses and so on. These are remarkably similar to spells found as far apart as modern Africa, Victorian England and ancient Asia. Unlike Druids, who were the priests and magistrates, witches have always existed outside the establishment – they are not even as acceptable as the tribal shaman. They have always been considered dangerous and suspect, and people are generally wary of them.

With the old witches, learning from books and serving time as a witch counted for nothing. The only true measure of initiation was contact with the otherworld spiritual teachers. Julia used to say she knew when the candidate was ready when they repeated some part of the tradition that had never been written of or taught to them, and that could only have come from the coven's otherworld guides. This ensured that the degree status was not an empty title, but rather a true measure of inner-plane initiation.

In ancient times, initiates called themselves the "twice born", signifying that they had undergone the death of the old self and a rebirth of the new. Initiation is not a single event, but a journey – one I described in my book, *The Sacred Circle Tarots' Journey of the Fool*; a journey from ignorance to true inner knowledge. "Know Thyself" was the instruction written over the doorway to the ancient Mysteries of Eleusis.

Many people believe that witches are "born", and that they are "called" to The Craft – unless they are born into a family of witches. Do you consider yourself to be a natural-born witch?

Maybe everyone is a natural-born witch. I think the talent to be a witch or shaman, to travel in the world of spirits, is latent in everyone. Some are born fully invested with this gift, and for others a particular experience awakens it. In others, the ability is never realized but is repressed.

For as long as I can remember, my moments of deepest joy and fulfilment have come from communion with Mother Nature. For me, each tree, each stream and each rock has spirit; is alive. Despite the best efforts of my adoptive parents and the Church, I have always known this to be true.

The "world view" of the witch and Pagan is essentially different from the normally accepted materialistic view of Western society. Pagans believe that everything possesses spirit, a living force within it. I learned to recognize and work with this force, knowing that because this force is spiritual, all things that contain it are sacred: in other words, manifest Nature is sacred.

This is perhaps the great difference between Paganism and other religions. We believe that the divine is manifest in nature, and is imminent: we can walk out and speak to it, communicate with it. We can touch our gods. We do not believe that this world is a place of suffering – rather, it is already a paradise if only we have eyes with which to see it. It is marred only by human greed and insecurity. To borrow another myth, Adam and Eve never left the Garden of Eden, but just became so blinkered that they couldn't see it anymore, like the developer who looks at a beautiful landscape and sees only the money he can make when he covers it in concrete.

In 1986 you were instrumental in founding the Hearth of Arianrhod and the popular Pagan magazine, Silverwheel. How did your path lead you to this particular goddess, and how do you experience deity?

In 1985 Sara Lees-Smith and I founded the Coranieid in Leicestershire. When Sara moved to Dorset, she founded the Hearth of Brigid and I kept the original group, which became the Hearth of Arianrhod. We were the first covens to use the term "hearth", which had previously been restricted to groups of the Northern tradition; now many covens call themselves hearths. As the dwelling place of the living flame, the hearth is a holy place, a threshold between this world and the realm of the gods. Its rising smoke takes prayers to the gods of the upper world, while the gods of the worlds below may be contacted through the hearthstone. In other words, the hearth is a cosmic axis.

I dedicated the hearth to Arianrhod after seeing her in a vision after Sara's hive, but that is personal and is not something I would like to share, except to say that Arianrhod has a particular resonance for me.

The name "Arianrhod" may derive from the Welsh words *"arian"*, meaning "silver", and *"rhod"*, meaning "wheel", though her name is also given as Arianrhod from "aran", meaning "immense" or "round". She is usually associated with the moon, and, like most moon goddesses, with regeneration, since the moon regrows after its monthly dissolution.

The circumpolar stars known as "Caer Arianrhod" – the Corona Borealis or "Caer Sidi" – are her spiral castle, where she houses and passes judgement on the souls of the dead. These stars are also her spinning wheel, and she spins the patterns of the universe and the thread of life, death and rebirth, an eternal thread with no ending and no beginning. She controls the maelstrom of creative forces at the heart of the cosmos.

Arianrhod is also a goddess of hard-won initiation. The famous poem of Taliesin states that he was three times in the castle of Arianrhod, or in other words, three times he underwent a death and rebirth initiation experience under her auspices, when he travelled in spirit-flight to her domain. Her son Llew was forced through three initiations at her hands: his naming, his arming and his marriage to the flower bride.

You are a well-known author of numerous books and tarot decks. How has teaching others through your work changed your life?

My books are a by-product of the face to face teaching I do in my coven, outer circle and workshops, and the experience that I have gained during my years as a priestess. I write them when I feel I have something that must be said, something that should be passed on. I don't think writing books has changed my life; it is the real work in The Craft that has done that. Hopefully, the books contain information that others will find useful in their own spiritual quests.

Many of your published works concern the faery world. Can you describe your first and most memorable experiences with the faery beings?

I'm not sure I can remember my first experience of the otherworld, though I have always been aware of it.

I think I'd better explain what I mean by "faeries" here, in case anyone gets the impression I'm referring to Tinkerbells and cute garden gnomes! Amazingly, similar stories of faeries, under a variety of names, exist around the world, from Africa to the Americas; they are white and shining, they can appear in animal form, they live in the underworld with the dead or in an otherworldly paradise; they are responsible both for the fertility of the land and can also cause disease, blight, decay and death. Their names, more often than not, simply mean "spirit", or else "shining", and sometimes just "lord" or "lady".

In these legends of faeries we can trace pre-Christian concepts of gods and nature spirits, along with the principles of dealing with them. Both the ancient Celts and Saxons had gifted individuals who were able to journey at will into the world of the spirits. In later times, these people were called witches, a name that comes from the Anglo-Saxon "wicce", or "wise one".

Saxo, in *The History of the Danes*, written between 1182 and 1210, said that one had to be a gifted person to see spirits, and went on to explain that such people had probably experienced prophetic dreams in childhood or had later undergone a sickness that opened the world of spirits to them, thus describing a classic shamanic initiation. Even into the 19th and early 20th centuries, the good Christian farmers of Europe believed in spirits of land and water that could affect the growth of the crops and the fecundity of the land itself. There is plenty of evidence in Britain, Ireland and the rest of Western Europe that regular offerings were made to the faeries on stones in the corners of fields; on the hearth; in special places outside the farm and on the house door. These offerings were given both to placate the faeries and to prevent them from doing harm, and to win their friendship.

In the practices and taboos surrounding faeries there are many parallels with shamanic cultures. These include working with animal totems and familiar spirits, the feeding of the familiars, travels to the otherworld, the association of the spirits of the otherworld with the ancestors and the spirits of the dead, and the various offerings made to the spirits. These beliefs were not confined to the witches and Cunning Men, but were shared by the general population – even by its most learned and distinguished members, as is evidenced by the writings of King James I. It is in these beliefs and traditions that we find the real roots of modern witchcraft.

You currently organize various witch-craft gatherings, including seasonal celebrations such as the Mercian Gathering. Why are these gatherings important and what can people expect if they are new to the path of Paganism and witchcraft?

Many people are interested in Paganism, but don't know any other Pagans. They are often afraid to take the step of joining a coven or committed group, so informal moots and Pagan camps, like the Mercian Gathering, are a good way of meeting others in a safe environment. In addition, such events are a great opportunity to meet up with old friends and exchange views and ideas.

Most Pagan camps will have talks, work-shops and some entertainment and group rituals that anyone can join, even without previous experience. We often get people emailing us beforehand who say they are really worried about coming to their first camp, but who then go away having made lots of new friends and having had a life-changing experience – and that's really what it's all about!

MICHAEL THOMAS FORD

✳✳✳✳✳✳✳✳✳✳✳✳✳✳✳✳✳✳✳✳✳✳✳✳✳✳✳

How did you begin on your path to the Old Ways? Did you have a teacher? Describe your first experience with witchcraft.

I've been interested in Paganism since I was a child and discovered myths and legends, particularly the Norse ones. I have read books on Paganism and witchcraft throughout my life, but my first concrete encounter with them happened in 1997, when I attended a retreat put on by the EarthSpirit Community in Massachusetts. The leader of my particular group was a gay man, and we subsequently became friends. Through him, I became more involved in actually practising the things I had come to believe.

What do your family and (non-witch) friends think of your spirituality choice? Has it caused any problems or changes in your life?

Oddly enough, it never comes up. Because I wrote a book about my beliefs, a lot of people are aware of my spirituality. I also have a number of tattoos related to Pagan spirituality, so occasionally the topic will arise when people ask about them. But mostly I don't talk about it with my friends or family, not because I'm afraid or ashamed to, but because there's no reason to unless someone asks.

In your book, The Path of the Green Man, you introduce a new tradition of witchcraft in which gay men can celebrate the seasons, worship the Old Gods and connect with each other on a spiritual level. How did the "Green Men" develop?

The Green Men came about in the way such things usually do: by a happy meeting of like minds. A friend of mine in Boston started holding drumming circles for gay men. I went to those meetings, and there I met a couple of men who were interested in Pagan spirituality. We decided to do something more formal than the drumming, so we began holding monthly circles where we worked with various traditions simply as a way to explore our spiritual lives as gay men. We were never overly formal and our rituals were a mixture of many different things.

Many traditionalist witches argue that gay men and witchcraft do not mix, as the female gender is needed for balance and harmony in rituals, worship and in covens. What is your response to this argument?

I think that this assertion is the biggest fallacy in modern Paganism. It developed primarily because so much of the early Pagan/witchcraft revival was about reclaiming the female presence in spirituality, which of course was and is an important thing to do. But the notions of masculine and feminine energy are far too limiting. What are they, exactly? Which characteristics of energy are special to women and which are special to men?

Energy, to me, is defined by intention, and that originates in the mind. Personally, with the exception of Sybil Leek's ridiculously homophobic comments claiming that gay men can't fully participate in witchcraft because we don't participate in the creation of children (which in itself is a falsehood), I have only heard this argument voiced by heterosexual men. Almost without exception, these men are more interested in holding rituals with naked women than they are in exploring spirituality, and the idea of gay men either seeing them naked or somehow interfering with the heterosexual sexual energy these men crave is threatening to them.

Why do you think witchcraft appeals to gay men, and what can it bring into their lives that other religions cannot?

I think witchcraft appeals to gay men because it allows them to be who they are without judgement. Once you remove the restrictions on worthiness that are demanded by most religious paths, you allow participants to explore themselves more fully. Having said that, I must also say that I think there is the same percentage of bigoted, closed-minded people in Paganism as there is in any other religion. Gay men can't expect to walk into any Pagan group and be welcomed with open arms. We have to find the right group. Again, it's about finding and coming together with like-minded people.

Which deities do you feel particularly drawn to and why?

The deity I am most drawn to is Kali, the goddess of destruction and rebirth. For me, following the path is about destroying the parts of myself that prevent me from becoming who I am and allowing myself to grow.

I am also very fond of the deity I call simply the god of the wood. To me, He is the embodiment of male sexuality and a symbol of creation and wild magic. He isn't any specific deity, but rather one who symbolizes everything I wish to be.

How does the practice of Green Man spirituality manifest in your daily life?

Green Man spirituality is much less a rigid system of practice and more a way of thinking about the world. For me, it means trying to constantly be aware of my place in creation, my connections to everything else in creation and my responsibility to make the most of this

life. It also helps me on the path to becoming who I'm meant to be, and also, whenever possible, helps me to help others do the same.

Do you think it is necessary for partners to share the same spiritual beliefs in order to live a happy and fulfilling life together?

No. My partner has no interest in Pagan spirituality and probably views it with more than a little scepticism. This is not a problem for me, though, as I think that each person in a relationship needs to be himself, and because I know that we all have individual ways of exploring and expressing what we believe. The only time a partner possessing different beliefs from my own would be a problem in a relationship is if the other person actively ridiculed my beliefs or prevented me from expressing them, either by directly interfering with them or by causing me to self-limit my participation in order to keep peace.

Your book, The Path of The Green Man, takes the reader through one full cycle of the Wheel of the Year. How do you feel you have grown and changed over the many turns of the Wheel since the inception of The Green Men to the present day?

Have you learned any important lessons along the way?

I've changed a great deal since the early days of The Green Men. For one, I've entered middle age, which is bound to change you. Most important, perhaps, is that I've let go of a lot of worrying about whether I'm doing things the "right" way. I no longer care if people say my path isn't "traditional". What works for me works for me, and what works for others isn't going to be the same. Other than that, I think I'm always changing, so every turn of the Wheel brings along something new.

The Green Men is a spiritual tradition for gay men. Is there a similar place for lesbian witchcraft?

There have always been lesbian traditions within Paganism and witchcraft. The Dianics, of course, are the most obvious example. I think there's a place for everyone. Some people criticize The Green Men for being gay-male centered. But this is not because we don't like women or straight men; it's because we like being with other gay men.

There is something undeniably powerful and useful about starting from a foundation of sameness. When a group of people have a common background and similar experiences and world views, this creates an atmosphere in which the personal work you want and need to do can happen more effectively.

The Craft is changing and adapting to survive and prosper in the modern world. How do you see gay witchcraft developing over the coming decades?

I think we're going to see, as we have with every other spiritual tradition, an opening up of what it "means" to be Pagan or Wiccan, or whatever anyone wants to call themselves. People are starting to discover that spiritual traditions, whatever they are and however ancient they are, are simply manmade constructs that have been created in order to support and popularize particular world views. Not one of them is empirically provable.

You cannot prove, for example, that after death the soul enters heaven or hell. Similarly, you cannot prove that following the teachings of Buddhism leads to nirvana, or that devout Muslims will receive 72 wives when they enter paradise.

What you can know, however, is whether following a particular set of beliefs or precepts makes you a happier, more productive, more alive person who works hard to create positive changes in yourself and also in the world around you. If you are indeed such a person, then whatever you're doing is working for you, and you should keep at it.

The problem tends to be that so many traditions are almost obsessively focused on ensuring that a person is happy, and also that he or she is given some sort of reward after death. This seems to me to be completely beside the point. The idea that a person must suffer throughout his or her life in order to attain peace in some sort of afterlife seems a bit unrealistic to me. Doesn't it make more sense, and isn't it more productive, to work hard in the present in order to make the life that you have – possibly the only life you'll ever get – a happy, fulfilling and ultimately rewarding one?

THE GRIMOIRE

"Secrets in a sacred book;
If you dare, now take a look."

GLOSSARY – THE WORDS OF THE WITCHES

ABRACADABRA
Magickal invocation

AFTERWORLD
Alternative term for Summerland

AICME
Group of five Ogham symbols

ALDEBARAN
Lord of the Watchtower of the east

ALEXANDRIAN
Witchcraft tradition named after Alexander
Sanders, often noted in the media as the
"king of the witches", who mixed together a
variety of different practices to form his own
tradition of witchcraft

ALTAR
Sacred space created by a witch at which to
honour deity and perform magick

THE ANEMOI
Collective term for the gods and deities of
the winds

ANKH
Egyptian symbol of life

ANTARES
Lord of the Watchtower of the west

APELIOTES
Tempest deity of the south east

APOLLO
Greek god of music and the arts

ARADIA
Daughter of the goddess Diana

ARCHIVIST
Keeps the coven library

ARIANRHOD
Welsh Celtic moon goddess

ARTEMIS
Greek goddess of hunting

ASPERGER
Tool used to sprinkle consecrated water

ASTARTE
Phoenician goddess of fertility and war

ATHAME
Magickal ritual knife

BANE
In wort cunning, a poison

BANISHING
Magickal conjuration with the intention of
sending something away

BAPHOMET
Deity worshipped by the Knights Templar

BARD
Coven entertainer

BARLEY MOON
September full moon

BAWMING THE THORN
Act of decorating living trees for ritual
celebration, including adorning the maypole
at Beltane and the Yule tree at Yule

BCE
Before (the) Common Era

BELTANE
Greater Sabbat on 1 May

BESOM
Witches' term for a broomstick

BINDING
Magickal conjuration with the intention of
stopping something

BLASTING
Magickal conjuration with the intention of
causing infertility

BLOOD MOON
October full moon

BLUE MOON
Second full moon in the same calendar
month

BOLINE
Sickle-shaped knife used for magickal
preparation

BOOK OF SHADOWS
Handwritten book of magickal records

BOREAS
Wind god of the north

BRIGID
Celtic triple goddess of fire

BURIN
Tool used to inscribe and engrave writing
and sigils

CARTOMANCY
Divination by playing cards

CAULDRON
Large metal pot used for magick

CE
Common Era

CENSER
Incense holder

CERNUNNOS
Celtic god of animals and the wildwood

CERRIDWEN
Celtic triple goddess

CHALICE
Goblet or cup that holds consecrated wine

CHARGE
Act of imbuing something with magickal
power

CHARMING
Creation of magickal amulets, talismans
or objects

CHASTE MOON
March full moon

CINGULUM
Magickal cord worn by a witch around his
or her waist

CONE OF POWER
Energy perceived as cone-shaped, raised in a
magick circle

CONSTRUCTING
Magickal conjuration with the intention of
creating something new

CORD MAGICK
Magick performed with cords

CORN MOON
August full moon

CORRESPONDENCES
Magickal connections between seemingly
unconnected things

COVEN
Group of witches who meet to celebrate the
Sabbats and Esbats, make magick, honour
deity and learn from each other

COVENOR
Member of a witches' coven

COVENSTEAD
Building where a coven meets regularly

CRYSTAL BALL
Orb of crystal or glass that is used for
scrying

CUNNING MAN
Man who practised folk magick

CUNNING SHOE
Magickal charm that protects its owner

CUNNING WOMAN
Woman who practised folk magick

CUPS
Suit of 14 cards in the tarot deck

CURSING
Another term for hexing

DARK MIRROR
Mirror made of obsidian or black glass that is used for scrying and magick

DARK MOON
Black moon phase

DEGREE
Level of achievement and experience in The Craft

DEITY
Supreme force

DEMETER
Greek goddess of agriculture

DEOSIL
A Scottish Gaelic word, adopted by witches for sunward movement (clockwise). Associated with positive magick and invocation, as moving in the same direction as the sun – east to west – was believed to be auspicious in ancient times

DIANA
Roman goddess of the hunt

DRYAD
Secondary Elemental of earth

DYAN MOON
June full moon

ELEMENTAL
Preternatural spirit creature associated with an element

ELEMENTS
Five forces of nature – earth, air, fire, water and spirit

ELEUSIAN MYSTERIES
Yearly cult initiation ceremonies held at Eleusis in ancient Greece

EQUINOX
When day and night are of equal length

ESBAT
Witches' gathering at the full moon

ETHER
The fifth element, also known as spirit

ETRUSCAN PERIOD
Relating to Etruria, the period began in 800 BCE

EURUS
Wind god of the east

EYEBITING
Form of hexing by looking at the victim with ill intent

EYE OF HORUS
Egyptian symbol of protection

FAERY
Preternatural creature or witchcraft tradition

FAMILIAR
Witch's animal that might be present during magickal workings

FIREDRAKE
Secondary Elemental of fire

FOLK MAGICK
Ancient magick the origin of which lies in Cunning people and hedge witches

FORMALHAUT
Lord of the Watchtower of the north

FREYA
Nordic moon goddess of fertility, love, sexuality, war and death

FULL MOON
Moon at its full potential

GAIA
Earth Mother Goddess

GARDNERIAN
Witchcraft tradition named after Gerald Gardner who, in the mid-20th century, mixed together a variety of different practices to start a new form of The Craft

GAST
Place where all benevolence has been driven out leaving other, potentially harmful, forces to dwell

GENIUS LOCI
The spirit of the place. This manifests as an atmosphere that can be tangibly felt, even by those without magickal faculties

GLAMOUR
Magickal conjuration with the intention of changing perception of appearance

GNOME
Primary Elemental of earth

GRAMARYE
Book of magickal lore

GREEN MAN
An archetypal image of the God represented as a male face surrounded by, or springing from, vegetation

THE GRIGORI
Collective term for the four Lords of the Watchtowers

GRIMALKIN
Also "Graymalkin", a witch's feline familiar derived from the words "grey" (the colour), and "malkin", an archaic word for "cat"

GRIMOIRE
Ancient term for a book of magickal lore

GUNDESTRUP CAULDRON
A cauldron dating from 1st century BCE, found in Denmark in 1891

HADES
Greek god of the underworld

HAG STONE
Naturally holed stone that is magickally potent

HALLOW
To bless, consecrate or sain

HALLOWEEN
Modern term for Samhain

HANDFASTING
Witches' ceremony of magickal marriage

HARE MOON
May full moon

HECATE
Greek goddess of the night

HEDGE WITCH
A solitary nature witch

HERA
First Greek goddess

HERBALISM
Magickal or medicinal use of herbs

HERNE
Spirit god of nature and the wild hunt

HEXAGRAM
Sigil to command spirits

HEXING
Magickal conjuration with the intention of ill wishing

HIDDEN COMPANY
Discarnate witches who act as spiritual teachers

HIGH PRIEST
Male leader of a coven

HIGH PRIESTESS
Female leader of a coven

HOLLY KING
Legendary aspect of the Horned God manifest as the spirit of the holly tree, who reigns between Litha and Yule

HORNED GOD
The many named and horned witches' god

HOUSEL
Sharing of food and drink between witches, both sentient and unseen

HYPNOS
Greek god of sleep

IMBOLC
Greater Sabbat on 2 February

INITIATION
Ceremony of acceptance into witchcraft

INVULTUATION
Act of sticking pins into a wax poppet to cause pain and injury to a person whom the poppet represents

ISIS
Egyptian mother goddess of magick

JACK O' LANTERN
American term for a hollowed out pumpkin, lit with a candle

JOHN BARLEYCORN
Manifestation of the Horned God at Lughnasadh

KAIKIAS
Tempest deity of the northeast

KALI
Hindu goddess of war and destruction

KEY OF SOLOMON
Book of magickal sigils and rituals

KUTHUN
An artefact given by a dying witch to another to bequeath their powers at death

LABYRINTH
Shamanic symbol that can induce a trance

LAMMAS
Christian term for Lughnasadh

LITHA
Midsummer solstice and Lesser Sabbat on or around 21 June

LIVOS
Tempest deity of the southwest

LOKI
Nordic trickster god

LORD OF THE WILD HUNT
Manifestation of the Horned God in winter

LUGH
Irish Celtic god of light and harvest

LUGHNASADH
Greater Sabbat on 1 August

MABON
Autumn Equinox and Lesser Sabbat on or around 21 September

MAGICK
Power used by witches to affect the worlds; different to "magic", which refers to tricks and illusions

MAGICK CIRCLE
An invisible sphere of power in which witchcraft is practised

MAGUS
Gratuitous title given to a high priest

MAIDEN
Assists the high priestess and priest in ritual

MAJOR ARCANA
22 primary cards of the tarot deck

MAN IN BLACK
Male organizer of a coven, sometimes referred to as the magister

MAYPOLE
Hawthorn trunk that is danced around at Beltane

MEAD MOON
July full moon

MIDSUMMER
Alternative name for Litha

MINOR ARCANA
56 lesser cards of the tarot deck, which are split into four suits

MORPHEUS
Greek god of dreams

THE MORRIGAN
Irish goddess of war

NEW MOON
First crescent moon phase

NOTUS
Wind god of the south

OAK KING
Legendary aspect of the Horned God manifest as the spirit of the oak tree, who reigns between Yule and Litha

OAK MOON
December full moon

ODIN
Nordic father god of war and magick

OGHAM STAVES
Woodcuts upon which the symbols of the Ogham Tree alphabet have been carved

OSTARA
Spring equinox and Lesser Sabbat on or around 21 March

PAN
Greek god of the wild

PARACELCUS
16th-century alchemist

PELLAR
Cornish term for a magick maker, meaning "one who repels malevolent spells and charms"

PENDULUM
Weighted string that can be used for dowsing

PENTACLE
Magickal five-pointed star sigil; the most important symbol in witchcraft

PENTACLES
Suit of 14 cards in the tarot deck

POPPET
Representation of a person made from wax, pottery or cloth, for use in sympathetic magick; usually stuffed with herbs and bodily elements from the subject such as hair, fingernails or photographs

POSEIDON
Greek god of seas and rivers

PRETERNATURAL
That which is beyond the accepted natural order of things

PRIAPIC WAND
Phallic-shaped wand

PRIAPUS
Greek god of fertility

PURSEWARDEN
Coven accountant

QUARTERS
Four cardinal directions – north, east, south and west

RA
The sun god and creator, sometimes depicted with a falcon head

REGULUS
Lord of the Watchtower of the south

ROBIN GOODFELLOW
Manifestation of the Horned God in early spring

RUNES
Set of magickal symbols that double as an arcane alphabet

SABBAT
Seasonal gathering of witches

SAIN
Act of hallowing, consecrating or blessing a place, person or object by ceremony

SALAMANDER
Primary Elemental of fire

SAMHAIN
Great Sabbat on 31 October

SCRIBE
Coven record-keeper

SCRYING BOWL
Bowl in which liquid is held in order to scry

SEAL
Drawn, carved or inscribed magickal sign

SEED MOON
April full moon

SEPTAGRAM
Seven-pointed star symbol used in faery-based magick

SIGIL
Magickal sign, from the Latin "*sigillum*", which means "seal"

SKEIRON
Tempest deity of the northwest

SKYCLAD
Act of being naked, clad only by the sky

SMOOR
Act of putting out a ritual fire

SMUDGING FEATHER
Feather used to waft around sacred smoke

SNOW MOON
November full moon

SOLSTICE
Longest or shortest day of the year

SPIRAL
Celtic symbol of the Goddess

SPIRIT BOARD
Flat device with the alphabet depicted on it, used to contact the spirit world

SPIRIT HOUSE
Cage of twigs in which spirits dwell

SPRITE TRAP
Magickal device that traps mischievous spirits

STALE
Handle of a besom

STANG
Forked staff that represents the horns of the Horned God

STORM MOON
February full moon

STREGHERIA
Italian witchcraft

SUMMERLAND
Place where the spirits of the dead go after leaving their physical bodies

SUMMONER
Summons covenors to gatherings

SUN CROSS
Represents the four seasons

SUN WHEEL
Wheel of The Year as a symbol

SWIMMING
Form of torture used to test for witchcraft

SWORDS
Suit of 14 cards in the tarot deck

SYLPH
Primary Elemental of air

SYMPATHETIC MAGICK
Magick that uses the principle that like affects like, for example, poppet magick

SYRINX
Alternative name for pan-pipes

TAROT
Deck of cards with esoteric meanings

TASSEOGRAPHY
Divination by tea leaves

THANATOS
Greek god of death

THEBAN SCRIPT
Arcane alphabet, also known as the Witches'
Alphabet

THIRD EYE
Invisible eye in the forehead that operates
second sight

THURIBLE
Hanging censer

THYRUS
Alternative name for a priapic wand

TRADITIONAL WITCHCRAFT
The tradition of English pre-Gardnerian
witchcraft

TRANCE
State of alternative, magickal consciousness

TRIPLE GODDESS
Many-named witches' Goddess who has
three aspects: Maiden, Mother and Crone

TRIQUETRA
Symbol of the Triple Goddess

TRISKELION
Early Celtic symbol of reincarnation

UNDINE
Primary Elemental of water

VERDELET
Term for the dual aspects of the God: the
Green Man for the abundant spring and
fruitful summer, and the Man in Black
for the dark of autumn and icy embrace
of winter

WAND
Tool of invocation

WANDS
Suit of 14 cards in the tarot deck

WANING MOON
Diminishing moon phase

WARD
Spiritual guardian of a place

WARDING
Magickal conjuration with the intention of
repelling

WARLOCK
Ancient derogatory word meaning "oath
breaker"; often incorrectly used to describe a
male witch

WATCHTOWER
Magickally invoked tower from where the
Grigori watch

WAYFARER
Coven events planner

WAXING MOON
Increasing moon phase

WHEEL OF THE YEAR
365-day yearly cycle observed by witches

WICCA
A modern term for a specific witchcraft tradition that was created by Gerald Gardner

WIDDERSHINS
Scottish Gaelic word meaning the opposite of deosil: moving anti-clockwise. Associated with banishing

WIND ROARER
Device that raises energy when whirled around in the air

WITCH BALL
Reflective orb that wards against evil

WITCH BOTTLE
Ritually created spell that wards against evil

THE WITCHING HOUR
Midnight on the night of a full moon

WITCH POST
Carved timber that wards against evil

WITCH PRICKING
Form of torture used to test for "witches' marks"

WITCH QUEEN
A third-degree high priestess who has had three covens hive off as a result of her teachings

WITCH'S CRADLE
Ancient method of torturing witches to extract a confession. The accused would be bound in a sack, tied up and swung continually back and forth over a tree branch to create intense disorientation

WITCH'S LADDER
Knotted cord into which magickal intent is tied

WITCH'S WHISK
Bundle of dried blackberry stems bound together. When the ends are lit it can be used to whisk away negative energies from a ritual space

WOLF MOON
January full moon

WORT CUNNING
Magickal use of plants

YULE
Winter solstice and Lesser Sabbat on or around 21 December

YULE LOG
Log that is ritually burned at Yule

ZEPHYRUS
Wind god of the west

THE WITCHES' WEB – INTERNET RESOURCES

Here is a selection of the best websites dedicated to the true path of witchcraft. You will find teaching sites, magickal suppliers, experienced witches, online communities, magazines and sites of interest. The Internet will never replace books and practical experience, but it is a good place to begin exploring the world of witchcraft.

UK General Suppliers

13 Moons www.13moons.com

Abaxion www.abaxion.com

Amulets By Merlin www.amuletsbymerlin.com

Arsenic www.arsenic.com

Avalon www.avalon-cornwall.co.uk

The Awareness Shop www.awarenessshop.com

Boscastle Studio www.boscastlestudio.co.uk

Caduceus Jewellery www.paganjewellery.com

Cornish Pagan Wheel www.cornishpaganwheel.co.uk

Cornish Witchcraft www.cornishwitchcraft.co.uk

A Coven of Witches www.covenofwitches.co.uk

The Creaky Cauldron www.drbombay.co.uk

Crowhaven Corner www.crowhavencorner.net

Enchantments Inc. www.enchantmentsincnyc.com

Fire Dragon Pewter www.firedragonpewter.co.uk

Gaia's Garden www.gaias-garden.co.uk

The Goddess & The Green Man www.goddessandgreenman.co.uk

Gothic Image www.gothicimage.co.uk

Hedingham Fair www.hedinghamfair.co.uk

Hocus Pocus www.hocuspocus.co.uk

Lucky Mojo Curio Company www.luckymojo.com

Magical Omaha www.magicalomaha.com

Magick Rose www.magickrose.co.uk

Merry Meet www.merrymeetuk.com

Mysteries www.mysteries.co.uk

New Moon www.newmoon.uk.com

The Occult Art Company www.theoccultartcompany.co.uk

Pendle Hill Wands www.witcheswands.com

Pendle Witches www.pendlewitches.co.uk

The Psychic Piglet www.thepsychicpiglet.co.uk

Raven Corvus www.raven.karoo.net

Sacred Mists www.sacredmists.com
Silverlight Source www.silverlightsource.com
Sorcerers Apprentice www.sorcerers-apprentice.co.uk
The Speaking Tree www.speakingtree.co.uk
Spirit of the Forest www.spiritoftheforest.co.uk
Star Child www.starchild.co.uk
Stone Age www.stoneage.co.uk
The Stone Pentacle www.thestonepentacle.com
Traditional Cornish Witchcraft www.geocities.com/cronnekdhu/index.html
Voodoo Authentica www.voodooshop.com
Wiccan Way www.wiccanway.com
Witchcraft Ltd. www.witchcraftshop.co.uk
Witches Galore www.witchesgalore.co.uk
Witches of Salem www.witchesofsalem.com
Wychbury www.wychbury.org
The Wyrd Shop www.wyrdshop.com

Handmade Ritual Tools
Achaman Ritual Tools www.achamanritualtools.com
Caduceus Jewellery www.paganjewellery.com
Haunted Wood Crafts www.hauntedwoodcrafts.com
Rod Matless www.interknife.co.uk
Spirit of Old www.spiritofold.co.uk
Stagman Creations www.stagmancreations.co.uk
Wiccan Wood www.wiccanwood.co.uk
Witches Moon www.witchesmoon.net

Statuary
Baroque Designs www.baroquedesigns.net
The Black Broom www.theblackbroom.com
Cerridwen Ceramics www.oracle.pwp.blueyonder.co.uk
Dragonesque www.sharpe-designs.com
Dryad Design www.dryaddesign.com
Goddess Gift www.goddessgift.net
Jay W Hungate Sculptor www.jwhstudio.com
Mythic Images www.mythicimages.com
Mythographica www.mythographica.com
Carl Newman www.carlnewman.co.uk

Sacred Source www.sacredsource.com
The Stone Circle Sculpture Studio www.stonecirclesculpture.co.uk
Windstone Editions www.windstoneeditions.com

Books and Books of Shadows
Capall Bann Publishing www.capallbann.co.uk
Green Magic Publishing www.greenmagicpublishing.com
Llewellyn Publishing www.llewellyn.com
Mandrake Press www.mandrake-press.co.uk
Oak Magic Publications www.oakmagicpublications.com
Witches Inc Publishing www.witches-inc.co.uk
Witches Moon www.witchesmoon.net

Spirit Contact
Speaking with Spirits www.speakingwithspirits.com

Ritual Robes
Ivy Moon Design www.ivymoon.co.uk
Stagman Creations www.stagmancreations.co.uk

Wands
Pendle Hill Wands www.witcheswands.com
Willowroot Magic Wands www.realmagicwands.com

Candles, Incense and Oils
7th House www.7th-house.com
13 Magickal Moons www.13magickalmoons.com
Alchemical Magickal Oils www.twilightalchemylab.com
Black Phoenix Alchemy Lab. www.blackphoenixalchemylab.com
Herb Moon Hollow www.herbmoonhollow.com
Magical Scriptorium www.magicalscriptorium.com
Pan's Pantry www.panspantry.co.uk

Herbs
Nicky's Seeds www.nickysnursery.co.uk
The Herb Garden & Historical Plants Nursery www.historicalplants.co.uk

Pagan and Witchcraft Greetings Cards

Astrocal www.astrocal.co.uk/cards.html
The Goddess & The Green Man www.goddessandgreenman.co.uk/prod/2/Cards/
Hedingham Fair www.hedinghamfair.co.uk
Mandrake Press www.mandrake-press.co.uk/acatalog/Greeting_Cards.html
Moon Dragon Cards www.moondragoncards.com
Witch E Cards www.witchecards.com
Witch Hollow Cards www.witchhollowcards.com

Magazines

Pentacle Magazine www.pentaclemagazine.org
New Witch Magazine www.newwitch.com
Witchcraft & Wicca Magazine www.witchcraft.org
Pagan Dawn www.paganfed.org/pdawn.php

Pagan Art

Meraylah Allwood www.meraylah.co.uk
C. J. Bloomer www.nydwyngreendragon.com
Faerywolf www.faerywolf.com
Steve Fox www.gothicangel.co.uk
Neil Geddes Ward www.neilgeddesward.com
Theresa & Ann Keegan www.wildwood-designs.co.uk
Timothy Lantz www.stygiandarkness.com
Judith Page www.judith-page.com
Marc Potts www.marcpotts.com
Joanna Powell Colbert www.jpc-artworks.com
Jana Souflova www.maffet.cz
Anne Sudworth www.annesudworth.co.uk
Sarah Vivian www.geniusloci.co.uk/sarahvivian/index.htm
Ken Williams www.shadowsandstone.com

Well-known Witches

Rae Beth www.raebeth.com
Gavin Bone & Janet Farrah www.wicca.utvinternet.com
Raymond Buckland www.raybuckland.com
Laurie Cabot www.cabotwitchcraft.com
Phyllis Curott www.phylliscurott.com
Ellen Dugan www.geocities.com/edugan_gardenwitch

Olivia Durdin Robertson www.fellowshipofisis.com
Michael Thomas Ford www.michaelthomasford.com
Anna Franklin www.annafranklin.co.uk
Gerald Gardner www.geraldgardner.com
Raven Grimassi www.ravengrimassi.net
Professor Ronald Hutton www.bris.ac.uk/Depts/History/Staff/hutton.htm
Amber K www.amberk.com
Cassandra Latham, Village Wisewoman of Cornwall www.cassandralatham.co.uk
John & Caitlin Matthews www.hallowquest.org.uk
Edain McCoy www.edainmccoy.com
Dorothy Morrison www.dorothymorrision.com
Christopher Penczak www.christopherpenczak.com
Silver Ravenwolf www.silverravenwolf.com
Doreen Valiente www.doreenvaliente.com
Kate West www.pyewacket.demon.co.uk

Moon Phases and Calendars
www.astrocal.co.uk
www.childrenofartemis.co.uk
www.goddesswithin.co.uk/moons.html
www.new-age.co.uk/moon-dates.htm

Events
Beltane at Thornborough Henge www.sacredbrigantia.com
Butser Ancient Farm Wicker Man Beltane Burning www.butser.org.uk
Green Man Festival of Clun www.clun.org.uk/greenman
Lammas Games www.lammasgames.org
PaganCon www.shared-earth.org.uk/pagancon.htm
Pagan Festivals, including The Beltane Bash www.paganfestivals.com
Pendle Witch Camp www.penwitchcamp.co.uk
Witchcraft Seminars www.witchcraftseminar.com
Witchfest Festivals www.witchfest.net

Museums and Locations of Interest
Bats & Broomsticks Gothic Bed & Breakfast
http://freespace.virgin.net/batsand.broomsticks/index.html
The Highwayman Inn www.thehighwaymaninn.net

Icelandic Sorcery & Witchcraft Museum www.vestfirdir.is/galdrasyning/english.php
Lime Tree Farm Spiritual Sanctuary www.limetreefarm.co.uk
The Museum of Witchcraft www.museumofwitchcraft.com
Salem Witch Museum www.salemwitchmuseum.com
Salem Witch Village www.salemwitchvillage.net
Voodoo Museum www.voodoomuseum.com

Music
Clannad www.clannad.ie
Llewellyn www.llewellynandjuliana.com
Loreena McKennitt www.quinlanroad.com
New World Music www.newworldmusic.com
Tim Wheater www.timwheater.com

Organizations and Communities
Pagan Federation & Pagan Dawn Magazine www.paganfed.org
Pagan Federation North West www.pfnw.org
The Witches Voice www.witchvox.com

Teaching Sites
The Alchemy Website www.alchemywebsite.com
Cunning Folk www.cunningfolk.com
Faenation www.faenation.com
Faeriecraft www.faeriecraft.co.uk
Folk Magic www.apotropaios.co.uk
Hearthstone www.hearthstone.co.uk
Hedgewitchery www.hedgewytchery.com
The Modern Antiquarian www.themodernantiquarian.com
Sea Witchery www.seawitch.org
Stonepages www.stonepages.com
Stregheria Italian Witchcraft www.stregheria.com
Tasseography www.tasseography.com
The Witches' Sabbats www.geocities.com/Athens/Forum/7280/

Gay Witchcraft
Gay Love Spells www.gay-lovespells.com
Gay Witch www.gaywitch.org

BIBLIOGRAPHY AND FURTHER READING – THE WITCHES' LIBRARY

An ABC Of Witchcraft Past & Present by Doreen Valiente

An Abundance of Witches by P. G Maxwell Stuart

Ancient Ways by Pauline Campanelli

Aradia Gospel of the Witches by Charles G. Leland

The Archaeology of Ritual & Magic by Ralph Merrifield

Autumn Equinox by Ellen Dugan

Beltane by Raven Grimassi

The Book of Charms by Elizabeth Villiers

Book of Shadows by Phyllis Curott

The Book of Spells by Nicola de Pulford

The Book of Spells 2 by Marian Green

Bud, Blossom and Leaf by Dorothy Morrison

Buckland's Complete Book of Witchcraft by Raymond Buckland

By Oak, Ash & Thorn by D. J. Conway

Call of The Horned Piper by Nigel Aldcroft Jackson

Candlemas by Amber K & Azrael Arynn K

Cat Spells by Claire Nahmad

The Celtic Wisdom of Trees by Jane Gifford

Charge of The Goddess by Doreen Valiente

Circle, Coven & Grove by Deborah Blake

Colour Magick by Raymond Buckland

Complete Magician's Tables by Stephen Skinner

Cornish Witchcraft by J. MacLeay

Cottage Witchery by Ellen Dugan

Covencraft by Amber K

The Craft by Dorothy Morrison

The Craft Companion by Dorothy Morrison

Craft of the Wild Witch by Poppy Palin

Creating Magical Tools by Chic Cicero & Sandra Tabatha Cicero

Crone's Book of Charms and Spells by Valerie Worth

The Dream Book by Gillian Kemp

Dream Spells by Claire Nahmad

Druid Magic by Maya Magee Sutton & Nicholas Mann

The Druids by Ronald Hutton

Earth Magic by Claire Nahmad

Eight Sabbats for Witches by Janet & Stewart Farrar

The Element Encyclopedia of Witchcraft by Judika Illes

The Elements of Ritual by Deborah Lipp

The Enchanted Cat by Ellen Dugan

Encyclopedia of Wicca & Witchcraft by Raven Grimassi

The Encyclopedia of Witches & Witchcraft by Rosemary Ellen Guiley

Entering the Summerland by Edain McCoy

Everyday Magic by Dorothy Morrison

Every Woman A Witch by Cassandra Eason

Fairy Spells by Claire Nahmad

Fire Burn by Ken Radford

The Fortune Telling Book by Gillian Kemp

From Stagecraft to Witchcraft by Patricia Crowther

Garden Spells by Claire Nahmad

Garden Witchery by Ellen Dugan

Gay Witchcraft by Christopher Penczak

Gerald Gardner & the Cauldron of Inspiration by Philip Heselton

The Goetia by Samuel Liddell Macgregor Mathers

The Goodly Spell Book by Lady Passion Diuvei

The Good Spell Book by Gillian Kemp

Good Spells for Creativity by Witch Bree

Good Spells for Good Friends by Witch Bree

Good Spells for Great Sex by Witch Bree

Good Spells for Healing by Witch Bree

Good Spells for Love by Witch Bree

Good Spells for Peace of Mind by Witch Bree

Good Spells for Prosperity by Witch Bree

Green Witchcraft by Ann Moura

Green Witchcraft 2 by Ann Moura

Green Witchcraft 3 by Ann Moura

Grimoire for the Green Witch by Ann Moura

The Grimoire of Armadel by Samuel Macgregor Mathers

Halloween by Silver Ravenwolf

Handfasting & Wedding Rituals by Raven Kaldera & Tannin Schwartzstein

The Heart of Wicca by Ellen Cannon Reed

Hedge Witch by Rae Beth

The Hedge Witches Way by Rae Beth

Herbcraft by Susan Lavender & Anna Franklin

The History of Magic in the Modern Age by Neville Drury

The History of Witchcraft by Lois Martin

The Illustrated Encyclopaedia of Fairies by Anna Franklin

The Illustrated Guide to Witchcraft by Graham Wyley

Inner Magic by Anne Marie Gallagher

The Inner Temple of Witchcraft by Christopher Penczak

In The Circle by Elen Hawke

Invoke the Gods By Kala Trobe

The Key of Solomon the King by Samuel Liddell Macgregor Mathers

Lammas by Anna Franklin & Paul Mason

Lancashire Witchcraft & Magic by John Harland & T T Wilkinson

Light From The Shadows by Gwyn

A Little Book of Mirror Magick by Patricia Telesco

The Little Book of the Green Man by Mike Harding

Living Wicca by Scott Cunningham

Lord of Light & Shadow by D. J. Conway

The Love Spell Book by Gillian Kemp

Love Spells by Claire Nahmad

Mabon by Kristin Madden

Magical Animals by Claire Nahmad

Magical Gardens by Patricia Monaghan

The Magickal Year by Diana Ferguson

Magickal Arts by Sally Morningstar & Laura Watts

Malleus Maleficarum by Jacobus Sprenger & Heinrich Kramer

Midsummer by Anna Franklin

Modern Magick by Donald Michael Kraig

Moon Magic by Lori Reid

Natural Magic by Doreen Valiente

The Natural Magician by Vivianne Crowley

Natural Witchcraft by Marian Green

Natural Witchery by Ellen Dugan

The New Book of Goddesses & Heroines by Patricia Monaghan

Ostara by Edain McCoy

The Outer Temple of Witchcraft by Christopher Penczak

The Pagan Book of Living & Dying by Starhawk

Pagan Christmas by Christian Ratsch & Claudia Muller-Ebeling

Paganism by Joyce & River Higginbotham

Pagan Pathways by Graham Harvey & Charlotte Hardman

Pagan Rites of Passage by Pauline Campanelli

The Path of The Green Man by Michael Thomas Ford

The Pendle Witches by Christine Goodier

The Pendle Witches by Richard Catlow

The Pendle Witches by Walter Bennett

Phoenix From The Flame by Vivianne Crowley

Practical Magic by Marian Green

Principles of Wicca by Vivianne Crowley

The Quest for The Green Man by John Matthews

The Real Halloween by Sheen Morgan

The Real Witches' Book of Spells & Rituals by Kate West

The Real Witches' Coven by Kate West

The Real Witches' Craft by Kate West

The Real Witches' Garden by Kate West

The Real Witches' Handbook by Kate West

The Real Witches' Kitchen by Kate West

The Real Witches' Year by Kate West

The Rebirth of Witchcraft by Doreen Valiente

Ritual Use of Magical Tools by Chic Cicero & Sandra Tabath Cicero

Sabbat Entertaining by Willow Polson

The Sabbats by Edain McCoy

Sacred Drumming by Steven Ash

Sacred Journeys for Women by Sally Griffyn

The Sacred Round by Elen Hawke

Scottish Witchcraft and Magic by Raymond Buckland

Solitary Witch by Silver Ravenwolf

Sons of the Goddess by Christopher Penczak

Spellcraft for Hedge Witches by Rae Beth

Spellweaving by Sally Morningstar

Spirit of the Witch by Raven Grimassi

The Stations of The Sun by Ronald Hutton

The Summer Solstice by John Matthews

The Temple of Shamanic Witchcraft by Christopher Penczak

To Light A Sacred Flame by Silver Ravenwolf

To Ride A Silver Broomstick by Silver Ravenwolf

To Stir A Magic Cauldron by Silver Ravenwolf
The Triumph of the Moon by Ronald Hutton
True Magick by Amber K
West Country Witchcraft by Roy & Ursula Radford
West Country Witchcraft by Gillian Macdonald & Jessica Penberth
Popular Magic by Owen Davies
Wheel of The Year by Pauline Campanelli
Wheel of The Year by Teresa Moorey & Jane Brideson
The White Goddess by Robert Graves
Whispers From the Woods by Sandra Kynes
Wicca by Scott Cunningham
Wicca by Vivianne Crowley
Wicca For Life by Raymond Buckland
Wiccan Beliefs & Practices by Gary Cantrell
The Wicca Garden by Gerina Dunwich
The Wicca Handbook by Sheena Morgan
The Wiccan Handbook by Susan Bowes
Wiccan Magick by Raven Grimassi
The Wiccan Mysteries by Raven Grimassi
Wiccan Roots by Philip Heselton
Wicca Spellcraft for Men by A. J. Drew
Wiccan Wisdomkeepers by Sally Griffyn
Wild Witchcraft by Marian Green
The Wildwood King by Philip Kane
The Winter Solstice by John Matthews
Witch by Fiona Horne
A Witch Alone by Marian Green
The Witch Book by Raymond Buckland
Witchcraft a Beginner's Guide by Teresa Moorey
Witchcraft a Complete Guide by Teresa Moorey
Witchcraft a History by P. G. Maxwell Stuart
Witchcraft & Practical Magic by Susan Greenwood & Raje Airey
Witchcraft A Secret History by Michael Streeter
Witchcraft by Evan John Jones & Doreen Valiente
Witchcraft For Tomorrow by Doreen Valiente
Witchcraft from the Inside by Raymond Buckland
Witchcraft in Cornwall by Kelvin I. Jones

Witchcraft in England by Christina Hole
Witchcrafting by Phyllis Curott
Witchcrafting by Willow Polson
Witchcraft The History & Mythology by Richard Marshall
Witchcraft Theory & Practice by Ly De Angeles
Witchcraft Today by Gerald Gardner
Witches by Michael Jordan
Witches by Nigel Suckling
The Witches Craft by Raven Grimassi
The Witches' Familiar by Raven Grimassi
The Witches God by Janet & Stewart Farrar
The Witches Goddess by Janet & Stewart Farrar
The Witches Sabbats by Mike Nichols
The Witches Way by Janet & Stewart Farrar
Witchfinder General by Craig Cabell
A Witch's Bible by Janet & Stewart Farrar
A Witch's Guide to Faery Folk by Edain McCoy
Write Your Own Magic by Richard Webster
A Year of Ritual by Sandra Kynes
Yule by Dorothy Morrison

Index

ABC of Witchcraft 140
Abracadabra 53-5, 164
Abraxas 54
Acthnici 49
Afterworld 164
Agama Hindu Dharma 10
aicme 117, 118, 164
Air 48-9, 128
Alban Eilir 76
Alban Hefin 79
Aldebaran 50, 164
Alexandrian tradition 14, 141, 155, 164
alphabets 117-18, 126, 174
altar 108, 164
layout 109
amulets 64, 129
Amun 101
Amun-Ra 101
Anemoi 51-2, 164
Angurboda 104
animal worship 7
ankh 127, 164
Antares 50, 164
Apeliotes 52, 164
Apocraphya 62
Apollo 92, 94, 164
apprenticeship 98
Aradia 100, 164
Aradia - Gospel of the Witches 100
Aradia di Toscano 100
Archivist 45, 164
Ares 94
Arianrhod 10, 99, 157, 164
Artemis 92, 94-5, 165
Arundel, Thomas 18
asperger 113, 164
Aspinall Arms, Mitton 62
Astarte 102, 165
athame 112-13, 165
Australian Aborigines 116
Avagdi 98
Aztec 116

Bacchus 93
Baldu 104
Bali 10
bane 165
banishing 55, 63, 83, 165
Bannister, Nicholas 22
Baphomet 105, 165
Bard 45, 165
Barley Moon 84, 165
Bartmann's bottles 56

bawming the thorn 165
BCE 165
bees: three bee charm 66
Bel 76
bell 111
Bellarmine, Robert 56
Bellarmine bottles 56
Beltane 76-9, 165
besom 114-15, 165
Beth, Rae 9
Bible: on witches 18, 20
binding 55, 63, 165
Bishop, Bridget 32, 33, 35
Black Paintings 124
blasting 55, 63, 165
Blight, Thomasine (Tamsin) 29
Blood Harvest 82
Blood Moon 84, 165
blue moon 85, 165
boline 113, 165
Bone, Gavin 140, 143-8
bone fires 83
bone rings 40
Bonemen 155
bonfires 83
Book of Shadows 41, 114, 152, 165
Book of Thoth 9
Booth, Elizabeth 29
Boreas 51-2, 165
Boscastle: floods 151-2
Bowen, Laurence Llewellyn 152
Brigid 75, 99, 112, 165
Brigid's Cross 75-6, 99
Bromley, Sir Edward 22
broomsticks 107, 114-15
Buckland, Raymond 9, 41, 140
Bulcock, Jane and James 22, 23
burin 113, 165
Burning Times 7, 115
burnings 7, 19
Burroughs, George 31-2, 32

Calamy, Edward 26
calendar 71-85
Callaighe 146
Calling the Quarters 49-50
Candlemas 76
candles 64, 110, 112
Capricorn 91

cardinal directions 47-50
Carrier, Martha 33
cartomancy 119, 122, 166
Cases of Conscience Concerning Evil Spirits Personating Men 34
Cathars 119
cats: mummified 61-2
cauldron 107, 114, 122, 166
cave drawings 7
CE 166
Celts 14, 158
alphabet 117-18
deities 97-100
spiritual philosophies 128
censer 111
Cernunnos 7, 11, 97-8, 166
Cerridwen 98, 166
chalice 114, 166
charge 166
Charles, Prince 152
charming 55, 64-7, 166
Chaste Moon 84, 166
Chattox (Anne Whittle) 21-2
chilli pepper charm 65-6
Christianity 7, 14, 19, 72, 96
festivals 72, 73-4, 76, 80, 82
Christmas 73-4
Christmas trees 74
Chrysocomes 92
Churchill, Sarah 29
cingulum 125, 166
Clarke, Elizabeth 24
Clarke, Helen 24
Cleito 91
cloaks 124-5
Clonegal Castle 102
clothes 123-6
Cloyce, Goodwife 31
Clutterbuck, Old Dorothy 41
Cone of Power 47, 166
conjuration 19, 20
consecration 108-10
constructing 55, 63, 166
cord magick 125, 166
cords: magickal 125
Corey, Giles 34
Corey, Martha 31, 32, 34
corn dollies 75, 80
Corn Moon 84, 166

correspondences 166
coven 44, 166
roles in 44-5
covenor 166
covenstead 166
Creed 8, 15
Creirwy 98
Crow, Elizabeth 39
Crowley, Aleister 9, 41, 54, 149, 152
Crowther, Patricia 9
crystal ball 118, 166
Cunning Folk 28-9, 35, 43, 57, 58, 155, 158, 166, 167
Cunning shoes 62-3, 166
Cups (suit) 122, 167
cursing 64, 83, 167

Daphnis 91
dark mirror 118, 151, 167
dark moon 83, 167
Davidson, Nic 112
Davies, Dr Owen 60
dead man's candle 64
Dee, Dr John 118
degrees 45-6, 144-5, 167
deities 87-105, 147, 167
Celtic 97-100
communication with 7
Egyptian 101-2
English 88-90
Greek 90-7
Hindi 103
Italian 100
Norse 103-5
Phoenician 102
triple goddesses 96-7, 98, 99
worship of 11
Delphi 92
Demdike, Old Mother (Elizabeth Southern) 20, 21-2, 23
Demeter 95, 167
deosil 167
Device, Alizon 20-1, 22
Device, Elizabeth 21, 22
Device, James 21, 22
Devil 25, 105
Devil's List 25, 26
Diana 14, 95, 100, 167
Dianics 95, 162
Dionysus 92, 93, 112
dolls: "Fums Up" 151

dolls *see also* poppets
dowsing 115
Drawing down the Moon 51
Drawpnir 103
drinking horn 113-14
Druids 10, 14, 74, 97, 113, 154, 155-6
drum 111
Dryads 69, 167
Dumb Supper 82-3
Duncan, Helen 20
Durdin-Robertson, Lady Olivia 102
Dyan Moon 84, 167

Earth 48, 128
Easter 76
Eastey, Mary 31, 32
Echo (nymph) 90
Eclectic Witchcraft 138-9
eggs 76, 80
Egyptian deities 9-10, 101-2
Eight Sabbats for Witches 142
Elementals 48-9, 50, 109, 167
elements 48-9, 167
Eleusian Mysteries 95, 167
Elffin, Prince 98
Elizabeth I 19
English gods 88-90
Eos 93
Eostar 76
Eostre 77
equinox 81, 167
eras: labelling 72
ergot 35
Esbats 0, 8, 167
full moon names 84
Ether 49, 167
ethics 8
Etruscan period 167
Eurus 51, 52, 167
Evans, Ian 60
Eye of Horus 129, 168
eyebiting 167

faeries 49, 158, 168
Faery traditions 14, 127
Fairclough, Samuel 26
fairy stones *see* hag stones
familiar 21, 24, 35, 114, 168
Farrar, Janet 9, 139-48
Farrar, Stewart 9, 141, 142-3

Faunus 91
Fellowship of Crotona 41
fertility magick 112
fertility rites 115
Festival of the Dead 83
Festival of Light 75
Fire 49, 128
Firedrakes 49, 168
folk magick 168
Ford, Michael Thomas 159-63
Formalhaut 50, 168
Foulds, Ann 23
Fox, Hannah 59-60
Franklin, Anna 153-9
Freemasonry 144
French, Dawn 152
Frey 104
Freya 103, 104, 168
Freyja 104
Frigga 104
Fuld, William 123
full moon 84-5, 168
Esbat names 84
Fylde Witch 35-6

Gaia 8, 96, 168
Gardner, Gerald 9, 15, 39, 40-1, 141, 149, 152, 155, 168
Gardnerian tradition 14, 41, 141, 155, 168
garlic and ribbon charm 66
gast 168
Gaule, John 26
gay men 159-63
Geb 101
genius loci 168
George II 20
Gillow, Joseph 35
glamour 55, 168
glossary 164-75
Gnomes 48, 168
God of the Witches 9
Godbolt, Sergeant John 26
Goddess 8, 9, 14, 41, 49
union with God 77-8
gods and goddesses *see* deities
Good, Dorcas 31
Good, Sarah 31, 32
Gooding, Elizabeth 24
Goya, Francesco de 124
Gramarye 168
Greek gods and goddesses 90-7
Green, Marian 10

Green Man 14, 15, 75, 89-90, 168, 174
Green Men (group) 160-2
Greybeard's bottles 56
Griggs, Dr William 30
Grigori 50, 168
Grimalkin (Graymalkin) 168
Grimassi, Raven 100
grimoires 114, 168
Gundestrup Cauldron 97, 169
Gungnir 103
Gwion 98

Hades 95, 169
Hadrian's Wall 101
hag stones 66-7, 169
Hale, John 34
hallow 169
Halloween 82, 169
Hallowmass 82
hand of glory 64-5
handfasting 77-8, 115, 145, 169
hangings 7, 19, 23, 26, 32, 34, 35
hare 76, 77
Hare Moon 84, 169
harvest festival 7
hat 107, 124
Hathorne, John 31
hawthorn 78
Haydock Papers 35
Head, Richard 37
heart: pierced 63
Hearth of Arianrhod 155, 157
hearths 157
Heathenism 14
heathens 9
Hebe 94
Hecate 96-7, 169
hedge witch 9, 169
Hedge Witch: A Guide to Solitary Witchcraft 9
Hel 104
Heliopolis 101
Helios 93
Henry I 18
Henry VIII 19
Hephaestus 94
Hera 94, 169
herbalism 69, 169
herbs 68-9
heresy 19
Hermes 90
Herne 88, 169
Herne's Oak 89

Hess, Rudolf 39
Hewitt, Katherine 22, 23
hexagram 127-8, 169
hexing 55, 64, 83, 169
hidden company 169
High Magic's Aid 41
High Priest/Priestess 4, 169
Highwayman Inn 39-40
Hilton, Margery (Meg) 35-6
Hindi goddesses 102
history 16-41
Hoggard, Brian 60
holey stones *see* hag stones
Holly King 73, 80, 169
Hopkins, Matthew 23-7
Horned God 7, 8, 9, 14, 15, 41, 49, 81, 83, 87, 97-9, 169
Horsemen 155
horseshoe: upturned 15
horseshoe charm 65
Horus (the elder) 101
Horus (the younger) 102
housel 169
Howe, Elizabeth 32
Hubbard, Elizabeth 29, 30
Hugin 103
Hyperion 93
Hypnos 97, 169

Imbolc 75-6, 112, 169
initiation 45-6, 98, 141, 169
degrees 45-6, 144-5, 167
invocations 50-1
invultation 170
Ireland 145-6
Isis 9, 10, 11, 101-2, 170
Isle of Man 39
Italian goddesses 100

Jack O'Lanterns 82, 170
Jacobs, George 32
James I 19, 23, 25, 158
jewellery: magickal 125
John Barleycorn 97, 170
Juno 94

Kaikias 52, 170
Kali 103, 161, 170
Karl, Jason 152
Kells 145-6
Kelly, Aidan 81
key of life 127
Key of Solomon 170
Kildare 99

King, Graham 39, 40, 59–60, 148–53
Knaresborough 36–7
knife:
boline 113, 165
white hilted 113
Knights Templar 105, 119
knitting: magickal 68
Kronos 91, 94, 95, 96
Kuthun 170

labyrinth 129, 170
Lady Day 76
Lammas 80, 170
Lascaux, France: cave drawings 7
Last Harvest 82
Lavina 135–9
Law of Threefold Return 15, 53, 55, 83
Leech, Anne 24
Leek, Sybil 9
Lees-Smith, Sara 157
Leland, Charles Godfrey 100
lemon charm 65
Lenkiewicz, Robert 150
Leto 92, 94
Levi, Eliphas 105, 126
Lewis, Mercy 30, 31–2
Litha 50, 79–80, 170
Livos 52, 170
Loki 104, 170
Long Meg Stone Circle 62–3
Lord of the Wild Hunt 80, 97, 170
Lords of the Watchtowers 50
Lowes, John 25
Lucifer 100
Luciferian witches 155
Lugh 80, 100, 170
Lughnasadh 80–1, 100, 170
Lughnasadh Funery Games 145

Mabon 50, 81, 170
Maenads 93, 112
magick 15, 17, 170
making 53–5
methods of practising 67–9
spellcasting 53
sympathetic 64
timing 53
types 55–67
white 53

magick circle 46–7, 49, 170
closing down 51
magus 170
Maiden 4, 170
Mains Hall, Lancashire 59–60
Major Arcana 119–21
Man in Black 171, 174
Maoris 116
Martin, Susannah 32
Massey, Dr Alan 58
Mather, Cotton 30, 32
Mather, Increase 34
May Day 76
maypole 78, 171
maypole dance 78
Mead Moon 84, 171
Medusa 91
Memorable Providences Relating to Witchcrafts and Possessions 30
Mercian Gathering 159
mermaids 49
Metis 94
Midsummer 79, 171
Mills, Frances 25
Minor Arcana 121, 171
mirror: dark (scrying) 118, 151, 167
Mischief Night 81
mistletoe 74
mistletoe pouch 65
Mitton, Henry 23
Molay, Jacques de 105
mole foot charm 65
Moon 7
blue 85
Esbat names 84
phases 53, 83–5, 167
Morpheus 97, 171
Morrigan 10, 11, 171
Moses 119
Mother Goddess (Mother Nature) 8, 14, 87, 97, 98
Mother Shipton's Cave 36–7
Munir 103
Murray, Margaret 9
Museum of Witchcraft 29, 38–9, 40, 58, 59–60, 68, 148–9, 150–3
floods 151–2
library 152
publications 152–3

Naiads 49
Navajo 116
Neptune 91
New Age Wicca 137–8

new moon 84, 171
Notus 51, 52, 171
Nowell, Roger 21–2
Nurse, Rebecca 31, 32, 33–4, 35
Nut (goddess) 101
Nutter, Alice 22–3
Nutter, Christopher 22

Oak King 74, 80, 171
Oak Moon 84, 171
Odin 103, 104, 171
Odinism 14
Ogham staves 117–18, 171
Old Ways: survivals of 15
Olympia, Greece 12
Oracle 92
orange charm 66
Osborne, Sarah 31
Osiris 9, 101, 102
Ostara 50, 76, 171
Ouija board 123

Paganism 8–9, 14, 115, 129, 155, 156, 159, 160
definition 9
festivals 76, 81
Pan 10, 90–1, 171
Paracelsus 47, 171
Parker, Alice 32
Parker, Mary 32
Parris, Betty 29, 30, 31, 35
Parris, Elizabeth 29
Parris, Samuel 29
Parsley, Edward 25
Path of the Green Man 160
Patrick, St 146
Patterson, Steve 59, 116
Pearson, Margaret 22, 23
Pellars 28–9, 171
Pendle Hill 12, 62
Pendle, witches of 20–3
pendulum 116, 117, 171
pentacle 110, 125, 126, 171
Pentacles (suit) 121, 171
Persephone 95, 96–7
Petrifying Well 36–7
petroglyphs 129
Phaethon 93
Phillips, Mary 25
Phipps, Sir William 32, 34
Phoebus 92
Phoenician goddesses 102
Pitt Rivers Museum 58, 59
Pitys (nymph) 90
playing cards 122
poppets 33, 53, 75, 80,

112, 171
sticking pins into 170
Poseidon 91, 95, 172
Postgate, Nicholas 59
Potts, Thomas 21
Pow Wow 136–7
Preston, Jennet 22
preternatural 172
priapic wand 112, 172
Priapus 92–3, 112, 172
Proctor, John 32, 34
Progressive Witchcraft 143
Pudeator, Ann 32
pumpkin carving 82
Pursewarden 45, 172
Putnam, Ann 29, 30, 31, 33, 34
Putnam, John 29

quarters 48–9, 172
calling 49–50

Ra (Re) 101, 102, 172
Raglan, Lady 89
Redd, Wilmott 32
Redfearn, Anne 21–2, 22
Reed, Julia Isobel 153–4
Regulus 50, 172
Rhea 91, 94, 95
Rich, Robert 25
Richard II 88
Rivers, Augustus Pitt 59
robes 123
Robey, Isobel 22
Robin Goodfellow 75, 172
Rollright Stones 12
Rosicrucians 119
rowan 59
rowan tree charm 65
runes 117, 172
Ryedale Folk Museum 59

Sabbats 8, 9, 71, 73–83, 172
Sacred Circle Tarots' Journey of the Fool 156
sacred sites 8
sain 172
Salamanders 48, 49, 172
Salem 29–35
salt 111
Saltonstall, Nathaniel 33
Samhain 81–3, 172
Sanders, Alex 9, 132–4, 140, 141, 152
Sanders, Maxine 9, 132–4, 141
Satan 14
Satanism 126, 135

Satyrs 90
Saven 81
Scott, Margaret 32
Scribe 45, 172
scrying bowl 122, 172
scrying mirror 118
sea salt 111
sea witchery 68
seal 172
Seal of Solomon 127-8
Seed Moon 84, 172
Selene 93
Selkies 49
septagram 127, 172
Sergiev, Gilly 62
Seth 101, 102
Shakespeare, William 89
Shamanism 14, 158
shamans 7
Sheldon, Susannah 29
Shipton, Mother 36-7
Shipton, Tobias 37
shoes: concealing 62-3
shrine 108
sigils 107, 117-18, 126-9, 172
signs and symbols 107, 117-18, 126-9
Siguna 104
Silverwheel 157
Skeiron 52, 172
skyclad 125-6, 172
Slieve na Callaighe 146
smoor 172
smudging feather 111-12, 173
snail shell charm 66
Snow Moon 84, 173
solstice 173
Southeil, Ursula see Shipton, Mother
spellcasting 53
spells: making up 9
spiral 128, 173
spirit board 122-3, 173
spirit houses 61, 173
sprite trap 61, 173
staff: forked 110-11
stale 115, 173
stang 110-11, 173
stars: elven (faery) 127
Stearne, John 24, 25
stone 111
Stonehenge 7, 80
Storm Moon 84, 173
Stregheria 14, 100, 173
Summerland 173
Summers, Montague 26-7
Summoner 45, 173

Sun 83
sun cross 129, 173
Sun god 79, 80
sun wheel 79, 129, 173
swimming 25, 26, 173
sword: magick 113
Swords (suit) 121, 173
Sylphs 48-9, 173
sympathetic magick 64, 173
Syrinx (nymph) 90-1, 173

Taliesin 98
talismans 64, 75-6
talking sticks 110
Tarot 118-21, 173
tasseography 122, 173
teacup 122
Tegid 98
Thanatos 97, 173
Theban Script 126, 174
Theia 93
Themis 94
third eye 174
Thomas, James 29
Thompson, Sally and Bruce 40
Thor 103
three bee charm 66
Threefold Law 15, 53, 55, 83
thurible 111, 174
thyrus 112, 174
Titans 96
Tituba 29-31, 34-5
tombs: chambered 145, 146
tools 107, 110-23
consecration 108-10
divinatory 117-23
magickal 115-17
ritual 110-15
torture 24, 175
touching wood 15
traditional witchcraft 15, 174
trance 174
The Tree: The Complete Book of Anglo-Saxon Witchcraft 140
trees: spirits of 68-9
"trick or treat" 82
Triple Goddess 9, 73, 75, 83, 174
triquetra 128, 174
triskelion 128, 174
Trivia 96
Trois-Frères cave 7
Typhon 94

Undines 48, 49, 174
Uranus 96

Valiente, Doreen 9, 41, 51, 124, 140
verdelet 174
vervain 64

Wade, Charles Paget 27-8
Walcott, Mary 29, 30
wand 112, 174
priapic 112, 172
Wands (suit) 122, 174
waning moon 84, 174
ward 174
warding 55-63, 174
wardrobe 123-6
Wardwell, Samuel 32
warlock 174
Warren, Mary 29, 30
Watchtowers 50, 174
Water 49, 128
water nymphs 49
waxing moon 84, 174
Wayfarer 45, 174
West, Anne and Rebecca 24
What Witches Do: A Modern Cover Revealed 9, 142
Wheel of the Year 9, 71-85, 97-8, 129, 175
whistle up the wind 68
Whitby Museum 65
white magick 53
Wicca 8, 41, 155, 175
witchcraft and 15
widdershins 175
Wilcox, Gwen 38-9
Wildes, Sarah 32
Willard, John 32
Williams, Abigail 29, 30, 31, 35
Williamson, Cecil 27-8, 38-9, 40, 110-11, 115, 149-50, 151
willow witching branch 115
wind roarer 115-16, 175
winds:
magickal 51-2
whistling up 68
Wise Women 155
Witch Alone: Thirteen Moons To Master Natural Magic 10
witch balls 55-6, 175
witch bottles 56-8, 175
Witch is Born (LP) 142

witch posts 58-60
witch pricking 24, 175
Witch Queen 175
Witch-finder General see Hopkins, Matthew
witch-hunts 7, 15-27
witchcraft:
contemporary 8
derivation of word 6
developments 147-8
history 16-41
modern revival 40-1
progressive 143-4
test for 24
Wicca and 15
Witchcraft Acts 14, 18-20, 24, 39, 41
Witchcraft Research Centre 39
Witchcraft Today 41
witch(es):
Creed 8, 15
definition 6
derivation of word 6
hereditary 8
reasons for becoming 8
solitary 9-10
wardrobe 123-6
Witches' Way 142-3
witching hour 84, 175
witch's cradle 175
Witch's Garrett 27-8
witch's ladder 67-8, 175
witch's whisk 175
witchwood 59
Wolf Moon 84, 175
Woodplumpton 35-6
worship 7, 11
wort cunning 68-9, 175
Wunderfull Discoverie of Witches in the Countie of Lancaster 21
Wytte, Joan 150-1

Xanthus 92

Yggdrasil 103
Yorke, Jane 20
Yule 72, 175
Yule log 175

Zephyrus 51, 52, 175
Zeus 91, 92, 93, 94, 95

ACKNOWLEDGEMENTS

For their help in creating this book I must offer my deepest thanks to:

Morianna Ravenswood, for a wonderful personal foreword.

Willow Silverwheel for her research concerning the gods and goddesses.

Graham King and Hannah Fox at The Museum of Witchcraft for a wonderful interview, for supplying information on Cecil Williamson and the Witches Garrett and for their general on-going help in other areas too! www.museumofwitchcraft.com

Lavina, for an insight into New Age Wicca.

Maxine Sanders for sharing her magickal life with me through interview.

Janet Farrar and Gavin Bone for their fascinating and revealing joint interview.

Anna Franklin for introducing the faery world and traditional witchcraft in her inspiring interview.

My partner Simon for cooking the dinners while I was tucked away in the secret world of witchcraft writing this book; my Mum, Liz; and lastly I must thank the Goddess, the Horned God and the Hidden Company, who, upon being asked, provided guidance and support throughout this project.

As Merry We Have Met,
and Merry We Have Been.
So Merry May We Part,
and Merry Meet Again.